Kidney Bean Sandwich

Jody Randle

© 2021 by Jody Randle. All rights reserved.

ISBN 9798985038002

These memoir stories reflect the author's present recollections of experiences over time. Some events have been combined and some dialogue has been recreated. I recognize that some individuals' memories of the events described in this book may be different from my own, and the names of some have been changed to respect their privacy.

Cover Illustration © 1965 Ann Randle

Book design by Roy Cordell

Editing by Darinda Sharp for Sharper Prose Communications

Illustrations and photographs © 2021 Jody Randle, except where noted

Once, having accepted an invitation to a get-together, I was then asked, "Will you be bringing a grownup?"

We both knew what she meant.

Thanks for being the grownup, Kelly Marie.

Contact the author at jodyrandlebooks@gmail.com

Contents

An Introduction 8

Growing Up

Who and Where.. 12
Ride to Live, Live to Ride 14
One of Mom's Favorite Party Stories..................................... 18
Yum!... 19
A Fire Down the Street... 20
The Use of Deflection Tracking When Simulating
    Aerial Bombardment with Pub Darts 22
Hot Air Balloons... 25
Nouveau Cuisine.. 27
Let's Make the Water Turn Black 28
FWTiB.. 30
A Summer Job at the Feed Store... 32
A Real-Life Cowboy 39
Never Trust a Raisin 48

The Exchange Student

Mitt Kompisgäng.. 52
An Exchange Student in Sweden 54
Lightning Round 56
Tristesse Chapeau.. 69
A Bloom of Moon Jellies 70
Adventures in Thomas' VW 72
Krimminy... 75
A Boy Named Julius 76
I Met a Møøse Once 77
Fred Flintstone Meets Gene Simmons 80
Drosophila 84
I May Have Met a Forest Sprite 85
What a Knucklehead 87
Black Dog Folklore... 89

Vagabonds in Europe

Tågluffa with Jerry... 92
German Sounds Like Danish 94
Americans in Paris... 100
Essential Oil... 105
A Night in Brittany 106
The Train in Spain... 109

Learning to Bargain in Tangier 113
Dine and Dash Casablanca 120
The Man in Black Goes to Ipanema 125
The Long, Long Road to London 126
Mrs. Moorehead and the Tower of London 130
Frank Zappa and the Mothers of Immigration 133
Back to Sweden 138
Snow Day at Home 142

An Academician

A Scholarship for College Track 144
The Karl and Andy Totem Pole 146
McCabe's Lectern 148
A Degree in Mischief 149
A Rat Race in the Subaru 158
Crossington 161
Booze and Bobsledding 162
Shot At and Missed 164
Short Tales, Fun Facts 168
Momentary Hooligans 178

Rock and Roll Bedtime Stories

"I'm Not a Musician; I'm an Entertainer" 180
The Bull Pen 183
Rumble at Club Nitro 186
Swanson's Lament 190
Tales From The Sip 191
I Believe That 196
Dead Raccoon 197
Rolling Ant Farm 198
Like a Rolling Stone 200
I Stared Down David Allen Coe's Posse 202
Lucas 209
Rollins Meets Ong 210
The High-Concept-Art Band 212
Meet My Friend Scooter 214
An After-Gig Photo 217
Pareto Improvement 221
You Get Bored, Ya Know? 222
Jackson's Last Fight 224
Apology 228

Adulting

Kell and Jode 230
We Had Abby at Home 237
Observations While Following the Wife
    Around the Grocery Store 242
A Bank Robbery! 243
They Burned Our Church 245
Zapped 248
I've been a 251
Captain of a Pirate Ship 252
Hardee's and the Terrible, Horrible,
    No Good, Very Bad Day 259
Your Mother Can Roll 264
Warm Cup of Coffee 268
They Found a Mammoth 269
I Have Seen a UFO 273
Alfred P. Murrah 276
A Saint Croix Christmas 282
The Randle Christmas Curse.. 283

An Introduction

I come from a family that loves to tell stories.

I was lucky, as a very young boy, to spend time with my great grandmother. When I'd get fidgety she'd tell me stories from her childhood, and her tale of a grassfire during her move to Kansas in a covered wagon was able to keep me spellbound, even as an inattentive grade-schooler. My dad's parents spun a great yarn too, even though our age difference sometimes made it another language, with strange words and a different meter. All of my grandparents knew a lifetime of songs, and I learned as many as they could teach me.

My mom's parents were younger, and all of the grandkids called her dad PopPop. He was a former fighter pilot, who slipped exciting nuggets into his conversations, about fast airplanes and .50 caliber guns. His wife had a big, infectious laugh, and you knew from the other room that she'd told the grownups a whopper when you heard it ring out. PopPop once told me he didn't like comedians that laughed at their own jokes, but he didn't seem to mind it at all when he heard my grandmother cut loose.

I think that's where Mom got her "party voice." She and Dad would finish each other's sentences as they worked a crowd at a party. I may not have inherited their skill, but I love telling crazy tales every bit as much as they did.

One night while relating yet another of my personal parables, of stupidity that nearly caused a disaster, one son-in-law said, "Man, you sure seem to have a lot of stories like that."

I guess I do. Everyone has had their scrapes, their near misses, and I don't mind spinning mine for a group. My wife, Kelly, is okay with hearing them all again as long as it doesn't become a hostage situation. She has a secret signal to tell me that everyone has heard this one, and it's time to go check on the turkey. As a buffer for boredom during some pandemic downtime, she talked me into writing some of them down.

I did feel like there are things that my girls (and my friends) might not know about me, and there was a motive for telling some of these stories. That perspective also gave me an audience to write for.

It doesn't take much to *tell* a story, you just rely on your memory of the random details about life, and string together the most absurd ones. And as you retell your favorites—they evolve over time. You refine, you modify, and without realizing it, you're working toward what comedians call a "Tight

Five." You emphasize the parts that got laughs or a gasp, you chuck out the parts that snoozed. You change the rhythm, add a detail, and after thirty years of telling it you begin to wonder: Did all of that really happen?

It is much harder to *write* a story. You can't use physical cues, waving your arms and making faces. You have to describe the scene, and a funny voice isn't going to be there to help you. And if your editor doesn't get the joke, you have to start over.

When I decided to commit my stories to writing, I felt like I needed to make sure that at least the *plot* of the thing was factual. The internet will let you dig into just about any documented event. It was fun to find facts that corroborated a memory, like an itinerary from 1980 that confirmed that Jimmy Carter *was* in Madrid at the same time we were.

Why name the book "Kidney Bean Sandwich"? My mom painted abstract impressions with oil on canvas in college, and after. Some were actual things, some were scenes, a few were ideas she had about color and shape. She preferred that you make up your own mind about what you saw in them, and so, only named them when pressed to do so. In those cases she'd assign them a non-sequitur, like "kidney bean sandwich". That one is probably my favorite, and I wanted it on the cover.

I owe my friends and family a debt for letting me bug them endlessly to contribute details that had become hazy. I let a few read the stories they were in and was told that I probably combined a couple of incidents into one event, or maybe got the order wrong. I was told that I describe every gal in every story as good-looking, and the one just *wasn't*. So, I changed a few things to get some facts straight, but I've left others as they were. These are memories after all, and *how* you remembered something can be its own story.

Sorry if I missed that one that you really wanted to hear. I still have a thousand of them, and if I don't swear off typing forever after this, I'll get around to it.

Oh, and yeah, that one really did happen.

Growing Up

Who and Where

you can't tell the players without a program

Mom and Dad, Ann and Bill, were from small Kansas towns that weren't too far apart. They were freshmen in college at Kansas State when I was born—and I had been a bit of a surprise.

Dad grew up on a farm and wanted to be a veterinarian for as long as he could remember. Mom was an art student who painted and drew beautifully. Her dad owned a car dealership and was a former fighter pilot. They met one night when Mom honked her horn at Dad and his friends from her shiny new convertible.

When my folks finished school, we lived in Kansas, Kentucky, and New Jersey while Dad did his medical internship. I have a few murky memories from a trailer house and apartments in several cities.

I saw a fistfight in the courtyard of one apartment building. Two teenage brothers had been arguing, and their dad hauled them out for everyone to see, then goaded them into a physical altercation. The father screaming, "You said you were mad, hit him," left a deep impression.

Moving from internship into practice, Dad found a vet in South Oklahoma who was willing to take him on, and our family moved back west with high hopes—I was five.

Duncan was a booming, middle-sized town with an oil-based economy and a growing population. It is close enough to Texas that there's not much difference in temperament, but don't get caught saying something so blasphemous—by Texans or Oklahomans. It was a great place to grow up, and the town's growth attracted educated, optimistic people. We settled into a house on Lakewood Boulevard in a brand-new neighborhood on the east edge of town, and in a couple of years I had a brother, Barry, and about a year later a sister, Jen.

Dad's new partner, Dr. C. H. Wulz, was twenty years older and had a solid veterinary practice on the south side of town. Dad did well enough to buy Wulz's half of the business when he was narrowly acquitted in a scandalous murder trial and needed to find a quieter place to live. Dad worked with vet-school interns for several years himself and finally found a kindred soul in Dr. Bob Cross, who became his long-time business partner.

Our neighborhood was crammed full of kids, from kindergarten to high school age. Barry and I made friends all up and down the street: Ralph, the twelve-year-old criminal genius from down the hill; Jeff, the daredevil who only showed up in the summer; Pammy; Allen; Dale; and others. It was a '70s version of *Our Gang*.

Sister Jen tagged along, playing split-lip football and crashing bikes with the boys. I remember warm summer nights, playing unsupervised until after the porch lights came on, when the sky was clear enough that seeing the Milky Way above us was just a normal thing.

During eighth grade we moved away from all of those friends to another house in Duncan on Fairway Drive. By then, I'd started to make new friends at school. Walt and Lee were Texas expats who lived on the other side of town, and I was never sure if it was their family that was eccentric or if it was mine. Their parents had a labyrinth of intricate rules and navigating them created a sort of frenzied fun for us and their siblings on a Saturday morning after a sleepover.

I met Roy around that time, and we became fast friends and conspirators at school. He helped me get a summer job working at the feed store for a local farmer/entrepreneur named Lyndel Strain. Years later, when I became suddenly homeless, Roy offered the extra bed in his apartment in Edmond, and we shared rent for years. After I was married and had moved to Oklahoma City (known to us locals as OKC), I commuted to Edmond to manage photo labs for a guy named Rick Rothwell. Roy and I have kept in touch all these years and are still good friends (I probably still owe him a couple months' rent).

Social media has put me back in touch with most of the characters in these "Growing Up" stories. My wife, Kelly, and I have an annual midsummer party to get everyone back together.

We reminisce about our adventures and watch our kids make their own.

Ride to Live, Live to Ride

it's not childhood without blood and stitches

I started riding with a learner bike. It was plain—red with old-lady handlebars and dorky fenders. They let me loose in the neighborhood, and when I taught myself to stay upright, I started riding it the mile or so to Lee school. When my brother, Barry, got old enough to ride the learner, it went to him as a hand-me-down, and Santa brought me something fantastic on Christmas morning: A brand-new Stingray!

It was a Schwinn "Apple Krate" with a fat back tire, a banana seat and sissy bar, ape-hanger handlebars, and chopper forks with a tiny front tire. I was the envy of Lee Elementary School for a while.

I taught Barry how to ride, and we took the training wheels back off of the learner soon after. We rode everywhere. It was common for me to ride from home to my buddy Walt's house or to Ward Mall, clear across town. What freedom we felt back then: Go as far as your legs could take you, just be home for dinner.

This was the early '70s, and every kid with a bike wanted to emulate Evel Knievel's daring motorcycle jumps. My siblings and I were fans, and we set up a ramp in front of the house to practice our epic daredevilry. It helped that we lived on Lakewood Boulevard, one of the steepest hills in town. Lakewood could always be counted on to help you get up enough speed to crash epically.

We lived for the thrill of weightlessness at the top of the arc, and the terror of the curb that was coming next. We went through the knees of a lot of pairs of jeans in our day, and we became self-taught experts at first aid and bicycle repair.

Barry had a friend from out of town named Jeff who hung out with us when he came to stay with his grandma. He was a great bike-jumper, and one evening after dinner, he used the old learner to try a dangerously long one.

He built up speed and when he hit the ramp hard, it yanked the front wheel back and forth, popping both of the old rubber grips off the handlebars. This left him in midair holding only the grips with no hope of controlling his landing. Jeff and the bike smashed down, and his face was forced onto the bare end of one handlebar. When he rolled over, his eyes were big as saucers. He was bleeding profusely from his mouth, and his face had swollen, so Barry and I calmed him down while sister Jen ran like hell for help.

Dad ran out, knelt down, and opened Jeff's mouth. His tongue was as big as a fist and had a neat hole the size of a handlebar pipe punched into it. Dad told me to look for any missing pieces of Jeff, and then rushed him off to the emergency room. They repaired his tongue, though he had to do a bit of work to learn to use it again. It left a circle-shaped scar, and you know that little crease that runs down the middle of your tongue? Jeff's was always just a little off-center after that.

Total destruction of the old learner bike meant that Barry needed a new one, and the next Christmas Santa delivered. In retrospect, that should have been the year we figured out who "Santa" was, because his taste in bicycles was *just like* someone who had grown up on a farm in Kansas!

Barry got a John Deere cruiser bike, complete with green and yellow paint and J.D. logos all over it. It was a fairly dorky model, more of a grown-up bike than cool. Its main attribute, as Dad told us several times, was that it was built as solid as a farm implement! With extra thick frame-pipe and big ol' welds, it weighed a ton-and-a-half.

"You knuckleheads will *never* be able to tear *this* one up," he said.

One thing we thought was cool, and that Barry had specifically asked for, was that John Deere had equipped the beast with a speedometer. This led to a big debate, and ongoing discussion, about how fast we could actually get the thing going, factoring in the steepest hill in town, the manliness of the two riders, and the sheer tonnage of the vehicle in question.

So, we set out one Saturday to do downhill trials and see if we could make a decent show of some speed. Barry clocked one run in the twenties, then walked it back up the hill. I ran one at twenty-four miles per hour.

We trusted each other to self-report what we saw on the meter. I think it was more about what the bike could do than a contest between us.

On the next run, Barry did twenty-eight, but it looked like that was going to be the top end. We tried a couple more runs and just couldn't beat that speed. We were getting tired and seeing diminishing returns with each new try. So, we went in for dinner, rested up, and I gave it one more go.

This one would be an all-out effort, and I bore down on the pedals. I watched the needle climb: fifteen, twenty, good speed going into the steep part of the hill, twenty-five, twenty-eight, head down intently watching the dial, thirty-two miles per hour—a new record! And...

WHAM! Out go the lights.

Thirty-two to zero in a split second. Mrs. Maddox lived toward the bottom of the hill, and sometime while we kids were up at our house eating, she had parked her car in the street. I ran into the back of that Buick Riviera at thirty-two miles per hour—hit so hard that I wound up flying all the way over the car and landing on the hood. Let me tell ya, we knuckleheads were able to ruin the John Deere. The crash permanently bent the bike's frame, and it never quite steered correctly after that.

It took some time before I steered correctly, too. My crotch hit the upright for the handlebars on the way over the car, and I walked like a cowboy for about three days. I was in enough pain that when Mrs. Maddox came out after hearing the noise, she let slide the fact that I'd put a big crease in her trunk. But she reminded me about it every time she saw me after that.

Many years later, we were having a busy night at the restaurant that I managed when a man came up to me in the lobby with a huge grin on his face.

"Jody Randle! How have you been?" he waited for me to answer. "You don't remember me, do you?"

I didn't.

"I'm Barry's friend Jeff!"

I paused a beat and said, "Stick out your tongue."

By golly, it was Jeff.

One of Mom's Favorite Party Stories

sleeping on the job

This is one of the stories I heard my mom tell more times than I can count. She always got a laugh.

Right after Dad finished vet school, when I was about four, our family lived in New Jersey, and Dad worked long hours doing his internship for a vet in town. One night, he wasn't feeling particularly well. He was tired, and he fainted in the bathroom.

When Dad fell backward into the tub, he grabbed the shower curtain with one hand, and with the other hand grabbed a huge ivy plant that Mom had growing in a pot (In the bathroom? Yup, sounds like Mom). She heard the big *KABAMAWHAM* and ran into the bathroom to find:

A wrecked ivy plant ...

On top of a pile of dirt ...

On top of a shower curtain ...

On top of Dad, who was snoring.

Yum!

Emu brisket silver fork

cold hamgravy with a Spork.

Slice that ketchup mighty fine

to lay upon some French-o-fryne.

Hedgehog Omelet, Gator-tots

calamari in three pots.

Crableg Biscuit, Broccoli Pie,

bean-soak water in my eye.

A Fire Down the Street

an early lesson in different perspectives

When I was nine or ten, I had a first-generation skateboard, made of a thick, inflexible hunk of plywood with metal wheels that made a horrible racket on the pavement, like a '78 Chevette dragging its muffler on the freeway. It was much smaller than the boards they began to make when the market took off a few years later, and it had a blue shark painted on the deck.

During a summer while we lived on Lakewood Boulevard, I was derping around on my skateboard in front of the house when I heard a loud, low "thump" from down the street. I continued playing, but when I heard sirens, I looked in the direction of the noise and there was dark smoke rising from down the hill. I skated down, and as I came closer, I saw a house burning and firemen scrambling, unloading hoses.

That night at dinner, I was still numb.

"A couple of teenagers were sniffing gas while they smoked dope and blew themselves up," my dad declared.

The newspaper was less judgmental, reporting that the fire originated in the garage with two men working on a lawnmower. Smoking while working, they had ignited the fumes from a five-gallon gasoline can and caused an explosion.

That afternoon, I'd skated down to the scene to stand with several neighbors across the street from the driveway of the house. After a while, two firemen emerged from the smoke billowing out of the open garage door, carrying a man by the shoulders and legs.

He was lifeless and smoky, and he was all one color. His face, clothes, hands, all completely black. They loaded him into an ambulance, but the ambulance just stayed there. I guess it didn't have a reason to hurry.

I heard some laughing and a squeal from the other side of the house, so I walked next door to find two of my classmates, boy and girl, running and playing on the lawn. The firemen were spraying the house from the uphill side, and it was blasting wood shingles off the roof up in the air and down into the next yard.

My friends were giggling and chasing each other while trying to avoid the falling chips and sprays of water. They grinned and waved and asked if I wanted to play.

"No. No I don't." I said and carried my skateboard back up the hill.

I never got very good at skateboarding.

The Use of Deflection Tracking When Simulating Aerial Bombardment with Pub Darts

okay, we'll have the SpaghettiOs

It was common for my parents to go out of town for a day and leave me, the eldest kid, in charge. It started when I was about eleven or twelve with some light daytime babysitting and progressed to entire weekend trips by the time I was fifteen and the sibs, Jen and Barry, were nine and ten, respectively.

We stayed out of trouble for the most part. I always cooked, and my entire repertoire was SpaghettiOs or La Choy canned Chinese. I really liked La Choy, but Barry and Jen dreaded it.

Mom and Dad left us for a weekend trip and told us to do our laundry. We slogged through that drudgery, but instead of folding it, we got into a pillow/snowball-type fight with it, throwing socks and underwear at each other.

We let the dishes stack up, and the cat tipped the garbage over. On that Saturday afternoon, we just went ape and decided it would be fun to TP the living room. We were sure that we had at least twenty-four hours left to clean up all this fun.

Of course, they cut their trip short, and came home to an absolutely trashed house.

Our transgressions weren't that bad, really. (Well, okay. Walking in while we were running wild, with toilet paper hanging from the living room ceiling beams was probably a shock.) But we survived the beatings, to frolic another day.

When Barry was about six and I about eleven, the folks left us for a day trip. We were living at the house on Lakewood, and they consented to having my friend Walt over while they were gone. Walt and I have always been into aviation, and at that age, we were experts on warplanes of all sorts. We were insufferable nerds for jets, fighters, bombers, anything that could be looked up at the library then built as a plastic model—I suppose we still are.

This particular day, we were discussing deflection shooting, a technique used by fighter pilots who have to shoot well ahead of a crossing enemy plane, so the bullets and the target meet as they cross paths. The discussion moved to bombers, who face a similar dilemma because they must release their bombs while flying at airplane speed. From far ahead of their target they had to factor in altitude and crosswind and rely on a large arc in order to hit a Nazi ball bearing plant.

I had a dartboard and some darts—the inexpensive kind with plastic fins and very sharp steel points. We got out the dartboard, laid it on the ground in the backyard, and started experimenting with aerial bombardment. How high could we chuck a dart and still hit the board?

We realized quickly this method was only an artillery exercise. To simulate bombing, we'd have to do it from above. What if we got up on the roof of the house? The parents aren't home to stop us.

We enlisted Barry to be our gopher so we wouldn't have to climb down and get the darts every time we used them up. He was eager to help—anything to be in the big boys' club. We warned Jen to stay inside, got out the ladder, and went to work.

Twelve darts. I had six green, Walt had six red. It took a little practice, but it was fun once we got the hang of it.

Six green, then six red.

Barry ran out from under the overhang and yanked the darts out of the board. Grinning ear to ear, he chucked them one at a time up onto the roof for us then ducked under, and we went again.

We were getting good!

Six green, then six red. We tried throwing them hard and straight.

Six green, then six red. We tried throwing them in a big arc.

Six green, then three red ... four ... five ... Barry lost count and ran out from under the awning just as Walt threw the last red dart in a high arc. Time slowed to a crawl as the entire morning's discussion about two objects meeting in the same spot came to pass.

The dart struck Barry in the lower back right before he reached the dartboard. We scrambled down the ladder to him as soon as it hit. He stood still with his back to us as we ran up, the red dart buried up to the hilt through his shirt.

He turned around, and with a look more of concern than anything else said, "Jode, I think you stabbed me."

He didn't seem to be in any pain, maybe from shock, or the wound being very localized.

Walt and I were in panic mode. Our main worry was the dart's proximity to where we thought a kidney would be. We took him inside to the bathroom and a wide-eyed Jen watched in silence as we pulled the dart out.

"Still doesn't hurt?" I said.

"No, not too much."

There was little bleeding, and that didn't help our panic. We knew that really bad wounds didn't hurt initially, and the lack of blood worried us about internal bleeding.

"Maybe it's like getting a shot with a big needle?" Walt said.

At a loss for what else to do, we put Nolvasan (one of Doctor Dad's miracle disinfectants) and a spot-sized Band-Aid on it.

When writing this, I asked Barry for his memories of the incident, and I'll paraphrase what he said. Barry's point of view: Walt said I'm sorry, I'm sorry, about a million times and the thing was, I could see he meant it. I had a strange new feeling come over me. I had been treated like the annoying little brother all my life, and now for the first time I had some power. I have to admit, I kind of liked it.

For the next few days, I quietly watched over the wound as it healed almost immediately. I kept Barry's Band-Aid changed for a week or so just to be sure, and the whole thing just went away.

And that's the thing; he never squealed.

Sure, there were a couple of times down the road when I'd be left in charge and want La Choy for dinner, when he'd say, "Look, I never told anyone about the dart-thing. The least you could do is make SpaghettiOs."

Looking back with him, Barry and I thought that maybe he never ratted us out because it would have squandered the power he had found that day.

Hot Air Balloons

unforeseen disaster, unexpected party

All grown up, with young kids of my own, and having dinner at my parent's house, I told them that the store I was managing was having a sales contest. The Edmond Chamber of Commerce had contacted me and asked if I wanted to do a tie-in promotion with the balloon festival they planned to hold on the college campus half a mile from my store. I agreed to participate, and my staff would sell tickets to the event. The person who sold the most would win a balloon ride.

I told Mom I was a little ahead of my crew and had a good chance at the ride.

Her eyes got wide. "You'd go up in a balloon?" she said.

I told her sure. I thought it'd be fun.

"Really? After what happened?" she said with an odd urgency, and looked my face over, waiting for an answer.

Suddenly, in a rush, an entire scene played in my head. I don't know if you'd call it a "repressed memory," but I certainly hadn't thought about it since it happened.

When I was nine or ten, we still lived on Lakewood, which was on a hill that gave us a good view of blue sky through our back window. It wasn't often you'd see hot-air balloons in our little town, and Mom called me to the window one morning to see one. She said it had climbed, then descended from the same area several times already and that we should get my brother and sister in the car and go see if we could find where it was.

We followed the balloon to a car dealership that was using rides as a promotion. We kids watched excitedly as the balloon brought its passengers back down while we pulled into the parking lot. Mom told me I could hop out while she got my sister and brother out of the car.

The balloon was somewhere around sixty-to-eighty feet high. As I ran up, I realized there was some kind of trouble up there. Some yelling, someone screamed, and a man hit the parking lot right in the spot I had been running toward.

He hit face down and landed like a sack of potatoes, just absorbed the energy without a bounce. As I stared, the pile of person didn't move. Didn't express pain, or surprise, didn't breathe fast, or slow, or at all. It was still as dirt. Mom ran up without my siblings, grabbed me, and put me in the car.

Between that moment and our dinner discussion, I had not thought once about the incident. I told Mom that maybe it would be a good idea to let one of my employees win.

On a happier note: One weekend, years after my sales contest, Mom and Dad were puttering around the yard and saw a balloon land on the golf course behind their house (we had moved across town to Fairway Drive by then). They looked up and the sky was full of colorful hot air balloons. They could hear the aviators shouting to one another while hovering low in the suddenly still air.

They were from a festival event that was passing over Duncan and had run into completely calm air. They couldn't progress to their destination and chose the north end of the golf course as a clearing large enough to set down in.

They descended in a huge flock all around the neighborhood and filled up the street and the fairway behind the house.

Mom and Dad took some pretty crazy pictures that afternoon, and they hosted an impromptu party for the stranded aviators while they decided what to do. If you knew my parents, this doesn't surprise you.

After the aeronauts radioed their chase vehicles to come join the party, they packed up their balloons and called it a day.

Nouveau Cuisine

Clambake Phillysteak

East Topeka pie

Loop fruit birthday suit

Spa ghet ti on rye

Let's Make the Water Turn Black

grade school bootleggers

I had a neighborhood friend while we were living on Lakewood, I'll call him Ralph, who seemed to be a reasonably intelligent grade-schooler, but who also *really* wanted to be a bad boy. He wanted to be bad so desperately that he checked books out of the library on gangsters, bootleggers, and outlaws and poured over them.

His encyclopedic knowledge of crime made him the idea-man for our badness, and periodically he would propose things like distilling our own whiskey or making a "zip gun." He was the big thinker of our team, and I was the details guy, so he'd lean on me to figure out how to make his schemes work.

One of his books said that gang members would break off someone's car antenna (in those days they were still made of hollow steel so they could telescope), then find a section of it that fit a .22 shell to use as the barrel of an improvised firearm, known as a zip gun. He proudly presented me with an antenna that he'd stolen from a neighbor's car.

"Now what?" He asked me.

I told him that if his antenna was thin enough to snap off a car, it was an extremely bad idea to expect it to contain a bullet's explosion. But he talked me into it, as he usually did, by appealing to my curious/creative itch.

I attached a four- or five-inch piece of the antenna to the top side of an L-shaped piece of wood. We filed the end of an Allen wrench to a pointy slant and rigged it so a stretched piece of surgical tube would slam the point into the rim-fire end of the cartridge and set it off.

To ease my fear of the contraption exploding in his hand, Ralph had wrapped the whole thing in nine layers of black electrical tape.

"Let's go try it!" he said.

Yeah, there was no way I was getting anywhere near that thing. "When they find you, do you want me to tell your mom exactly what happened to you, or should I just play dumb?"

He came to me the next weekend and said that he'd walked way out into the field north of our neighborhood and pointed the gun at a cow. He showed me our now-ruined handiwork. The nine layers of tape on the top of our infernal machine were a frayed mass, and the antenna had split all down one side. He said that my firing mechanism worked great, but the bullet had blasted out through the side of the barrel, making a screaming noise as it went who-knows-where.

Well, thank God on behalf of that poor cow.

During a long winter spent romanticizing Al Capone, Ralph decided we were going to be bootleggers and began to collect the bits and pieces of equipment we would need to distill our own whiskey. By spring, he'd gathered copper tubing from an air conditioner, a pot from his mom's kitchen, funnels, beakers, and a camp stove to heat the mess to boiling.

We had to wait until I returned from that year's stint of working on the farm in Kansas, as we intended to ferment our "mash" from the small grocery sack of wheat I skimmed off this year's harvest. We boiled and burned, spilled a batch, and set a corner of our backyard tent on fire.

Did I mention this was the mid-'70s, and unsupervised play was the norm? Extremely unsupervised in our case. My only parental guidance for the entire summer was "don't be late for supper."

We wound up with about a half-cup of clear liquid that didn't seem very alcoholic to either of us. We'd probably rushed the fermentation and wound up with mostly water. But the summer was about over, we were out of wheat, and we could say that we tried. And we didn't go blind drinking it.

The title of this story is homage to a song of the same name by Frank Zappa. It's about a small group of boys who are left, unsupervised, to get into all sorts of bizarre trouble in their backyard. They grow up to be various types of citizens, not all of them upstanding.

Ralph got into a little worse trouble as a teenager, but he turned his life around later, and grew up to be a preacher in a church in a small town nearby. After marrying and having kids, he died relatively young in a home-repair accident.

I think he would have made one hell of a grandpa.

FWTiB

but I can usually put it back together

One of my many careers has been managing photo processing labs. I ran a couple of labs in Edmond in the '90s for a guy named Rick, and some of my many worries were the very complicated processing machines. Not only was the chemistry involved tricky, but they were big, sloshing, mechanical contraptions with shoots and racks, pumps and sensors, two hundred gears, and seventy-five rollers.

I learned to keep costs down by doing a lot of the repair myself, mostly by trial and error, and a lot of time on the phone to the manufacturer. I kept a cabinet full of tools and spare parts. You can rescue a $3,000 day if you're able to change a gear out while the machine is running.

One day, while I had my head in one of the printers, I told Rick one of my wife's favorite stories:

When I was a kid, I was screwing around at the house unsupervised one afternoon and broke a lamp. Dad came home soon after and he was *pissed*.

Exasperated, he hollered, "You just gotta fuck with somethin' 'til it breaks, don't ya? That shoulda been your middle-damned-name, Jody Fuck-With-It-Till-It-Breaks Randle!"

He had me clean it up, and that was one time when it was a good thing that I stifled my laugh, or I would've got a beating to go along with it.

Rick was highly amused by the tale and had a T-shirt made for me that just had FWTIB in big letters on the front of it. He would see me with a wrench in my hand and say, "Just put the wrench down, and back away from my machine, *EffDoubleyouTeeEyeBee!*"

But I did have a good record of keeping things running for him.

You know, Dad gave me a hard time, but I think he understood how I thought. He knew that I was fascinated with how mechanical things worked and was good at taking them apart and putting them back together (it's the best way to learn). He wasn't very mechanical himself, but he bought me a toolbox and brought home things from his clinic like an old oxygen valve and other defunct devices, just so I could take them apart for fun.

One day, he came home and handed me a dissection kit with tweezers, pins, a scalpel, and such, like you have to buy if you take a biology lab at college. Somewhat puzzled, I thanked him, then when Mom had turned the corner, he pulled out a medicine bottle full of alcohol with an EYEBALL in it! He explained that it was from a dog who'd lost a fight, and the eye couldn't be saved. Did I want to try taking that apart? Heck yeah I did!

It was the grossest-coolest thing ever.

A Summer Job at the Feed Store

I don't remember hearing an explosion

I started working for Dad at the pet clinic on weekends for minimum wage when I was twelve. Soon after, I picked up a few lawns that I mowed regularly for neighbors. In my early teens, Mom and Dad began sending me up to Kansas to work on the farm for the summer, where I was paid with supper and a bed.

I had enough cash flow for a little gas money and to buy a girl a coke, but I decided that if I was going to save enough money to have a car, I needed a full-time summer job. When I was picked as an exchange student, my financial ambitions changed to money for travel.

As I've done many other times, I went to my friend Roy for help. He was working at Strain Seed and Grain, a place we first knew of from our route home together from junior high. Back then, it had a retail store where you could get chicken feed and other farm supplies. By high school, they had concentrated on just a couple of businesses—cleaning seed and servicing farms with fertilizer and weed killer.

The place had recently been bought by an entrepreneur/farmer named Lyndel Strain. It had been there since the '40s, built back then by a man named Eldon "Pick" Pickrell, a rascally old guy who had also been the mayor of Duncan for a term during the early '60s. He still ran the day-to-day operations and came from a time when The Boss didn't waste time telling you *how* to do something. He shouted that it needed to be done, and you figured it out.

There were lots of things to figure out, too.

He had kind of a code of bass-ackward ways of saying things, body language, and implied rules. I don't know, maybe that created plausible deniability. For instance, he'd never just tell us to go to lunch. He'd come back from *his* lunch and putter for a minute or two, then look up at us and say something like "What? I ain't hungry!"

Roy would elbow me and whisper, "That means go to lunch."

It took a while to learn, but it kept things interesting.

Pick had a group of friends who came by in the mornings and sat in a circle of chairs, talking and chewing tobacco. He had nicknames for them all: The Swede, Bigfoot Brown. He'd known some for longer than my dad was old.

In the center of their circle, on top of a piece of cardboard, was a five-gallon plastic bucket they used as a spittoon. For the first couple of months I worked there I never saw the thing move, let alone get emptied. Some kind of fungus was growing in there and that gawdawful stuff was getting closer to the brim. Roy and I drew straws and finally emptied it when it had reached about four and a half gallons. Pick never said a word to us about it one way or another.

We loaded trucks. Sometimes we filled a thousand-gallon tank truck with water and weed killer. Sometimes we loaded dry-pellet fertilizer into a truck that looked like the ones that spread salt in the winter. We'd drive the truck up under an overhead bin and dump in a few tons of pellets. Then one of our drivers would go out to a farm that had hired us to spread the weed killer or fertilizer.

Sometimes humidity could cause bridging—a dome-shaped gap in the middle of the bin. To get the pellets flowing again we'd have to station one of us in the truck's hopper, and one twenty feet up on the side of the bin. The low guy would poke at the dome with an iron pole and the guy up high would beat on the side of the bin with a big rubber mallet.

The clog would cut loose suddenly, and I once buried Roy up to his armpits in pellets before I could scramble down the side of the bin and yank the rope. It's actually pretty dangerous. An article I read recently said that there's no way to swim out of a situation like that, and that twenty-six farmworkers died in accidents similar to that in 2016.

The task we spent the most time at (besides endless sweeping) was cleaning seed-grain. Farmers brought their big ol' wheat trucks into a drive-through dump area and tilted the beds up to pour the grain out onto the floor. It would filter through a grate to a below ground tank we called "The Pit," to be brought up and directed to one of the storage bins.

The whole building-sized mechanism was built of wood and was a marvelous Rube Goldberg contraption that could move grain from bin to bin and direct it over to the cleaner and back. You'd open the little door on a "leg" and see an impossibly long leather belt with hundreds of steel cups, each with about a pint of wheat rapidly whizzing by on its way up to the top of the whole thing, to be dumped into the proper bin. After cleaning, the grain was routed to a storage bin, to eventually come out of a nozzle we opened and shut by hand, as we weighed out sixty-pound bushel-bags of wheat.

The cleaner itself was suspended on rollers by leather belts and a little smaller than a Volkswagen Bug. It shook back-and-forth to vibrate the seed down through big, interchangeable screens, and the holes in the screens stopped or passed debris of various sizes.

One load of oats came in with thousands of huge, shiny black beetles. They poured out of the cleaner and crawled the floor, and you couldn't get close enough to change the screens without crunch-walk-squishing a hundred of them.

The worst load we got was full of grasshoppers. Those locust-sized bastards filled the air, flying and hopping and getting in your hairdo. They caused me more than one bad dream.

Periodically, we'd need to clean the whole place from top to bottom. We were the more thorough of the two facilities in town, and farmers brought us "show wheat" to be cleaned so it could be graded. We had a vacuum, made from a big motor on top of a 55-gallon drum with a super long hose, and we'd put on breather masks and climb up in the rafters with the thing set to blow. Our task was to find and eradicate *every single grain* of wheat in the building. One old shrively seed could throw a farmer's assessment off and cost him money.

The recurring clean-downs were also a good idea because of another farm hazard—grain dust.

Eldon Pickrell

The dust from wheat is highly flammable, and in that form, it has an enormous amount of surface area that can ignite. That makes it a risk at places like ours, and there have been grain bin explosions powerful enough to destroy entire facilities.

Pick had us keep that place pretty darned clean. We used the blower and swept all morning, eventually routing everything we had dusted down into The Pit. Then one of us would climb down with his breather mask and goggles, and the hose to suck it all out of there. The other guy watched (and listened to) the vacuum.

In the dark of the pit, you'd suck up something big that you couldn't see. The vacuum guy would hear it clog the hose, shut it down, and start pulling the hose up. The pit guy would climb up and we'd fish out the treasure—usually a clump of bugs or a dead rat.

One time, we couldn't tell what was down in the hose, so we put the vacuum on "blow" and a desiccated pigeon shot out, traveling across the truck yard to smack into a grain bin: *Foom - BONG!*

When the Alfred P. Murrah building in Oklahoma City was bombed, it took a day or two of investigation for them to discover that the device used was a mix of nitrogen fertilizer pellets and diesel fuel. When I heard that on the news, I just nodded my head. I had first-hand knowledge of that chemical reaction, from my days at Strain Grain.

One afternoon, Lyndel showed up in a flatbed truck carrying three empty 55-gallon barrels. They'd once held axle grease, and he told us to clean them up to be used as trash cans. The barrels still had a film of the thick grease inside, and the side welts held a pint or so of the stuff as well. We knew we'd have to crawl inside to scrape and wipe the barrels, so we told Pick that we'd prefer to dress in something we didn't mind throwing away to do this particular job. He agreed, and the next day we showed up ready and dressed for a mess.

Roy and I traded off duties: He'd crawl and scrape for a while, and I'd put what he gathered in a bucket to use later to grease our trucks. Then, I'd climb in and try to keep it out of my hair. Whether the job needed to take that long or not, we managed to spread the three barrels out over an entire day, finishing the first by mid-morning.

We got just darn near all of the grease out, but there was still a thin film inside that resisted wiping. While Roy and I mulled over solutions, Pick walked by and said, "Burn it out!" with his usual lack of any instruction on how to get that done.

We took the stack of newspapers that Pick's friends left daily when they were through spittin' tobacco and reading, and wadded them loosely, filling up the barrel. Roy lit a match and the newsprint burned merrily as we continued on to the next barrel. While we worked, Pick came out and watched the ashes from our burn float all over the yard and through the building.

"Yer gonna burn my place down," he griped, then spat a tobacco fleck.

During our daily lunch buffet at Ken's Pizza, we decided that we'd roll the second barrel out to the middle of the truck yard and cover it with a screen from the top of one of the spreader trucks. That should keep the ashes contained.

The folks at Ken's were probably mad about the grease prints we left on their table and seats.

We finished the second barrel and realized that we'd used up the newspapers. We spied a stack of the double-walled paper sacks that we used to sack wheat that were rejects from previous weeks of sacking. We tore them up into manageable pieces and tossed them into our second barrel, now in the middle of the yard.

The newsprint had done a fair job of melting and burning the grease in the previous barrel, but we wanted a little faster, hotter fire this time. The truck yard had its own gas pump, so after placing the grate for the truck on top, we pumped a couple of squirts of gasoline in as an accelerant. I lit a match and *WHOOMP* the fire got going, after startling us both pretty good.

Scraping the third barrel went about like the other two. It was gooey, greasy work on a hot August afternoon. The wheat sacks had done a better job at finishing up the second barrel, and we figured it was the gasoline that helped the grease participate in its own consumption. But we'd used up that stack of sacks.

In a dark corner of the back room, we found a stack of sacks we could use. These had been used, then discarded during a project we'd done for one of Lyndel's friends. He'd wanted us to sell him Nitrogen fertilizer, but in sacks like you'd find at the garden store. All we had was the overhead bin stuff, but on Pick's orders, we stood in the back of a truck under the bin and loaded up a dozen bags to sell him. The friend decided he didn't want the stuff after all, so we'd dumped it in a truck and saved the bags to keep from wasting them.

As we shredded them, we noticed a *lot* of fertilizer dust and a handful of pellets in the corners of each sack. Didn't bother us much. We tossed everything into the third barrel and placed the five-foot-square cover screen on top.

Pick had gone to the store and had the key to the gas pump with him, so we couldn't get gasoline to use for our bonfire. We remembered that he had a metal coffee can in the shop he was using to soak tools in diesel fuel. We grabbed the tools out of the can and poured the contents on the bags. After the reaction of the last burn, I told Roy it was his turn to light the barrel. He started from far back.

Lit a match, tossed it ...

Missed.

Lit a match, tossed it ...

It went out.

Lit a match, tossed it ...

I don't remember hearing an explosion. I suppose the shock wave hit me before my ears registered it. I did know that they were now ringing, and I was unexpectedly on my back, looking up at the screen turning end-over-end in the sky with a big hole blown through it. I followed it as it came back down to land seemingly silently on the barrel, and saw Roy backed up against a grain bin with his hat gone.

My face felt like it had been slapped. The explosion had thumped a dent into the bottom of the barrel and bent it outward at its middle, splitting the seam where it was crimped. Windows in our building had cracked. The mechanics from the International Harvester shop across the street all came out onto the sidewalk to gawk, and people from around the neighborhood came by to see what had caused the big noise. The police station sent a cop over to check out the scene.

Pick grumbled and groused publicly about us being idiots, but was privately happy that we were okay.

I had a great summer, working with Roy. We were good friends before, but the sweat, fun, and explosions bonded us further. Pick was crusty, but like many old guys, he had a soft middle. I still have several letters he wrote to me while I was an exchange student.

A few years ago, someone posted on Facebook that the old place had burned down. A fire got up, spread quickly, and consumed the entire structure. The building and grounds had been abandoned for a few years, and one wag speculated that it might have been host to a meth lab, how else could it have burned so fast? Well, that old girl was made of pinewood with a tar roof, and it was full of gunnysacks, leather belts, fertilizer, and wheat dust. She would have gone up like a gallon of gas.

I wish I had been in town. It would have been a sad sight, but I would have liked to have been there.

A Real-Life Cowboy

our dad was a veterinarian

Dad grew up on a farm where they grew wheat and raised beef. He rode his horse to school every day, so he could ride—he could rope 'em and he could brand 'em, too. In fact, he kept up the registration for the family brand E∃ and passed it on. He had a nice Stetson but seldom wore it, and his weren't "dude" chaps, with fancy tooling and fringe. They were plain leather and had cuts and scrapes and a big rip he had sutured up himself.

He once told me a story about a winter storm setting in, and he and his dad riding out to round up the cattle so they wouldn't freeze. They got them all in except one stubborn calf, who would let them get close and then run off before they could rope it—my dad did a great imitation of a scared calf's moo. They kept chasing it farther away from home until long after the storm set in, and in low visibility, they finally got it. But a blizzard was raging, and they were far from home, so the nearest farm fed them and let them stay overnight.

Inside and warming up, my grandfather and the neighbors hadn't noticed that my dad hadn't come in with them. The men went back outside to find him struggling to get off his horse. His jeans had frozen to his saddle! A pan of warm water fixed it, but he had to sit through dinner looking like he'd wet his pants.

When I traveled to Europe in high school, I met all sorts of people, some who knew the U.S. only through movies. More than once, I was asked if there were still "Cowboys and Indians" in Oklahoma (yep, really). I'd reply that it wasn't like the movies, but that I did know one real-life cowboy very well.

For five or six years after we moved to Oklahoma (we arrived in 1967), Dad practiced large animal medicine. Of course, this means that he worked on farm animals—cows and horses, mainly, because he didn't like to work on hogs. He occasionally worked on sheep, but I remember him saying, "Woollies are about the dumbest animal God ever invented."

When we were in New Jersey during his internship, he subbed at a zoo, so he even had a little experience with elephants.

Quite a few people in Duncan called him "Doc," and I was proud of that (although he was awfully fussy about correcting my friends when they called him *"Mister* Randle" instead of *"Doctor"*). I've been told by several of his peers that he was the best surgeon in town.

The people who called him Doc obviously admired him and would occasionally ask me if I would follow in his footsteps. They were always taken aback by my adamant, "NO!"

You see, I had been on a few farm calls with him. Mom let me go occasionally to keep him company if I didn't have school the next day.

A farmer is usually certain he can handle any situation with his animals. He wouldn't have gone into farming if he weren't sure of himself, so it's not until he is completely tired and out of options that he'll call a vet to come help, and that means it is always two in the morning, and things have really gone to hell.

Dad and Dr. Wulz, his partner at the time, used a '37 Chevy as a company car because they liked its huge trunk (cow-berthing equipment is mighty bulky.)

One morning at about three o'clock, I was sitting in the Chevy watching while Dad was up to his shoulder in a very pregnant cow. I watched it poop all down the front of him. Of course, he couldn't clean up right then, or even move, until he finished helping the calf out. And the cow was not so happy with the help, so it stomped his foot so hard that he limped a little for a couple of days afterward.

I crossed one career choice off my list right then and there. That didn't stop Dad from bringing me into the family business anyway.

When I was twelve years old, he woke me up early on a Saturday morning and said, "Guess what, boy, you've got a job. Welcome to the working world" (this is why my knowledge of Saturday morning cartoons has a seven-year gap).

By then, he and Wulz had moved from next-door to the A&W, built a new clinic up on the north side of town, and left large animal medicine behind to specialize in dogs and cats. There was more money in it and as we saw before, cows are a pretty physical game. Mom was okay with him not being beat up quite as often. The new location was just blocks from where Mom and Dad would later decide to build a new house on Fairway Drive, which meant that Dad could walk home for lunch any day that he wanted, and that I could get up later on Saturday morning to make my contribution to "the working world."

My new job duties were to go in early, feed the animals, take a break to let nature do its thing (and eat donuts on the couch), then clean cages until lunchtime. Sometimes I'd get to assist Dad with shots or a surgery.

The Clinic had an area in the back where they examined and treated the animals that needed to stay for long-term care. In the center of that area was a long glass cabinet with drugs neatly catalogued for use, and on the opposite wall was a chalkboard. When Dad got low on a type of drug, he'd write it down on the chalkboard so that he'd remember to order more when the salesman came around.

His blackboard always had a bunch of odd names on it like "Nolvasan" or "Denamarin" waiting to be ordered. During the school year, I only worked a half-day on Saturdays, and every weekend when it slowed down and everyone else was up front, I would make up a new drug and add it to his board.

I'd add things like Nazbahgleen, Splammablan, or Thorma-spibbulin, and every week I'd come in and see he had erased last week's nonsense. He never said anything about them, I think it was just a little game we played back and forth. I thought about asking him about them once, long after I had kids of my own, but never remembered to ask when I was with him.

One of Dad's favorite games was to see how far, during dinner, he could take a discussion about the grossest veterinary procedure he could possibly describe before Mom shut him down.

Veterinarians are connoisseurs of gross. I think it is a by-product of the job.

Dad and Dr. Cross kept a running list of euphemisms for "throwing up" pinned (with a syringe-needle, of course) to the frame of the drug cabinet. Any employee could add to the list, but there were rules to keep participants from just making things up. All entries had to be documented in print or verified by two sources. Moreover, they discounted derivatives. All very scientific.

It was quite extensive: Upchuck, barf, vomit, hurl, ralph, purge, puke, hork, buick, spew, there are too many to list here. But it was a mighty fine day when someone brought in a new one.

One Saturday, I was in the back with my head in a cage.

Dad came back and told me, "Boy, you're doing a fine job. I think you're doing such a good job that I've decided to give you a raise! How does two dollars an hour sound?"

It *was* a raise, so I told him I thought it was great, and went on with my cleaning, quite impressed with myself. When we got home for lunch, he made sure that the newspaper was lying out in my way so I would see the story about minimum wage going up to two bucks an hour, starting that week.

Mighty generous of you, Dad!

Dad started his career doing whatever veterinary work called for—working on large and small animals, pigs, and birds, and even de-skunking skunks so they could be kept as pets. But as he got more comfortable with his own practice and his place in the community, he got choosier.

No snakes, no skunks.

He gave up treating large animals early in his career, and later, he made some ethical choices. He became adamant about not using mercury in medicine or thermometers because of its environmental impact. He stopped declawing cats because it leaves them defenseless if they ever go outside. He also stopped cropping the ears of breeds like Schnauzers and Dobermans when it was strictly for cosmetics.

But a while before he made that choice, he came back one day while I was scrubbing away, stuck his hand out, and said, "Just wanted to shake your hand for really making it shine back here."

Of course, he had hidden a pair of cropped-off ears in his hand. *YIKES.* You'd think I'd have learned by then.

Dad would get after-hours calls occasionally and would hang up the phone and walk up the hill alone to the clinic to meet a client. When I was in high school, Mom started sending me with him even if I had school in the morning.

One night, he took a call about a huge Great Dane that had been hit by a car and shattered its leg. In this and similar cases, he would put the dog under anesthesia and tie its limbs to the corners of his stainless-steel surgery table. He'd roll a stool up to the end of the table, tilt the table, and get busy.

This night, alone and a little sleepy, he set the bone pins he would use in the blood-groove that ran around the edge of the table. Bone pins come in various lengths and diameters. Some are threaded so they can be screwed in, but all of them had three-sided ends sharpened to a razor point so they could be pushed in through the muscle and bone easily. He laid out some that were quite heavy and forgot that they were there at the far end of the table pointed right at him. He tilted the table.

The pins slid down, of course, and one stuck into his thigh like a stainless-steel arrow. His reaction was to jump up, but the angle was such that it hit the underside of the table and jammed (as it was designed to do) all the way to the bone. All alone up there, he hobbled to the phone and woke Mom up.

When she got him to stop bellowing, he told her he couldn't get it to come out without help. The muscle had clamped tight around it and his hands were shaking now. We went up and helped him extract it (jeezus, *eww!*), and Mom decided on the spot he was not to go on any emergency after-hours calls without one of us going with him.

Since I was already on the payroll I was now on call.

One night, Dad took a call during dinner and told me I should go with him because this one was going to be interesting. The client was coming in with a gibbon.

If you've never seen a gibbon, they are a small ape about three feet tall, but they have a disproportionately long arm span of six feet, and weird long hands.

The gibbon had a broken jaw, and when the client arrived, he explained that he also owned a Saint Bernard (Dad called them Saint Barn-yards). He said the monkey constantly pestered the dog, and that night the dog got tired of it yanking his tail, put his mouth around the gibbon's head, and ... crunch!

So, the guy brings in a cage, lets this thing out in the exam room, and ...

It. Goes. BANANAS.

It's jumpin' and grabbin' and screechin' and hootin'. It's on the ceiling, then on top of the fridge. It broke a jar that holds cotton balls, and somehow the sink wound up running full blast. Then it slapped Dad's glasses right off his face.

That was the last straw I think, and with a loud growl Dad grabbed it and—
Wham!

He pinned it face-down on the table, holding its elbows together behind its back. He handed the elbows off to me and gave it a sedative while the owner held the ape's feet, which were still kicking furiously: KICK-KICK-KICK kick-kick-kick   kick   kick   ... kick   ... *snore*.

Dad set the jaw and taped up the gibbon's head, but he didn't think he had a cage that would keep him, so he and the client agreed that he'd send them home.

I imagine that monkey steered clear of the family dog from then on.

A farm dog had been kicked by a cow and the owner called late in the night. I went to the clinic with Dad to assist. After a quick diagnosis, we scrubbed up, then Dad quickly prepped and opened while I brought instruments to him.

The cow's kick had torn the dog's liver, causing massive internal bleeding. My task was to draw some anticoagulant into a 50-milliliter syringe, put the tip in the cavity, and suck up as much blood as I could. I had two syringes, and slowly turned them in my hands to keep them mixed while I waited for Dad to grab one and put the blood back into the dog's system. Things were moving quickly. I didn't have much trouble with being queasy. I'd seen some gross stuff.

The all-time worst is a C-section. They usually become necessary when one puppy in the chain dies. The dog's system has begun breaking down the body, and the green goo that results is horrifying and stinky. But the reward is standing with a towel as Dad hands you a tiny pup, rubbing it briskly until it yipps, then putting the pup that you've "brought to life" with the others in the warming drawer.

Anyway, I was used to working in bloody situations, and was doing okay with this lacerated-liver thing. I had blood all over the front of me, but I was okay. I was sticky and warm and smelled like, well, blood but ugh. I was okay. Dad was trying to suture the liver back together and said that it wasn't working. Each suture hole made another spot that bled.

The poor dog was tanking, and we were under pressure. Dad said he was going to try to just cauterize the wound to shut off the bleeding. He wanted me to hold a flashlight for him, but I had syringes in both hands.

He stuck the mini-mag between my teeth and said, "Get down there close, so I can see."

With my face right down close to the guts, he squirted a big stinky bunch of formaldehyde on the wound ...

I came to with my arms dangling behind me, and Dad talking at me to wake me up. He'd seen me falter and grabbed the front of my shirt just in time to keep my head from hitting the floor. He hoisted me up.

"Go out and get a suck of fresh air and get back in here. I need your help, boy," he said.

I recovered and we worked on. But we wound up losing the dog.

When my brother, Barry, was about three, a family friend made a present of a toy raccoon with a rabbit pelt as its fur, with a real raccoon tail. Barry named it Herman (we never knew why), and he went everywhere with it, usually dragging it by its tail.

It was common that a pet would get into household cleaners or get ahold of something else around the house that was toxic and would poison itself. For many of these cases the best way to treat it is to sedate and then observe them for a number of hours, to let them sleep off the ill effects of the poison.

One time, a client brought in a pet raccoon that opened and ate an entire bottle of aspirin. Dad sedated and medicated it, then brought it home late that night so he could get up periodically and check on it. He laid it in the living room on a blanket to sleep overnight.

Very early the next morning we were all woken up by an ungodly amount of screaming in the hallway. We came around the corner to see Barry with that poor raccoon doing a dance on the top of his head. We guessed that Barry woke up before everyone else, thought he'd found Herman, and tried to drag him off to bed by his tail.

Dad's next carpentry project was to build a cage just like the ones at the clinic to have at home so his observation patients could rest without being bothered. It was in the garage, and Barry and I locked Jen up in it when she was annoying us.

Ever after, Mom referred to the whole incident as "The Night That Herman Came Alive."*

---

* "The Night Herman Came Alive" was another of Mom's favorite stories to tell, and I can still hear her saying, "doing a dance on Barry's head."

The Clinic also boarded dogs and cats for people while they were on vacation or away for a holiday and would often have every cage full over Christmas. Dad let the *other* people that worked for him have holidays completely off, even though it was packed. He had us kids go with him to feed and walk the dogs, then clean the cages. Jen never minded much, I'm not sure what Barry thought. I was on Dad's payroll, and this was a freebie. Why didn't I get the day off?

A year or two after I married Kelly, we spent the holidays with my folks. After coffee on Christmas morning, Dad announced that we all were going to load up and go clean dog and cat poop as a Christmas morning treat (except for Mom, who was off the hook so she could get some turkey ready for him).

He ended his command with "*Haha*," so Kell kind of thought he was kidding. When he indicated that she was to go also, she got in the car with the rest of us, but when we were done, let me tell you, the *wife* was <u>done</u>.

She held her tongue, probably to make sure she wouldn't misspeak, until after the gift exchange, Christmas dinner, and all of the festivities were over. Then, she took my dad into the other room and told him in no uncertain terms that the "family cage clean" would not happen again. I think that if Barry's wife, Tonya, had been a member when he pulled that stunt, between her and Kell, Dad wouldn't have lived through the day.

My dad had cousins who were sent to the farm to help his dad in the summers, and I was sent up to help for a few summers, too. Dad had a lot of stories about working with them on the tractor, fistfights in the barn, and snapping towels when they showered.

Great memories like these were one reason why he liked to hire high school kids to work at the clinic—sort of a way to pass along his dad's tradition. My friends Walt and Nancy and sibs Jen and Barry all worked for him at one time or another. I'm sure they have their own stories to tell.

The ol' cowboy was a favorite of my friends'.

Never Trust a Raisin

In the sun, where I could see
one afternoon at rest:
a mince pie standing over me,
who seemed in some distress.

The pie repair facility
sent out a patch technician
who inquired about the warranty
while I shifted its transmission.

The mechanic climbed and sat on top,
his finger up his nose.
We rolled the pie down to the shop
where wrenches hung in rows.

He put the pie upon the jack
and creepered underneath.
He handed me a spatula
and mumbled through his teeth:

"Butter, flour, salted egg.
The apple came unwound!
Allspice, currants, and I beg;
your nutmeg needs re-ground."

"What is suet," the apprentice asked,
"but meat byproduct ooze?
Mincemeat isn't meat, alas,
it's raisins in some booze."

The craftsman creased his toque and smacked
the apprentice with a spoon.
Said, as he pushed his creeper back,
"Be done this afternoon."

I never saw the pie again
and stiffed them for the bill.
'Twas ever only my intent
to go back to my hill.

'Cause pastry like this cost you
just a finn at Pies R Us,
and a vagrant tart should pay its own
repair cheque, thank you much.

But

a bit of wisdom carried I
away from that occasion.
Back in my sun I philosophized:
You should never trust a raisin.

The Exchange Student

Mitt Kompisgäng

some friends you'll get to know

I spent a year during high school living and studying in Sweden as an exchange student. It was an amazing experience, made more so by the people I met. If I had to go back and do it again, I would choose it every time.

An exchange student spends their whole tenure meeting people. I met hundreds that year, and I remember thinking that not one of the people that I met had known me, or anyone that I knew, prior to my flight across the Atlantic. Coming from a small town where everyone knew everyone, my seventeen-year-old world expanded very suddenly.

The Emmaboda, Sweden, Rotary Club arranged for me to stay primarily with two families, so I alternated living with the Söderströms and the Wetterholms.

The Söderströms had a big family. Inger and Sverker had a daughter named Christina and three sons named Peter, Mikael, and Joakim. Christina, who was my age, was a Rotary Club exchange student that year and went to study in the USA soon after I arrived. Peter was younger than me, and Mikael and Joakim were older.

They had grandparents in Stockholm, so we visited there several times, and the family moved from Emmaboda to Stockholm while I was traveling Europe, so I lived the last few weeks of my year there—a six-hour drive from our little town in the south of Sweden. Sverker worked with Bo Wetterholm. He and his wife, Monica, had two sons, Johan and Martin, who were close to my age but younger, and a younger daughter named Susanna.

Johan, Martin, and Peter were good "brothers" to have, that far from home. And they are still.

I made friends my age at the two schools I attended, and in the social circles that sprang up there. Ann Marie, who was called "Ami" and Monica, from Bjurbäcks School, were best friends who hung out with our gang. I met Joakim and Gustaf at Åkrahäll School. We called Joakim, "Jocke" (pronounced yo-kee) and called Gustaf "Gurra." Jocke and Gurra were part of a troupe of gymnasts who did shows at events and art festivals. They were BMOCs (if there was such a thing at Åkrahäll) and befriended me on my first day at school.

Johan went to school with Ami and Monica, who knew Jocke. Jocke, Gurra, and Johan introduced me to the Emmaboda Boy Scouts. Jocke knew Thomas, who we'll meet later, and we all rode around in Thomas' Volkswagen Beetle. And we all knew the Söderström brothers, who were famous for their parties.

It was just another small town where everyone knew everyone, and it wasn't long before I was part of the gang.

An Exchange Student in Sweden

it all might have happened in New Zealand

My path to becoming an exchange student started with meeting one from New Zealand. Hamish attended our school in Oklahoma and was a great ambassador for the program. Rotary Clubs all over the world sponsor high-school-age students by pairing with a club in another country. Our club and district in Duncan, Oklahoma, was very active in the program and had made all of the arrangements with the club that sponsored Hamish. He talked up the idea when he toured our classes, although he didn't have to work hard to convince me.

I had enjoyed traveling since I was young, and I cut the grass for the local club's district governor, so when I asked him about the program, he put in a nomination for me.

There was a short interview where they asked me about school and my grades, and I talked about my willingness to try new things. My mediocre grades must not have been a showstopper.

The committee also talked to my parents and a couple of my teachers. Teachers usually liked me but found my laziness annoying. My parents told them I was the golden child, so please send me. Send me far away. Please.

For the next step, I was invited to camp for three days with a bunch of Rotary foreign students. A bunch of horny kids staying in cabins out in southeast Oklahoma, we mingled and talked about their experiences.

I was told later that the campout was an interview itself. I was being observed to see how I got along with people and if I could stay out of trouble (they'd made the cabin arrangements co-ed on purpose). On the last day of the campout, I went before a group of three or four Rotarians and talked about language barriers, homesickness, and what I wanted from my experience.

I passed!

I was set up for a slot in New Zealand, to leave in August, but in June they called and told me there had been an awful auto accident. An American student was killed in New Zealand, and it had soured relations between the clubs, so the deal was off. I went back to my regular high school plans. In late July, I received another phone call.

They had a slot open up in Sweden, was I interested?

Write me in!

Didn't I want to consult my parents before I answered?

No, write me in!

Do you know any Swedish?

No, please just go write me in already!

Lightning Round

FAQs: Swedish edition

A whole year is a lot to cover, so I'll do a question-and-answer format, based on things that I'm frequently asked.

How long were you there? I spent a full year overseas. I left in early August of 1979 and returned exactly one year later. I wound up cutting it somewhat close—my one-year student visa ran out on the day I left.

Is it cold? The summer in Sweden is glorious. The highs are in the mid-'70s, and at mid-summer, the sun is up almost round the clock for a couple of days. It is a time to celebrate and drink aquavit late into the night. In October, it started raining, in November, it was raining and snowing at the same time, and by mid-winter, it had snowed a meter deep.

The winter is pretty harsh. It is cold enough that the dirt is frozen like concrete, and they schedule no construction that has digging involved for months at a time. And it is dark all day. I mean, midnight-dark when you arrive at school and that dark again when you leave. At school, we'd go out and sit on the snow at noon, just being quiet and facing the sun with our eyes closed, while it made its lame, just–above-the-horizon appearance for the day.

But that spring! Just amazing after a dark winter. Maybe because nature knew it had to wake up and get busy, it seemed like all in a space of two days the flowers had bloomed, the forest was green again, and the girls were all tanned and beautiful.

Are Swedes as attractive as they are said to be? Yep. Denmark, Sweden, Norway too. All amazing people. And I come from Duncan, so I know a pretty girl when I see one.

Was everyone tall and blonde? The higher percentage of blondes was noticeable, but not all were. The Scandinavian look is definitely a thing. I was 6-foot-2 and seemed about average height for my classmates, so yeah, they were tall.

What about learning Swedish? I knew no Swedish at all before I left. I ordered a cassette tape of lessons, and it sounded like *The Muppet Show*'s Swedish Chef to me.

The Emmaboda Rotary Club arranged a tutor for me, whom I met with every day for about three weeks at the local middle school. He was an art teacher there, and we spent more time discussing cultural differences than working on my Swedish. I think we assumed we'd have all the time in the year to learn Swedish, but he was fired from his job after being caught smoking pot. I was told to fend for myself.

My Swedish is very basic, and it really isn't anybody's fault but my own. I was lazy and learned enough to hop a train or buy a beer, but since it was self-taught, I was teased by my friends for speaking "like an immigrant" ("*Fan jävla turist!*"). I learned from my friends how to curse like a Swedish sailor, and I can hold a decent conversation. *Men kom ihåg att prata långsamt, tack* (But remember to speak slowly, thank you).

A girl named Anna-Lena who hung out with our group told me one night, "*Håll käften!* Do you know what dat means?" (I did, it means "shut up") "You talk English, English, English, and when you talk Swedish, it makes my head hurt."

Well, I gave up on *that* crush ...

What was your town like? I went to school in a different town than I lived in, and one of the two families I lived with moved twice, so I lived in three different towns.

Emmaboda was where I spent the most time and made the most friends, so I always think of it as "home" in Sweden. It was a community of about 10,000, in a dense forest that looked a lot like Minnesota, with a couple of major industries supporting it. One was a factory that manufactured industrial pumps. The headquarters for that company was also there, and the fathers of both my host families were executives there.

The other major industry was glass. That area of Sweden is famous for many factories that produce hand-blown crystal for dining ware and décor. I have seen Örrefors crystal from just north of Nybro for sale in Dillard's here in Oklahoma. Emmaboda also had a window-glass plant in town. Like Halliburton in Duncan, everyone you knew had a parent at Flygt (the pump company) or at one of the glass factories.

Emmaboda had the feel of a modern, small town. Everyone knew everyone, and the kids all grew up together.

My school was in Nybro, which was a slightly larger town of 13,000. It had a more European feel, with the typical town square and cobblestone streets. I'd visited Stockholm many times, and it is definitely an old-school European town. When Swedes say old, they don't mean "cowboy days" like we do, they mean *Viking* old—Storkyrkan, the oldest church in Stockholm, was consecrated in 1306.

Geographically, Sweden is roughly the size and shape of the West Coast states: California, Oregon, and Washington stacked together. But with respect to weather, think Alaska. Most of their population lives in the southern third, and the northern quarter is in the Arctic Circle.

Isn't Sweden a *socialist* country? Socialism isn't the boogeyman that we've been scared into believing it is, but Sweden isn't *really* a socialist country, either. Neither Sweden's economy nor their government fit the definition of socialist.

Economists consider it a *democratic capitalist* country. They do have an extensive government-provided social safety net that may give the impression of socialism. The reason Sweden can afford all those benefits is that their businesses are given a lot of economic freedom, so their market is productive enough to cover the expense.

Their system of free (or nearly free) health care, and higher education, is based on government contracts with for-profit companies. They pay high taxes, but most Swedes are proud to. Many consider it a patriotic duty to care about their fellow Swedes. Another reason it works is they don't let medical costs go bananas. Seventy-five cents worth of gauze costs seventy-five cents, not $300. Drugs are marked up to a reasonable profit, not ten thousand percent. Their universities aren't paying some schmuck $5 million a year just to coach a sports team, either.

Many members of the Rotary Club that sponsored my stay in Sweden were entrepreneurs. They owned and operated small businesses and factories, which seemed to be common in that area. Several of the club members invited me out to spend a day working at their businesses, and I visited some of their homes. Their standard of living appeared to be as high as that of the self-made oilmen back home.

What was school like? When I arrived for what would have been my senior year, I got the impression there had been confusion about my age. I was scheduled to go to school in Emmaboda at Bjurbäcksskolan, which is what we'd call a middle school. It soon became apparent that I had been placed in a group that was a bit young for me. When we lost the Swedish tutor, who worked at Bjurbäck, the club arranged for me to begin class in Nybro at a *gymnasieskola* (high school).

Young Swedes are expected to make a decision about continuing their education at the end of ninth grade. If you decide to go to *gymnasieskola*, you can choose from eighteen programs. Some are vocational, and some are prep for university. Some examples of the programs are sociology, building and construction, business administration, hotel and tourism, and technology.

I was placed with the *naturvetenskap* (natural sciences) second-year group. The thought was: Science was my area of interest (along with art), and they were nerdy enough that they all spoke English well. My new classmates were great, and very patient with me. I introduced myself to the school director and gave him contact information for my principal back home, who told him that all I needed to graduate was one semester of English. The Director told my principal it could be arranged.

To earn my credits, he gave me two semester-long assignments. The first was that I would substitute for the two English teachers when either called in sick. The kids take English as their main second-language classes, much like we take Spanish. Back then, you could tell how old a Swede was by their accent. You tend to try to say everything in the first accent you pick up, and before World War II Swedes took German, so older Swedes spoke with a bit of a German inflection. I think they switched to English soon after Armistice Day.

If it were the first time I was subbing with a group of students, we'd use the hour to talk about life as an American high school kid. If their regular teacher was out for longer, we'd work on the differences between King's English and American. They were taught very proper English and were always interested in slang. One odd thing I found was that if a Swede had trouble understanding me, it helped to temporarily adopt an English accent.

Side note: *The Muppet Show* was being shown on TV over there, and Swedes thought the Swedish Chef was hilarious.

My second task for English credits was to take three shelves in the school library and fill them with American books I thought someone my age would like to read. I took a class back home on American Nobel Literature winners, so I had some basis to start my purchases. I bought Steinbeck, Hemmingway, Poe, Pearl S. Buck, and Faulkner. I bought a slang dictionary, *Green Eggs and Ham*, and other classics. Before my budget ran out, I got them a subscription to *Rolling Stone*, and to *MAD* magazine.

The Director liked my work, and I got my credit, which is good because in every other class I was just useless. With no good grasp of technical Swedish, I wasn't able to do a lot of my homework, and the teachers let me slide on my good looks. The Director knew that I was expected to spend some of my time working and hanging out at the Rotary Club members' businesses, so he cut me a lot of slack. I took advantage of that more than I should have.

The Director was also in charge of another school that was in town: Riksglasskolan, the National School of Glass. He told me about it one day and asked if I was interested in spending some time there.

"You are certainly not getting much done here," he said.

My art background kicked into high gear, and I spent two weeks at the school watching, learning, and doing a little hands-on glass work. I loved it.

The Director came out one day to check on me. He told me that the school fed students to the local glassworks and asked if I would be interested in being at one. I could take the bus out to Johansfors instead of school and be an apprentice for a couple of days. Oh man, that sounded like heaven.

It was terrible!

It was 102 degrees on the shop floor and was lit by nothing but the open glass-furnace doors. It was nothing like the brightly lit, easygoing atmosphere of the glass school. There were people with jobs to do—jobs that I was screwing up with my incompetence, and they were yelling at me in a foreign language over the sound of the furnaces.

I burnt my hands on the iron glass blowing tube while running back and forth getting them hot glass, then cut myself busting waste glass off of that same tube when they were done. It was like being an apprentice in Hell. I was glad to go back to school and doubled down on trying to understand my chemistry homework.

I really did enjoy some of the jobs that I worked when I visited the Rotary Club members' businesses. One guy owned an IKEA-style furniture factory.

Another had a big plant that manufactured cans for beans and soup and the like. At the can factory, I loaded blanks into a machine that was as tall as I was, and five feet in diameter, with eight arms sticking out of a hub that rotated, doing a different operation at each stop: Roll the blank, crimp the rolled can, solder the crimp, etc. It was an amazing, noisy, gobstopper-makin' gadget.

I worked for a guy making headlamps for orienteering enthusiasts, and I worked in a paper mill. One guy had a little factory in a barn on his property with two machines, each the size of a dining room table. They molded a medical-grade plastic doohickey he held a patent for. He said that he went out a few times a week and boxed up enough to fill his orders, then took the rest of the week off. I told him that was the American Dream.

He said, "Ja. Mebbie deh Swedes invent dat dream first, you know?"

I didn't have a green card, so I couldn't be paid for my work, but getting another day out of school was good compensation. Many times, I'd go in in the morning, get a tour and a talk about the business side, then have lunch at the hotel in Nybro with the club-member/factory-owner. Then I'd spend the afternoon working on the shop floor.

Did you have spring break? Spring break at *gymnasieskola* isn't going skiing at Padre Island. You must set up a short internship and spend the two weeks working. Presumably at something related to your line of study, but they told me it could be anything.

I knew a guy in town who was a chimney sweep, and I talked him into letting me work with him. It would have been a gas, but he got sick and had to renege on his commitment. At the last minute, my host-dads set me up working at their pump factory in the Warranty Repair Shop. The shop had two guys, a foreman and a repairman, and Repairdude was going on vacation.

The Foreman took me in and showed me the routine:

You'll hear a bell,   *—DING!*

and a pump will appear on the conveyor belt.   *—A nasty, beat up pump.*

Find the model number on the plate.

Find the manual for it.   *—Over on this huge bookshelf of them.*

Turn to the fold-out exploded-view diagram,

and use it to take the pump completely apart.   *—The grody, stinky pump.*

The broken part will be obvious.   *—It was almost always the impeller.*

Type the part number into this keypad.

Use the sand-blaster cabinet to blast each part clean.   *—Man, that was fun!*

While you're doing that, you'll hear another bell,   *—DING!*

and the part you asked for will arrive on the conveyor belt.

Put it all back together.

Paint it Company Gray.

The tools are here, the hand-cleaner's there.

The Foreman walked back into his office and left me alone for a couple of days to merrily wrench and sandblast and paint.

When the third day ended, he came out and said, *"Reparerade du fem?"* (You did *five?*)

"Yeah, I guess so," I shrugged.

"Well, slow down. You're making my regular guy look bad," he said and went back to his office.

Were there school sports? There weren't organized sports sponsored by high schools or colleges like we have in the States—so, no Åkrahällskolan Aardvarks, or whatever. We had gym class and played sports that are popular there—basketball, soccer (or *fotboll* to them, and they always seemed to stick me at goalie), track etc.

I also learned a couple of sports that I'd never seen, like *innebandy* and *handboll*.

Handboll is an odd mashup of soccer and basketball. As a part of a team of seven, you dribble and pass (like you would in basketball) a small volleyball and throw it at a soccer-type goal—but you can't kick it. *Innebandy* is hockey with a rubber ball, and we had a great time running around the gym, smacking each other with sticks. I played some innebandy during the winter with friends, sort of an intramural thing. I also participated in a big area-wide open invitation track meet in the spring.

The gym teacher asked me to teach the class to play American Football, and I did my best with the limited time we had. They had a rugby ball to play with, and they figured out how to throw a good spiral pass pretty quickly.

They were used to soccer, where the players fake and dodge to avoid each other. So, it took a while for them to get the concept of running into each other to stop the ball, but once they did, goodness. They were kinda vicious.

What are Swedes like? Well, just like everybody, they have all personality types. Overall, you'll find they are quiet. It's not shyness, they are glad to meet you and eager to talk about things that interest them. But American gregariousness wears them out. Talking and laughing loudly and everything being "Just Awesome!" is not their style. Social distancing was already a thing there, long before our modern plague. Two concepts that are very Swedish will help you to know them better: *lagom* and *allemansrätt*.

Lagom means "just right." As a concept, it can also be translated as "in moderation," "only enough," or "balanced." It's not a matter of depriving yourself but more the idea that it is comforting to have just the right amount—not too little, but not too much. The proverb associated with the concept is *Lagom är bäst*, which is literally "The right amount is best," but another popular translation is "Enough is as good as a feast."

The Swedes have latched onto *lagom* because they place high value on equality, and of consensus, if it benefits all. In the workplace, they hold work/life balance dear, and the companies they work for promote it because their execs hold it dear, also. I mentioned earlier that they are not economic socialists. Nevertheless, *lagom* can be seen as refuting consumerism and greed and is a matter of national pride.

Allemansrätt means "freedom to roam." In Sweden, you have the right to traverse any land. It has been written into law, and of course, there are some exceptions: You can't stomp across private gardens or farmland under cultivation or go within seventy meters of dwellings if you aren't invited. You can fish any lake or beach, you can camp on any land, and you can pick blueberries and *lingon* wherever you find them.

The other side of this concept is that they are very respectful of others' property. A national slogan is "Don't disturb, don't destroy." *Allemansrätten* is a gift they are determined to preserve.

I've mentioned a couple of examples of "national pride," and most Swedes will tell you they aren't patriotic. But that's ridiculous. They are very proud of their country and of their fellow Swedes. Maybe the notion of patriotism goes against their tradition of modesty. Folks back home puff out their chest and declare "Ahm a *PATRIOT!*", as though only a certain political party from a certain country could be. I've learned that just about everyone everywhere is.

Did you have a girlfriend? Emmaboda was a small town, and as "The American Kid" everybody knew me after a couple of months—or had at least heard of me. It wasn't hard to get a girl to talk to me or hang out at the disco, but most of it was fleeting, superficial. I was a curiosity, and once they had checked me out, they moved on. I can't say that I had a *girlfriend* in Sweden, but I did have some fun.

Were there rules for exchange students? Of course, as a guest in someone else's home, you want to follow their household rules. In addition, we were given a quick class in common Swedish laws and customs at a clinic we attended at the beginning of the year. Two things forbidden of Rotary Exchange Students at the time: Driving a car and drinking.

I attended an overnight party that my class threw and got horribly sick-drunk. When I came back the next day, it was obvious what had happened. I felt, and smelled, terrible. I was told to go sleep it off and we'd discuss it that evening. I awoke to find my host family at the table with officials from the club. They had discussed sending me home but decided to give me the benefit.

Bo (my host dad) said, "Besides, you look like you may have been taught a lesson already."

From the references to beer or a nip of aquavit in some of my other stories, I obviously didn't learn the *desired* lesson, but I *did* learn to be a little more discreet.

The different families that I stayed with differed slightly in their approach to the rules. I think it partly concerned the age of their own kids, and what they'd had to deal with. In one family, I was suddenly their "oldest" kid. In another, I was a fifth kid, the second youngest. By the time parents have seen that many kids get in and out of trouble they can get a little glazed.

One night, as I left for a party where there was sure to be drinking, Inger (mother to the larger, older group of kids) thought about her translation for a moment then said, "Just don't come home as someone I don't know."

Were you lonely or homesick? Once in a while. A year is a long time. Ninety-nine percent of my time was exciting and fun. I was surrounded by people who wanted my experience to be positive. It's amazing that I wound up with such a good support-net of people I had never met before August of that year.

I made friends with my "siblings," and I keep up with them on Facebook. It wasn't just the adults of the families who put up with me. My "brothers" in the host families, Peter and Joakim Söderström, Johan and Martin Wetterholm were great friends to have. They helped me make friends, told me what *not* to say, and played wingman on occasion.

But you get tired. Not being fluent in the language wears you out. It can make homework hard-to-impossible. Many spoke English, and many wanted to help, though. Being a guest in someone else's home for an entire year is tricky. They tell you to make yourself at home, but you want to be a courteous boarder, also—in conflict with my state as a moody teenager.

The darkness of Swedish winters can get anybody down. What a good idea it was to have us students end our year abroad during the amazing weather of summer.

Weird-danged food could be fun in the right frame of mind, but you do daydream about a decent hamburger after a few months.

What is their food like? As with most countries, one could spend an entire chapter writing about just their food. We ate a lot of normal things that I recognized: Roast beef, chicken, green beans, and pea soup, but the list of things I'd never seen in Oklahoma is long. I'll take it one meal at a time.

For breakfast, we would have an open-faced sandwich on crisp bread. You can buy Wasa bread in Oklahoma. It's not so much *crisp* as it is *crunchy*. We'd put some butter on it, and cheese. Their everyday cheese was *always* good. Like the stuff we pay out the nose for now at Whole Foods.

We'd top that with boiled egg slices, cucumber, or caviar. We'd mix and match. Their *"kaviar"* comes in a toothpaste-type tube and isn't expensive. It's usually smoke-flavored, and one kind I liked was swirled with cream cheese. Sometimes we'd have granola-type cereal, but instead of milk, they put plain yogurt or *filmjölk* on it. *Filmjölk* is pasteurized sour milk. It is an acquired taste, but I could get with it, when we had strawberries and a lot of sugar.

We ate lunch in the cafeteria at school and had fish of some kind a couple of times a week. There was a pot of boiled new potatoes at the end of the food line every day. We had Swedish meatballs occasionally—they are as ubiquitous as you'd think. One thing they served too many times for my taste: *rotmos*. It is boiled, mashed rutabaga. If you boiled cabbage, carrots, and potatoes and mashed it up together, you'd get a similar meal. They ate it with sausage on the side and spicy mustard. Luckily, the mustard was hot enough it was all you tasted. A lot of Swedes like it. *Yeesh.*

A sandwich of boiled egg slices, lettuce, tomato, and cucumber piled high with boiled shrimp is a *räksmörgås*. I had a friend whose mum used to make us smoked horse sandwiches for lunch. Sliced thin with mustard and cheese like a ham sandwich, they were pretty darned good.

Dinner was often something familiar. A baked chicken or salmon, mashed potatoes, and asparagus. Occasionally, one of my families had *blodpudding*, (called black pudding in England), which is a sort of blood sausage they fried and served with *lingon* on the side. Make mine well done, please.

The famous Swedish *smörgåsbord* is an opulent holiday table set with cold cuts and sandwich fixings. It translates figuratively to "sandwich table," but "*smörgås*" (sandwich) is literally "butter-goose." Back in the days when you churned butter, the first blobs to pop up looked like little geese. An impatient sandwich maker would take the first "butter goose" and spread it on his sandwich.

I had moose at one fancy dinner, which was served with gravy, like roast beef. *Lingon* jam is the Swedish ketchup. It is tart, like cranberries, and very versatile. It works just as well with meat or on toast. Try it with your meatballs next time you're eat at IKEA.

Speaking of fancy dinners, many begin with a toast, and tradition holds that you toast with aquavit, a distilled spirit flavored with herbs. The flavor is somewhat like licorice, and every Scandinavian country has its famous brand: Linie in Norway, Aalborg in Denmark, and O.P. Anderson in Sweden.

The Swedes do like their licorice. A favorite candy there, *saltlakrits*, is salted licorice and kind of a "shock" candy like Sour Patch Gummies are here. They are so salty they make your jaw lock!

Their chocolate is very good, and their ice cream is light and sweet. One candy you won't find there? Swedish Fish. Nope, none. The gummies that are closest are shaped like cars (Bilar), and there are not many red ones in a bag.

Strawberry Yoplait always reminds me of riding the train home from school. A little store next to the station sold it in a liter carton. I'd buy one and drink the whole thing, right out of the carton on the walk home.

Another favorite snack was Swedish pancakes, which we made for *"fika."* The English are famous for teatime, and the Swedes for *fika*. *Fika* is a coffee (or tea) break they traditionally have at three o'clock in the afternoon. They like their coffee *very* strong and have cakes or sweets with it. The opportunity to stop for a few minutes in the afternoon and let everything go while they talk with a friend, is as much a part of their culture as anything else you can know about them.

Food at holidays and special occasions could get weird. Americans from the states that Swedes and Norwegians settled in know about *Lutefisk*: Whitefish that has been dried-out to jerky using lye, and then reconstituted by boiling it. It makes a horrid, soap-flavored, gelatinous fish pudding. One lady I knew fixed it as a comfort food. A dingdong from Wisconsin tried to tell me that lutefisk is a "Swedish delicacy", but not many swedes that I knew ate, or liked it.

One infamous Swedish "treat" is *surströmming*. Herring is canned, and then allowed to ferment for at least six months. Canned, rotten fish. I tried a small bite at a holiday party, then tried to make sure they couldn't find me to ask what I thought.*

Now *pickled* herring, I can endorse. It took a while, but I became a fan, especially of the type made with onions (*löksill*). Pickled herring is an essential component of a *smörgåsbord*. Swedes also have a season for, and parties dedicated to, crawdads. And you thought it was only a Cajun food.

There wasn't anywhere to get a good burger back then. Odd to think, from an American point of view, where there's a burger joint on every street corner. I wowed my host family by cooking a couple of things that weren't common there yet. I made them a big pot of Tex-Mex chili, and they talked about it for a month. One of their favorite of my gifts to them was the industrial sized bottle of chili powder that Mom shipped over for that pot of beans. We also made banana splits one fine evening, to great reviews.

I returned to Emmaboda a few years ago with my wife, Kelly, and we made a point of visiting a grocery store so I could compare my memory to what is available there today. We saw some "American" items that would not have been there back in 1979. Taco shells, ground beef, and barbeque sauce are

---

* *Another Scandinavian "food" that must have been based on a bar bet is Hákarl. Meat from the Greenland Shark is so full of uric acid that it is poisonous, so of course Icelanders eat it anyway. They prepare it by putting the shark in a hole in the ground until it ferments, then they dry it until it has a texture kind of like hard cheese. That gets rid of the toxic effect of the uric acid, but not the taste of it. Anthony Bourdain described Hákarl as "the single worst, most disgusting and terrible tasting thing" he had ever put in his mouth. My son-in-law Thomas and I tried it recently—he's a go-getter and adventurous soul, so I figured if anyone was up for it, he was. Then, we washed it down with shots of Brennivín, which is a distilled drink that Icelanders nicknamed "Black Death." The shark left a taste in my mouth like I'd eaten a dirty diaper, then thrown up.*

now easy to find. Burger joints have also become a lot more common. It seemed to us that the cost of living was high for most things, but that groceries were relatively cheap. Inexpensive food and healthcare—basic rights, maybe.

As for what Swedish food is available *here*, it can be hit-and-miss. Wasa bread and *lingonberry* jam are available in most stores. Rutabagas are readily available, but I ain't gonna mash one!

There are specialty shops in a few American cities where you can find other items. Some IKEAs have better grocery stores than others do, and some refrigerated or frozen items can be bought there, like meatballs or a tube of *kaviar*. The scarcity makes my favorites taste better when I find them.

Were you sad to "lose" your senior year of high school? People put a lot of stock in the ceremony of graduating and the traditions of cap-and-gown. I would like to have spent more time with my good friends, and there are a few friendships back home that would have been nice to develop further. Not having experienced my senior year, I guess I don't know what I missed.

Things like weddings and graduations and such produce wonderful memories, but the highly planned moments in life are rarely as "perfect" as we'd like them to be. I feel like unplanned, spontaneous times come closest to perfection, and maybe I sensed that living five thousand miles from home would provide opportunities for a lot of those.

In a letter that my mom sent at the beginning of my stay she wrote, "Have fun, and try everything that your conscience will allow."

It was sage advice, and I had a great experience. I'd recommend it to any kid who is interested.

Tristesse Chapeau

Disillusion reinforced:

a ten-gallon-hat

only holds three quarts.

A Bloom of Moon Jellies

and a visit to a nude beach

The fall I was in Sweden, my friend Kalle invited me to go to his family's *stuga** at Torekov, a resort-town on the West Coast near Denmark. The West Coast of Sweden is on the North Sea, and it's rocky and wild. The Swedes have called those waters the Skagerrak since Viking times. Gnarly!

There is an island a mile-and-a-half off the coast called Hallands Väderö, and Kalle and I took a ferry across and explored for a day. We derped around, played skee-ball at the arcade, and had ice cream for lunch.

In the afternoon, Kalle said, "Oh, I know! Come with me, but be quiet as we go."

We crashed through about twenty yards of bushes and trees, before I saw that a clearing was coming up. We cleared the thicket and popped out onto a very populated nude beach. Swedes are normally very blasé about nudity, but it was obvious that we were not invited to this particular party (we were laughing our butts off), and we were quickly chased away.

We ran along the beach until we came to a peninsula pointing to a very small island (maybe fifty feet across) that was only a short swim away. The water was very clear and quite deep in the strait. I don't really like deep water. Seeing *Jaws* spooked me for good when it comes to the size of things that could come up from down there. But I could see most of the bottom, so I was talked into swimming over. The current was strong enough through the gap we almost missed the island.

We walked the perimeter of the tiny *skär*, threw a rock at a seagull, and saw there were anemones and other creatures living a few feet under the surface. It was very coral-reef-colorful on the seaside edges. While we were goofing off, a giant swarm of moon jellyfish (a "bloom") had been traveling on the current around the coast of the bigger island and had filtered its way through the gap between the peninsula and the rock we were standing on.

Now, when I say *swarm*, it is an attempt to convey just how big it was. It engulfed the smaller island and stretched back in the direction they were coming from (the same direction *we* came from) for as far as we could see. We might be there for a long while if we tried to wait it out. Kalle said that moon

---

* *A "stuga" is a little cabin in the woods with few modern appointments. Many have been passed down several generations.*

jellies don't sting, and that as far as he could tell, there wasn't anything else in there among them. We decided to just swim through them.*

They were thick!

The current was squeezing the swarm through the small strait and concentrated them to where there was almost no water between them. It was like swimming through a ball pit—if the balls were made of Jell-O blobs. Jell-O that hasn't quite set up yet. Or, the outside layer of each had set up, but the inside was still squishy. What would it be like to swim in a bowl of chowder?

I looked down into the water while I was swimming and could see jellies all the way down to the bottom. They varied in size from as small as a bottle cap to as big as a dinner plate, but most of ours were about eight inches across. We started as far on the up-current side as we could and were still carried way down the beach with the swarm.

We came up out of the water laughing, as some of them had stuck to us. Kalle had one on his head like a beret. It was a big one and took two hands to hold. Before I could get it into the sea, it broke under its own weight.

Squish. Splat!

They hadn't left a slime or film on us, but we still felt like rinsing off when we found a place farther down the beach.

After a late dinner with his parents, we went down to the shore by his family's cabin and walked out on a jetty. He wanted to get back in the water and swim. After eleven o'clock at night. After *dark*. In the deep dark North Sea. Where Jaws lived. Now don't get me wrong, the jellyfish thing was kind of fun, but there was no way I was getting back in the water.

In fact, I was done with swimming until next summer.

---

* *The Swedes call moon jellies öronmanet, which translates literally to "the-ear-man." Wikipedia says it's because the four rings in their center look like ears. I've also been told since then that all jellyfish have a sting, and that the ones we swam through may have been so mild that we didn't perceive it.*

Adventures in Thomas' VW

herr Porsche's durable carriage

After a few weeks at Bjurbäcksskolan, I was moved to a group a little more my age at Åkrähall. One problem that came up when I switched to attending school in another town was that it was thirty kilometers (about twenty miles) away, and I had no transportation. The Söderström brothers had a lot of connections and talked their friend Thomas into giving me a ride every day. Thomas owned a late-1960s Volkswagen—a little white go-buggy that he and his friend Pontus drove back and forth to Åkrahällskolan.

Most of the time I rode in the back of the bug. The legroom was dismal, so I often sat sideways with my legs extended across the bench seat, or sometimes laid on my back with my legs bent, knees-up.

One fine morning, early in the snow season, I was laying down for the trip with my eyes closed listening to Thomas and Pont crack jokes. I knew the turns in the road and could usually tell where we were. There is a long curve as you approach Nybro, the town our school is in, and the outside bank of that curve was piled high with snow that had been plowed. As we started the curve, I felt us begin to slip, and when I looked up, we were traveling sideways in a long slow slide through the curve.

"Whohhhhh!" is a universal expression, and all three of us gawked wide-eyed through the passenger side windows as the snowbank loomed. We slowed down enough that when we hit, it was fairly gentle, but the tires on that side slipped off the edge of the pavement and tipped the balance.

With a long *cruuuuuuunch*, we rolled slowly over into the snow—first on our side, then over onto the roof. It was a slow enough roll that we just sort of crawled out of our seats and into the roof. We all piled out of the door on the driver's side and stood laughing at the imprint the VW left in the snow as it rolled. It was an easy task to push it back upright and, true to the Beetle's reputation, a little coaxing started it up and off we went.

A group of us, including my friend Jocke (he knew everybody), loaded up in the bug and went ice fishing in the early spring. The lake was melting and had four or five inches of water on it at the edges, and almost none in the middle. We all had rubber boots or waders, and we set up some spring-loaded gizmos that reeled in the fish when they bit. It also fired a .22 blank, so we knew which one had a fish.

The water on top was heavier than the eight or ten inches of ice below it, so when we cut a hole, the water drained down through. It swirled like a bathtub drain, and after a couple of hours, each hole had a blob of slimy grey foam turning above it. They explained that the foam was from a very thin layer of pollution on the surface of the lake. They blamed it on Russian industry, but I'd bet money it was from the iron-smelter at the local pump factory.

Jocke and I walked out to the middle of the lake and fished with a lure, bobbing it at the right depth. He chopped a rectangle halfway through the ice to form a sort of tank that filled with water from the top. We were catching fish that he called *mört*, and he tossed them into this holding tank. Over time, each fish began to swim on its side, and I asked if they were dying.

"Nay, watch!" he said.

Eventually they all were swimming upside down but struggling to do so. Jocke said that he thought it was because they were so used to the ice being above them, they had to swim upside down for their world to make sense. Thomas called it a metaphor for modern politics.

We drank a liter of Jägermeister that day (ostensibly to keep warm) by sipping it out of the bottle. The cold of the water I had been standing in, combined with the Jäger and lack of legroom on the way home, made my legs too numb to walk on when I arrived. They helped stand me up and I wobbled inside.

Thomas' girlfriend, Madeleine, was a cute apple-cheeked blonde who wore her hair in Heidi-braids and hung out with us often. On the afternoon we met, Thomas asked me if it was okay to detour by her house on our way home from school. I didn't mind and stretched out in the VW's back seat. The warm sun made me sleepy, so I had my eyes closed when we stopped. She sat down in the front and asked who I was, apparently thinking I was asleep back there. Thomas answered before I could, so I just rolled with the "sleeping" thing.

Maddi asked Thomas about me in Swedish, and her questions went from general: "Where is he from?" "How does he like Sweden?" to a little more personal, "Does he have a girlfriend here?" It was all I could do not to laugh, and Thomas shot me a glance and a quick smile.

She kept up the questions, veering off into downright embarrassing.

"American, right? Is he an asshole?"

Right after that question (Thomas told her no, I wasn't *too* much of an asshole), she finally thought to ask if I spoke Swedish.

I answered this one from the back seat, *"Ja."*

Maddi whipped her head around toward me and turned bright red with embarrassment. Thomas and I laughed our heads off, and I forgave her. It was a good way to make friends.

I don't know why she stuck with Thomas. He was a cad. One night a group of us was at the local bar, and he asked me if I would walk her home. His side chick had showed up, and he wanted to go home with *her*. This happened a couple of times, and I was always happy to step in. I don't know why she put up with him. She could have done much better.

Me, for instance.

Krimminy

Jiminy Bimini zibbety zop

Cow walked over and left a plop

Spoon and a fork at the rutabaga shop

Wiggle worm puddle and the rain don't stop

A Boy Named Julius

and Yoo–Deh

I was told that I am named for a friend of my parents, a Jody who was a pre-med student at Kansas State. He became a famous doctor and helped develop an artificial heart. I'm not a shortened Joseph, just plain Jody. I've heard all of the military chants about "Jody" and yes, it was me who stole your girl.

Jody is spelled in a way that is puzzling for Swedes. The letters don't make sense to them in that combination. The closest easy pronunciation is "Yoo – Deh" which I wasn't wild about, but when they are calling supper, you roll with it. I once asked how to spell it phonetically in Swedish to get it said correctly and we worked it out to be "Djådi."

The Söderström family's great aunt had been employed for years as a nanny in England, and as such, she had a very proper English accent with only a hint of Swede. She came to stay for a week and heard the family call me Yoo-Deh. With ears trained for English, she assumed they were trying to say "Julie," and they were shortening "Julius." So, she called me Julius all week.

I thought it sounded cool, so I never bothered to correct her.

I Met a Møøse Once

no realli!

The Scout troop in Emmaboda had a small campsite they maintained out in the woods a few miles west of town. It had a lean-to that was about six-by-eight feet in a small clearing with a campfire pit. One weekend in the dead of winter, my friends Jocke, Pigge, Gustaf, and I decided we would go out in the snow and stay overnight.

It was a typical Swedish winter—supremely cold, and it had snowed about a meter (three feet), so the snow was waist-deep out in the woods and piled up into mountains next to the parking lots in town. We planned to follow the railroad tracks a good bit of the way out to the campsite, because that was the only path in the deep woods that was clear enough to hike on. We met at the train station and headed out.

After we hiked about forty-five minutes, I began to notice that Jocke was checking his watch. Not saying anything, just checking his watch, walking along a little bit, looking over his shoulder, checking his watch again.

We walked and spoke our mix of Swedish and English we called Swenglish, and about as suddenly as I noticed that the ground was shaking, Jocke shoved me off the tracks into the snowpack.

The train he had been expecting suddenly roared around the bend through our little area and then disappeared again up ahead of us around another bend, leaving the scene just as quiet as it was before.

A couple of things conspire to make Swedish trains very stealthy.

One is that they are electric, so they make no sound except track noise. There is a video on YouTube taken by a Swedish conductor from inside of his cab, of him and the engineer creeping up on two people walking along the tracks. A little bit of discussion, then they hoot the horn—and the two walkers just about jump out of their skin. That's how quiet the trains themselves are. Two is that the tracks snake through the woods with a lot of curves, so there aren't many sections of track where you can see far enough to get a good warning.

I wish he had told me that. Being shoved off into the fresh snow was like falling into a ball pit and I made a nice, neat, cartoon snow-angel-hole a couple of feet deep. The other guys had jumped off the tracks also, so we dug ourselves out, slapped the snow off our pants, cleared it out of our noses and ears, then continued on.

After another mile or so of that wonderful silence that only snowy woods have, I decided that I needed to pee. I stepped off into the snow and high-stepped a little ways over into the trees to where I thought I was somewhere where they couldn't see me. I don't know, I must have been looking at my feet, being careful where I was stepping. I sure didn't realize what I'd walked into.

I was standing there taking care of business when above and behind me I heard this I heard a large, low

SNORT

The back of my head was suddenly warm, and what I was doing just stopped in mid-stream. I stood there for a second holding my breath (and my johnson) then turned around with my face inches from the nose of a HUGE female moose!

I must have startled her when I turned around, because—*POOM*—she jumped like a scared cat, straight up into the air, hooves above my head, and then thundered off in a giant cloud of snow.

I stood there stunned, and then heard snickers that turned into giggles that burst into laughter up on the railroad tracks. They were almost crying. I was pretty mad and trying to calm down enough to finish what I went to do, while the boys he-hawed. I turned my back to the tracks, and we yelled back and forth.

"Well, yu are locky! She went de oder way, and not over da top off yu. Yu *could* be smashed."

"YOU COULD HAVE SAID SOMETHING!"

"Well, we yust want to see what yu going to do."

The campsite was white-blanketed beautiful. The lean-to seemed ancient and had a peat roof that grows moss on it in the spring (forty years later, I'll bet it's still there). The rest of the campout was uneventful, but cold.

When I say cold, I mean Sweden-in-the-winter, land-of-permafrost cold, which is never above freezing and often below zero—there were many times when I was waiting at the bus stop to go to school that the snot would freeze in my nose.

The peat roof was there to keep the lean-to cool in the summer but wasn't up to the task of keeping us warm that night. The four of us zipped two sleeping bags together into one big sleeping bag, and all slept in that one sack. The Swedes advised me that the warmest way to sleep in this Arctic-rated down bag was to strip down to our skivvies so that we would warm each other.

Was it warm enough? Only barely.

Fred Flintstone Meets Gene Simmons

bikers vs. punks

Emmaboda, Sweden is a smallish town of about ten thousand, but it was home to the headquarters of an international company back when I lived there, so it also had a couple of decent hotels. One hotel had a pizza pub and several small bars that were all interconnected. There was a disco, a little casino, and a beer bar that had bands sometimes. They also had a separate room for kids sixteen-to-eighteen, with a DJ. They called the whole thing "Bodega." The place drew patrons from all over the area and it was always hopping.

One night after a beer or two in Bodega I ran into (physically—he gave me the "looking for trouble" shoulder bump) a guy with a beard, stompy-boots, and a leather jacket. He was a lot stouter than I was—I was six foot two, but only 140 pounds at the time. He said something nasty in blurry Swedish, and when he got a few feet past me, I said, "Asshole," in English (loud enough for him to hear, as it turns out).

He whipped around and came back with *"Va' saaa du?"* (What'd you say?)

I smiled and said, *"Förlåt, ursäkta"* (Sorry, excuse me). Then after he turned around again I said, "Jackass!"

So, he whipped around and lunged at me.

Jocke, who was close by and was a well-built gymnast, put himself between the two of us, facing me, and said, "Yu must stope dis game, he next will hurt yu." Then, he turned and leaned into the guy, who left us alone.

Later, when I asked about the jackass, I was told, "Well he is *Raggare*. 'Tough-guy.' He thinks he is a biker."

In the United States, a town of ten thousand would have quite a few restaurants, at the least some fast-food places, but the tax structure in Sweden makes it difficult to run a restaurant unless you're paying for a hotel also. So, there were only two restaurants in town.

Filling the gap were three or four *gatukökar* (street kitchens). These were newsstands that sold magazines, smokes, and candy and had a little grill. Seems like they all made only one thing—a paper boat that held two plain scoops of mashed potatoes and two funky sausages, all of it covered with really hot mustard. A bizarre, meat-banana-split. But man, it made great drunk-food for the walk home from the bar.

Weeks after my brush with Mr. Biker, a few of us were standing at a street kitchen and heard the mosquito-buzz of a couple of mopeds coming down the road. Two guys pulled up, stomped down their kickstands, and got off these little scooters in full chains-and-leather biker regalia.

One of them was my buddy Mr. Biker.

My friends shushed my giggles and reminded me that though they look silly, they can still be quite violent. We started referring to them as Emmaboda's two-man biker gang. That he and his short, blonde sidekick reminded me of Fred Flintstone and Barney Rubble did nothing to help me take them seriously.

I've always liked Halloween, but the Swedes didn't really celebrate it back then. They did customarily have costume parties in February, and when I was invited to one in Värnamo, it gave me a project.

I whiled away the dark winter days working up a Gene Simmons Kiss costume. It had bat wings and platform boots, chains, and everything. In the time I had, the costume turned out okay, but when I heard there would be a second party later at Bodega I took the opportunity to improve the look of the boots and buy better makeup. I molded Gene's dragon boots on top of bases I had special-made at the clog factory with six layers of platform added. They turned out to be very impressive but weighed a ton.

The party night arrived and a bunch of us went down to Bodega. Jocke went as The Hunchback of Notre Dame, friends Ami and Monica dressed as harem girls (Oh. My. Gawd.), and I clomped down in my dragon boots and kabuki makeup. It was great fun.

The place was packed, and some of the costumes were hilarious. My favorite was a group of three girls in tuxedos, swim fins, and paper-cone beaks who were penguins. I was having a good night. I was getting a lot of attention because in the boots, I was a foot taller than everyone else in the room, and I was already semi-famous as "The American."

I made my way upstairs to the pizza place to look for Jocke and ran smack into Fred Flintstone (aka Mr. Biker). He looked me up and down and then started poking my chest.

Poke-poke, "*Vi har trettio, hur många du?*" Poke-poke-poke, "*Vi har trettio, hur många du?*" Poke.

What the hell was he going on about?

"We have thirty guys. How many are you?"

His friend Barney was over there half-heartedly whamming an empty bottle against the edge of the bar as if he'd been told he should break it so he could be ready to shank somebody. Now why I thought I could sort the situation out by talking English at him, I don't know.

"Well now, hey there, feller, I think we could—"

WHAM! The world exploded.

Fred Flintstone Vespa Scooter Biker had become tired of me not taking him seriously and pounded me in the side of the head, knocking me straight out.

A roar in my ears like radio static woke me up. My head HURT, and I realized that I had fallen backward onto a table full of guys. I was pushed back upright onto my boots and saw Jocke and Gustaf grab the guy and hustle him out the front door with his fists swinging.

Gustaf hollered, "Fix your makeup and head downstairs, the costume contest has already started!" (Well, he hollered it in Swedish, anyway).

A quick note: Evidently, in late-'70s Stockholm it was common for biker-types to have gang fights with punk-rocker gangs. This was an offshoot of the violent reaction that Rockabillies had to the Punks in London. When I told the story the next day, the best we could figure was Fred and Barney had mistaken Gene Simmons for a Punk Rocker, and decided they'd start themselves a rumble right there in Emmaboda, just like they do in the big town. Where he thought they'd find 28 other bikers to help take me on was left undetermined, but I was flattered by his estimate.

The costume contest at Bodega was set up where people would yell out nominations so the audience could then pick between the three best. Up on the stage they already had a man dressed as a baby and a girl dressed as a Christmas tree (ornaments and all), and as I came down the stairs the crowd started chanting "Yoo – deh, Yoo – deh."

Gene Simmons was a hit!

After several rounds, the applause-o-meter determined that I had the best costume, and they handed me and my throbbin' noggin a check for three hundred Kronor (about seventy-five bucks)—not a bad payout for my first professional fight.

Although I really thought the penguins flapping around in their swim fins were better.

Hotel Amigo and its Bodega bar

Drosophila

Aviator navigator aggravator fly

Buzz around your nogginwig

without a reason why

Here's a small confession

for you, from I

I would like that pesky little sumbich to die

I May Have Met a Forest Sprite

or it might have just been a frog

The Wetterholms' grandparents had a *stuga** a couple of hours north, in the forest east of Jönköping. The weather was finally getting warmer, so we decided to drive out there to stay for a rainy spring weekend.

I'm told that many *stugas* date to the nineteenth century, built by former soldiers to live out their retirement in peace. They traditionally don't have electricity or plumbing—many have outhouses—and I visited one that had only a fireplace for cooking. Most have hardwood floors, and they are one of the few places where you aren't expected to take off your shoes when you enter. The lack of modernity inside a *stuga* is partly due to the expectation that you will spend a lot of your visit outside. The Swedes spend a long, dark winter inside and love to get outdoors for the few short summer months.

A diminutive soldier must have built the Wetterholms' *stuga*, as I was unable to completely stand up in any of the rooms but one. The rain stopped as we arrived, so we decided to go into the woods and pick chanterelles, wavy yellow mushrooms, to brown in butter for lunch.

The springtime forest in Sweden is fairy-tale pretty. You can find apples and mushrooms and strawberries, and you can crouch in one spot and pick enough blueberries to make a pie. We foraged all we needed to make a lunch, and as we walked back, we came across a small clearing full of three- or four-foot diameter boulders. Everything was completely carpeted with fuzzy green moss. One egg-shaped Boulder that was about waist-tall was directly under an elbow in an ancient tree's branch. Rainwater dripped from the elbow for years (Decades? Centuries? Who knows? One thing about the deep forest, it gives you the feeling that, for the millennia it has been there, you are the only human to ever have wandered through. And that when you leave, it will retain no memory of your visit.)

Water dripping on the rock had worn a bare spot through its moss and wore a little bowl into the granite. I was so fascinated with what I saw that I told Bo and Monica to go on. I knew the way back.

The top of the rock was its own little ecosystem—a gnome-shire scene with a perfectly round pond no bigger than a tea saucer, with a granite bottom and a green mossy shore all around. Little ferny plants sprouted along one edge, and a red-capped mushroom about an inch-and-a-half in diameter

---

* *little cabin in the woods*

grew on the opposite side. The rain that dripped into the center of the little pond three or four times a minute (*blip!*) was the only sound.

A tiny frog peeked out from under the mushroom, looked at me, and then paused, silently sizing me up. I must have seemed to be no threat. The froggy hopped in and swam around in the pond for a lap or two then crawled out and stretched one leg. I sat on another soft-mossy rock for a full half hour, not wanting to leave that little world.

Of course, the forests in Sweden are known to have elves and sprites (*älvor*) and every sort of forest gnome. That's where they come from. *Tomte* figurines were in every Christmas shop in the 2020s. (They're the little old men with long beards and pointed red caps.) If you treat them with respect, they'll help you keep an orderly farm, and look after the horse during the long winter night. However, you'd better leave a bowl of *julgröt* (Christmas porridge) on Christmas Eve for your *tomte*, or he might play pranks on you.

Swedes call the little red mushroom that I saw *Röd flugsvamp*. They are *Amanita muscaria* and are *not* the ones we picked for lunch. *Amanitas* are famously poisonous.

So, let us segue to a little mushroom history: A thousand years ago, Vikings swished amanitas around in their mead, so they could hallucinate while they got drunk—that is, if you didn't overdo the mushroom part and die. Waking up with a horrible hangover, but still hallucinating, put them in a *foul* mood, and well, they were Vikings, after all. Smashing and destroying everything in their path from an LSD hangover while still in their pajamas is where the word *berserk* comes from. In Swedish, it's *"bärsärk."* *Bär* means wear, and a *särk* is a nightgown.

Just have some tomato juice and settle down, willya?

What a Knucklehead

*the true and painful story of how I friend-zoned
a Swedish blonde*

I had a little bit of a crush on Monica, but I don't think she was ever interested in me. I didn't let that deter me and chased her for a while anyway. She was a blonde Swedish teenager and every bit as attractive as that description alone would suggest. She spent a lot of time that year with her good friend Ami, so I showed up at Ami's house when I thought Monica might be there.

I think Ami guessed that I liked Monica, because she called me up many times to invite me to go to a party or to go out dancing with them. There was a time or two when Ami called and I came over, but Monica didn't show up. Ami had made strawberry crepes, though, so I stayed, and we sat by the fire and talked and talked. Her parents worked late, so we always had a lot of time alone when that happened.

I started enjoying our talks, and after a while I was going over just to chat with her—Monica or no Monica. Her English was great, and while I was at her school, she'd come find me to help me with my Swedish. She had an intelligent twinkle in her blue eyes, and she held my gaze as we sat on her couch and talked about life, girlfriends, love, and loneliness, there in the dark—seems like it was always dark that winter.

Boy, her crepes were great, what a friend.

Have you figured this out, are you getting it? Because I sure as hell wasn't. What a knucklehead.

I spent a few days back in Emmaboda saying goodbye to friends—Jocke, Gustaf, the Wetterholms—after a month of seeing Europe. I owed them all a lot more than I could say in a day or two. I attended a wedding party, which was a good place to make the rounds. I found out that Ami wasn't around though—I think they said she was on holiday with her family. I left a note in her mailbox and called it a day.

While I had been vagabonding, the Söderströms had finalized their long-planned move to Stockholm. They were expecting me up there, so I said my goodbyes and I loaded up for the six-hour ride north. I spent a week in the big town before I realized that I had a problem—my round-trip ticket back to Oklahoma was no longer valid. The airline had dropped that route. In addition, my visa would expire very soon!

I had to hustle, and both the Söderström and Wetterholm families helped me renegotiate a flight back. We got it fixed (kudos to Scandinavian Airlines System for their help). I packed my trunk and headed to Arlanda airport to end my year as an exchange student and get back home to the USA.

Sitting alone with my carry-on, waiting to board, I looked up and saw a familiar and pretty face. There at the gate, having ridden six hours by train just to say goodbye, was Ami. She was crying. We said our goodbyes and hugged, then she turned to go ride six hours back home.

As I walked down the ramp to the plane, the lightbulb finally came on in that dark, dim noggin of mine.

I went home, I went to school, and corresponded with my Swedes for a while. Johan and Jocke were exchange students in the U.S. themselves, and came to visit Oklahoma during my college days. When I left college, I went into a long selfish period and let a lot of relationships slide. Ami is just one example of the great friends who I should have done better by. I owed my Swedes much more than that, and wish I'd done better. I wouldn't change anything about who I am now, but I might change a couple of things about the way I got here.

Monica and I are Facebook friends now. Johan and Martin, and several other of my classmates are also. I haven't found Ami again, but that's okay, I suppose. When Kelly and I visited a couple of years ago, my friends were very good to us. It's amazing that after all these years, they allowed me to pick back up where we left off and welcomed us so warmly.

I'm still in debt.

Black Dog Folklore

a hound in the churchyard

An interesting bit of North European folklore is the old belief that the first person buried in a cemetery *stays there*. The spirit doesn't cross over, but is fated to remain at the graveyard to help other spirits move on, and protect the Transitioning Dead from evil.

Naturally people wanted to avoid this fate for themselves or their loved ones, so before a newly-built church interred the first of the congregation in their cemetary, the elders would bury some poor hound. It would return in the form of a big black dog who would protect and guide the newly dead, and sometimes the living also, from evil spirits.

These were called Church Grims.

Vagabonds in Europe

Tågluffa with Jerry

planning to have no particular plan

When I arrived in Sweden in early August to begin my time as an exchange student, I spent a few days settling in and getting to know my first host family, the Söderströms. Then, I headed west to the small town of Grimslöv, where all of the Rotary Club exchange students met and stayed for a week or so. We bunked at a school that was on summer break and took the opportunity to build a support network among our fellow American kids while we learned rudimentary Swedish and a little Swedish culture, during the day. And at night, we *did* party.

I met a student from New York named Jerry at Grimslöv, and we hit it off. Jerry is originally from Saint Croix in the U.S. Virgin Islands, and he was fun to hang out with and always up for an adventure. He has a big personality and is, as they say, tall, dark, and handsome—we're talking six foot four, conspicuously tall, even in a room full of Swedes. So, when we'd meet up to barhop in Växjö, we'd wind up with a crowd hanging out with us.

I'd kid Jerry by asking, "Hey, mind if I stand next to you and pretend the girls are talking to me too?"

On one visit to Jerry's adopted town of Varnamö, we decided that we shouldn't live in Northern Europe for a year without spending some of that time traveling. It's common for kids in Sweden to take advantage of the Eurail Pass, which is a ticket (in booklet form) that allows you to travel by train all over Europe and North Africa. Students got unlimited miles for a month. The ticket-plan had only a few restrictions, one of them was you traveled lowest class available. The Swedes call it *tågluffa*, and we met a bunch of kids our age while riding the rails.

Along the way, we also learned that we didn't always have a good reputation. We heard of one scheme where college-age kids would start the summer in South France with no money in their pocket and follow the grape harvest north, picking and stomping grapes at vineyards for room and board (and wine).

Some travelers who fit our description behaved more like vagabonds or hobos, and authorities sometimes treated us as such. Despite the bad apples, most of the locals we met were very giving and kind. From working for Pick and other summer jobs back home, I had about $1,000 set aside to travel with, so I sunk what was left into traveler's checks.

We made our trip agenda partly by things we wanted to see: The German mountains, the Eiffel Tower, Gibraltar, the beach in Tangier, the Reeperbahn in Hamburg, and the West End of London. Our schedule was also planned to take advantage of Jerry's family's connections. His father was a politician in the Virgin Islands, and they knew a lady in England, a guy in Madrid, a married couple outside of Paris, and a guy in Morocco. I didn't know or have a chance to meet these people before we showed up, so I had to trust Jerry that they'd be there. He contacted most before we left but could only give them a vague sense of when we'd be on their doorstep.

Those were the days before cell phones, when you wrote a letter to Morocco and hoped for the best. That made our shelter plans fairly loose, but we planned for economy. If we didn't have a friend to stay with, hostels were cheap or free. If we couldn't find a hostel, we'd stay in a hotel. If all those failed us, we had sleeping bags for the park. We would eat where we found food, and as exchange students we'd learned to try anything they'd put on a plate.

Our plan started in Denmark. From there we'd go to Germany, France, and Spain, then cross the Mediterranean to Africa. Then, we'd go up through Belgium to England and finally back home to Sweden. In a month of travel, we could add seven or eight stamps to our passports. We decided to skip Italy and Greece this time.

There are only so many countries you can fit into one month.

German Sounds Like Danish

but the words are all wrong

When school let out for the summer in Sweden, Jerry and I met in the south-central hub of Växjö to set out on a month of adventure. We had both been to Denmark several times, so we didn't plan a long stay there. I had visited the Swedish town of Malmö several times, which is just a short ferry ride across to Denmark's capital.

The Wetterholms had family in Malmö and a cousin named Gunilla who was about my age. When we'd visited them earlier that year, Gunilla and I went across and hung out in Copenhagen. She told me that Swedish kids liked to take the ferry over and back as entertainment on a Saturday night. Øresund (the strait between Denmark and Sweden) is international waters, so it was possible to buy booze at a younger age in the ferry's duty-free shop, so long as you drank it on board. The kids would buy a bottle and party in the observation lounge without getting off in Denmark. Gunilla and I took a fast hydrofoil instead of the ferry and had a great time, talking and walking along the old harbor of Nyhavn.

When Jerry and I took the ferry over, we kept our partying down to one Tuborg each. The beers tasted fantastic after a year of the weak and tasteless stuff that had been available in the discos in Sweden. Swedes do have good taste in beer—they love their IPAs—but at the time, the laws kept what was available to my age down to a brand called Pripps Blå that was 1.8 percent alcohol.

We spent the first night of our adventure in a hostel close to Central Station in Copenhagen. It was a big room with cots set up in a matrix, like a shelter you'd see set up in a gym after a disaster. Nevertheless, it was clean, friendly, and close to the station. It cost ten bucks for the night, so it was an easy choice.

We had hot dogs on a park bench in Tivoli Gardens before turning in. Tivoli is a large, very green park in the middle of downtown. It first opened in 1843 and is billed as the world's oldest amusement park. The Nazis tried to burn it during their occupation, and the Beatles played there in 1964. Compared to American amusement parks it is very tranquil, and the elegant old Victorian-era rides take a back seat to the botanical garden itself. I'm not sure that I appreciated that as much as I would today.

Danish is a Scandinavian language, not as similar to Swedish as Norwegian is, but manageable when I tried to read it. Spoken Danish sounds like a drunk German speaking terrible Swedish and was almost indecipherable for me. We translated the platform displays at the central train station and hopped our next leg—outbound to Hamburg.

Denmark is made up of a bunch of islands, and it had one of the more modern trains we used. We wondered how they could run a train from island to island, and were surprised when our entire procession, engine and all, rolled onto the ferry through the back doors, then cruised across the gap. When we arrived, the front doors opened onto the tracks, and we headed off for Germany.

Hamburg was an industrial town—all cranes and smokestacks. The buildings downtown were new, modern warfare seemed to have wiped out the old-world charm we saw elsewhere. As our train passed the harbor, we saw the huge gantries of the shipyards that build oil tanker-sized ships.

Our walk from the station took us past a church that suffered heavy bombing by American planes during World War II. It had been reduced to ruins but was cleaned up and preserved in that condition as a reminder of the destruction caused by firebombing. It sat where it had been destroyed, with no fanfare and only a small sign. It was emotional, in part because I was from the country that blew it up.

We checked into a hostel and grabbed a map.

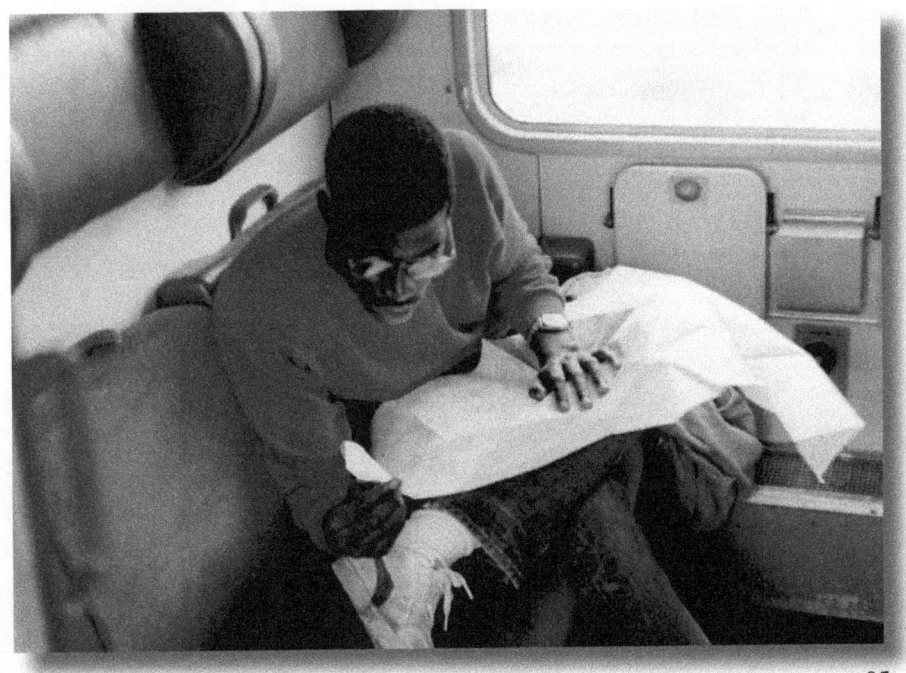

The main attraction for us was the famous Reeperbahn—the red-light district where the Beatles paid their dues playing in dives during their musicians' apprenticeship. That summer, it was still authentically grubby, and the St. Pauli nightlife lived up to its reputation. We felt like two naughty little boys, unsupervised and out on the town.

Along the way, we found a hat shop full of authentic nautical caps. It is a historic port town after all, and we discovered that the shop was where Daryl, of Captain and Tennille shopped (okay, that was a big deal *back then*). I bought a Greek fisherman's cap I wore for a total of two days before I left it on the seat of a train. Jerry later confessed that he was relieved when I lost it. It *was* pretty dorky.

Our hostel that night was set up like college dorms, with two sets of bunk beds to a room. We roomed with two Poles who were in Hamburg looking for work in the shipyard. They talked about politics and said that a bad economy was making it impossible for them to find jobs, and was the reason they had left Poland.*

The Hamburg Hostel was one of a few we encountered that summer that required that you eat breakfast before you leave, as kind of a social service program. "Breakfast" was only a croissant and coffee, but free always tasted good. During our breakfast, I mentioned the tattoo-parlor that we'd seen the previous night and suggested we memorialize our trip. Jerry said he was all for it and egged me on as we ate. I planned and plotted, trying to decide what would look good. Jerry's tattoo plans got more and more elaborate: Maybe he'd get a big dragon all down his arm. Maybe across his shoulder, too.

It finally dawned on me that he was pulling my leg, and I gave him the stink-eye, "You're not gettin' any stinkin' tattoo."

He burst out laughing, "I was wondering when you were going to catch on."

Our route to Munich took us through the German countryside, and we sailed through the rolling hills of the German Forest. Beech and pine trees whizzed by, and suddenly we topped a hill and could see far across the countryside over miles of green. An ancient castle poked through the canopy in the distance, and then we ducked back into the woods. We were particularly enjoying the ride today but weren't sure why.

Less than two months after we talked with the Poles, Lech Walesa led an "illegal" strike at the shipyard at Gdansk, Poland that soon spread nationwide and turned into the Solidarity movement. It brought about huge changes for workers in Poland, and an end to the communist government there. I hope our guys went home and did well for themselves.

That train sure was nice!

Trains varied a lot—condition, quality, comfort, amenities. We both traveled by rail regularly in Sweden and were used to a mix of old and new cars with many different designs. We encountered a great variety on this trip as well. Some of the newest were in France, and they were first-rate.

Because of the vast differences, we missed all the warning signs. This train was all new and very nicely appointed. It even had a restaurant. It sure was fast! The officials on this train were dressed sharp—with dark, military style uniforms slightly reminiscent of German wartime officers. The conductor came by to check tickets. When we pulled out pass-booklets, he suddenly got stuffy with us. We had accidentally boarded an expensive First-class Express train. The conductor had us thrown off after they made a special wheel-screeching stop for us at the next station - boot!

We stood there on the platform of a random, tiny village.

As I said, this was long before cell phones. We had no one we could call, anyway. The lone station manager ambled out to greet us (I think he wondered what prompted the train to stop) and told us that another train should be along within the hour. It would be coming from the other way though, as the train we had been on was headed for *Berlin*, not Munich.

At that time, East Germany was still Iron Curtain spooky, and you needed special visas and paperwork to even think about crossing through to Berlin. It was a stroke of luck we got tossed out before we got that far.

We made it to Munich and spent several days there, staying the nights in another hostel. We found we recognized many words in German. It and Swedish have a lot in common with English, so if you are competent in two, you can get by in the third (unless you're getting on a train to Munich, I guess).

We spent our first morning at the Deutsches Museum von Meisterwerken der Naturwissenschaft und Technik (the German version of the Smithsonian). The museum was immense, with rooms and rooms full of airplanes and machinery and an entire wing of musical instruments. We wished we had days to spend there instead of hours.

After lunch, we hitchhiked out to Dachau and spent a very somber afternoon touring the remnants of the concentration camp. The wire, the guard towers, and the famously ironic "Work Makes You Free" gate were reminders of the awfulness that people are capable of.

Most of the barracks had been reduced to just the foundations, but other buildings survive. We walked past a memorial sculpture of emaciated human forms entangled in barbed wire, into the administration building, which had been turned into a museum. The exhibits of personal effects taken from thousands of prisoners who met their deaths there was very sobering. The toughest thing to see was the crematorium's ovens.

We hitched a ride back to town, and our host was very talkative, but Jerry and I just couldn't find any words.

The next day, we visited the Olympiapark where the 1972 Summer Games were held. We skipped the apartments where terrorists killed two and held nine hostages.

Outside the bicycle stadium, I saw a handbill with a familiar face. Frank Zappa was going to be playing a concert soon, right there in the park. I wasn't able to convince Jerry that it was a show worth seeing, but I told him I HAD to see Zappa, and I bought myself a ticket, deciding that wherever we were on the day before the concert I'd ride the train back and see the show. It would be my first concert, and we'll see later that it was quite an adventure.

In the evening, we made our way down to Marienplatz, the Munich version of the town square that every European city seems to have. The Rathaus-Glockenspiel is there, and we watched street performers while we waited for the big clock to put on its show. A couple of guys were rocking out on a guitar and a small harp and entertaining their captive audience. They took a break when the glockenspiel started, and we watched as life-sized wooden figures appeared, rotating through the stage while the clock played a tune on a carillon.

The mechanism put on a pageant that told the story of the wedding of a sixteenth century duke. The wooden Duke wed his bride, carved revelers danced to the bells, and brightly-painted knights jousted.

As we headed back to the hostel for the night, we passed a little sweetshop and ducked in for some ice cream. I entered first, and the guy behind the counter made a quick move over to the door and locked it in Jerry's face.

"Oh, so sorry! Are you closed?" I said.

"Not for you. But ve are closed for him," the shopkeeper said.

This overt act of racism surprised me, but it only took a second to recover.

"Well, then you are closed for me too," I said, and left.

It didn't seem to ruffle Jerry at all. It wasn't his first time.

We had sampled the schnitzel, ate three kinds of wurst, and tried the potato pancakes and *spätzle*. But we realized, as we sat in the train station waiting for the train to our next adventure to roll up, that we were about to leave Germany without trying the beer!

We set out to remedy that and wound up with two of the biggest paper cups we'd ever seen, filled with bocks that were like, four-jillion percent alcohol. We caught an ear-thundering buzz. The train was late, so we got more. I remember going the wrong way through the back of the beer stand.

"*Raus*! *Raus*! *RAUS*!" a bardame hollered at us.

We giggled at her barking, then quickly chugged our second liter of beer as the train pulled up. We drug our backpacks—clinking with more smuggled-on bottles of beer—aboard. We snorted and guffawed under our breath as the conductor checked our passes, then settled into our compartment for an overnight run to Paris.

I have a blurry memory of a girl that appeared at our compartment door sometime in the middle of the night. There were no other seats, could she ride with us? We welcomed her in, and we laughed, talked, and offered her our beer.

When I awoke in France, she was gone.

Americans in Paris

feted by the locals

I woke up with the world spinning around me. Where *was* I? I sure wasn't home. Sweden? No, I was face down in some slobber on some kind of seat cushion. The sun was too bright through a window close by, and flickering. Telephone poles whizzed by at an alarming speed. Some kind of constant rhythm was pounding my head.

Kachunk-kachunk, kachunk-kachunk.

It was the wheels of a train on the tracks. I was sprawled across the seats of a compartment that was all bed. They were normally three facing three but had been pulled out and laid flat so we could sleep. Why was I alone?

Kachunk-kachunk, kachunk-kachunk.

The train compartment rocked and swayed like a ship at sea, and I rolled back and forth like an empty beer can on the floorboard of a pickup.

Kachunk-kachunk, kachunk-kachunk.

Reality was coming slowly into focus. We'd got very drunk the night before, and my morning was becoming ugly and nauseating.

Suddenly, I felt the taste in my mouth that meant I needed to find a bathroom quickly to throw up. As I scrambled for the door, I realized that I was alone because Jerry was already occupying one of the two toilets on either end of the train car. That gave me a fifty-fifty shot at an empty one on the other end.

I picked a direction and ran—bam-bam-bam—pinballing down the window-lined passageway, then through the door and around the corner and ... LOCKED.

Oh god, where to puke?

I wrestled open the latch of the train's outer door and barfed in the wind, with my head sticking out of the side of the speeding train. Jerry emerged from the restroom as I crouched on all fours. The wind felt good on my face. He said that he hadn't gotten sick, but that he felt horrible as well. Opening the train's door had summoned an angry conductor, and after some negotiation, we agreed to behave for as long as it took to make it into Paris.

When we arrived, the first order of business was to call Jerry's friends Marie and George who had a house in Saint-Germain-en-Laye, a pretty suburb northwest of Paris. Marie agreed to meet us at the station.

As we waited, hung-over on the steps, a thin man in a black and white striped long-sleeve tee shirt rode by on his bike with a beret on and a baguette in his basket. Jerry said that he guessed France must have been paying the guy to ride around and around the station, so tourists won't be disappointed. I said that if he started whistling *Frere Jacques,* I was going to knock him off his bike.

Marie pulled up, and as she helped us put our packs in her trunk, she said, with the cutest accent, *"Mon dieu, you steenk!"*

We explained our evening, and she told us we should shower and sleep, and we would have lunch when we awoke.

George and Marie were a delight. George was a compact man who had been a famous speedboat racer in the '60s. He'd had a horrible crash and retired, and now owned a company that supplied parts to racers. He was hilarious and animated.

Marie was fun too, though proper and pretty, and we suspected that she was the grownup of the couple. They were both generous to a fault. All of the people that we stayed with from Jerry's acquaintances were. It speaks volumes about what good people his family must be.

Their yard was very green, with trees as old as the city. Marie led us downstairs to the guest room to shower. There were two beds with feather mattresses and pillows. The basement room was built into the hill with an open window out onto the garden. It was cool and quiet, the best sleep we had the entire trip.

The tree outside our bedroom window was an ancient cherry tree, and Marie told us over lunch that if we'd pick enough cherries for a pie, she'd make us a real French dinner. They invited guests for the evening, and we had a fine meal. Marie fixed escargot with the traditional garlic sauce, in mushrooms as *l'entrée.*

Next up was the *plat principal* of steak tartare. I'd had the dish while living in Sweden and knew to expect raw ground beef served in a mound, with a half-shell of raw egg placed in the center. The Wetterholms had served it in the tradition—surrounded by chopped onion, capers, and diced pickled beets. This you mix together and top with a lot of salt and pepper. Like Sushi, it needs to be served carefully to minimize risk from the raw ingredients. Marie's ground meat was very red, and gamier tasting than I'd had before. George explained that it was Horse. Ever the explorers, Jerry and I tucked in.

I had a friend in Sweden whose mom liked smoked horse and made us sandwiches with it several times, so I was not new to the idea, but this seemed a little *carnivorous*.

After the cheese course, we had our pie in the living room and George told the group hilarious stories while he chomped a cigar. The other guests' English was minimal, so he entertained us in French, and his eyes twinkled as he acted out the parts with hand motions and sound effects. He had us laughing right along with the others, though we couldn't tell you what any of it was about.

There are just too many things to see and do in a single visit to Paris, and we spent several more days trying to hit the highlights. Our sidewalk café experience was rained out, so we settled for some coffee inside where it was crowded and a little too warm. The radio played "Funkytown," and it was the first time I'd heard it. I think of rainy Paris every time I hear it.

We did our traveling on the Métro, one of many subway systems we experienced. Most every big city on our trip had a subway, and often we'd know that we'd arrived in town when our train suddenly ducked underground and melded with the subway system.

Our fare-passes were always good while we were on a "train," but sometimes not when it was strictly a subway. We usually just got on and hoped for the best. When we ran into trouble, I'd employ the strategy of talking English in a sincere and apologetic tone, but just as fast as I could blather. It usually flustered the conductor enough that he'd just tell me to *please* just sit down and *shut up*.

I learned this strategy while riding back and forth in Sweden, as I forgot my school pass regularly. That is to say, my friend *Anders'* school pass. He gave me his when he quit school for a good job—foreign students didn't qualify for one. Luckily, there was no picture on it.

Jerry and I rode out to the Centre Pompidou, a brand-new museum built with ultramodern architecture. Every Parisian we talked to bitched about it, so we decided we had to go have a look. It was built with its ducts and escalators exposed and hanging from a scaffold-like main structure, so that it looks like the entire building had been turned inside out.

When Kelly and I visited in 2018, it had not aged well. We speculated that the French are used to letting their landmarks darken a bit, to "gather a patina," and grow a little moss. That hadn't worked so well with chrome and Plexiglas.

Next, we hopped the Metro to Ile de la Cité, the island on the Seine where Notre-Dame has sat for eight hundred years. It is an amazing piece of history, and I was profoundly sad to see it gutted by fire in April 2019. I hope I'll see it restored in my lifetime.

We ventured over to the Eiffel Tower, and in those days, you could just walk up, pay the man, and ride to the top. Now, you have to book your visit weeks in advance, and tell them what day and hour you will be there. As we stood on the perforated iron floor at the top of the tower looking 900 feet down, Jerry told me that he didn't really like heights.

"Then why the heck did you come up here?"

"It's just something you gotta do," Jerry said.

Paris is really not like anywhere in the U.S. It is *fifteen centuries* older than any town here, and some of its cobblestone streets predate the Mayan civilization. Even the newer (nineteenth century) buildings and bridges are from a time when works were erected on a grand scale. There is just nothing like seeing the Nymphs in the center of the Pont Alexandre Bridge with the Grand Palais in the background.

We spent a day with Marie at the Louvre, and the next day, her nieces joined us to tour the Palace of Versailles and the castle that Napoleon built for Josephine. The Louvre had oil paintings that were bigger than my front yard. As we gawked at the crown jewels, gold-filigree wall carvings, and ceilings painted by Jean-Baptiste, an odd thought struck me.

"Man. This was all just some guy's house."

The palaces and museums all have extensive gardens. The trees, ponds, and fountains of the garden behind the Palace of Versailles seemed to stretch all the way beyond the horizon, but the web will tell you that my view that day was only two miles. The back porch of the Philbrook museum in Tulsa is a miniature likeness of it—if you'd like to see it but stay closer to home.

Many years later, and after I'd played in a band for a while, I dreamt that I was hired to play a show with Frank Zappa on that back landing at Versailles. It was the typical half-nightmare where you blow the greatest opportunity of your life. Thousands of people out in that garden listening and I'm playing so badly that Frank is disgusted with me. But the setting sure was swanky.

Essential Oil

Orange pickle in a pot

salt it down with bergamot,

and as the Camptown ladies say

you'll de-do the livelong day.

A Night in Brittany

lost and hassled by gendarmes

At George and Marie's dinner party, one of the subjects that interested everyone was our perspective on France and the sights that Jerry and I had seen so far. With Marie translating for her friends, we were told that Paris was a fine city to visit but the true heart of France was the countryside, and to really experience it we'd have to get out of town.

We agreed that a side trip to the country was necessary and asked for suggestions. George offered Brittany, the area of the Northwest Coast of France, and after some debate, our hosts and their guests decided that the port town of Saint-Malo would meet the requirements they had set forth.

Our next scheduled city was Madrid, so we'd detour west for a stay-over on our way. After a three-hour trip, we pulled into the train station and realized we had no game plan. We scouted hotels, but it was high tourist season, and everything was booked.

Our "plan-B" had always been to camp out if we had to. We traveled with sleeping bags on our packs, and we could sleep under the stars in the park if need be. We met a group who said they were headed to a park where they allowed camping, and they offered us a ride.

A guy, two girls, Jerry, and I crammed into a Mini, with knees and elbows everywhere, and set out for the campground. Over hill and dale and passing hedgerows, we could neither see nor pay much attention to where we were being taken.

We piled out at a park near the sea and next to an old fort and explored the campground. The wooded area had many trailer-campers and tents, and quite a few people there. It was a place for migrant workers, travelers, and working people out for a weekend holiday. The atmosphere was cordial, and we heard about twenty different languages as we walked along.

On the way to the beach, we walked through the fort, which dated to the mid-1700s. During World War II, the Germans had used it as a garrison, and among the preserved historic pieces are several steel turrets, with walls a foot thick and full of terrifying shell holes. The Germans had retreated to Saint-Malo after the D-Day invasion and the town suffered a horrific bombardment. There were remnants of Roman fortifications here and there on our peninsula as well.

As we explored, we kept an eye out for a likely place to bed down after dinner and decided that we would come back to a tree in a grassy area close to the fort wall, after dinner.

A fellow camper told us that we could find something to eat along the waterfront, so we walked across to a harbor area to see what there was. We'd lost track of time, and it was getting close to dusk, so the only restaurant still open was just closing.

A little balding man in a white apron saw us coming as he pulled the window shade down, and smiled and waved us in. It was a mom-and-pop place with nice linens, and flowers in vases on the four or five tables. It was old, it was clean, and it felt very real. The owner's wife could see that the menus made absolutely no sense to us. She mimed for us to trust her, and brought out a cheese plate, some bread, and some wine. They sat down and ate with us, and we talked and watched the tide come in. He told us he had been there for *leu zhoor zhee* (what the French call D-Day), and he liked Americans.

It was well after dark when we made it back to the tree we thought we had picked out before. We rolled out our bags and dozed off.

The Gendarmerie is a police force in France that patrols rural areas and small towns. The local sheriff department would be the closest U.S. equivalent. The gendarmes are a branch of the military, though, and are recruited and trained like an army. They are some tough messieurs. Let's say their bedside manner is a bit rough around the edges.

These are the guys who woke Jerry and me up under our tree at two o'clock in the morning - by poking our sleeping bags and shouting, "*Passeport, PASSEPORT! Montrez-nous vos PAPIERS!*"

Their stick hurt, and I quickly produced a passport from my travel pouch. Jerry's was nowhere to be found. They'd started out grumpy and got angrier as he searched.

By the time they stood me up against our tree and started to frisk me, Jerry pulled his papers from the very bottom of his sleeping bag. They shined their flashlights in our eyes while they gave us a very serious lecture about being *clochards*. I whispered to Jerry *"klo-shar?"*

"Vagabonds," he replied.

The gendarmes left us, and we drifted back to sleep for another hour before

107

a drenching cold rain that came in from the sea dumped on us, and lasted until just before dawn. We dragged our now heavy, soaked sleeping bags out of the rain to under the arch in the wall. We shivered and tried to sleep sitting up so we wouldn't drown in the mud.

Dawn broke clear and beautiful that morning, and we decided we'd try to find some civilization at the end of the train line in Madrid. But, where were we? We'd been distracted by the French girls in our laps on the way out and had no idea where or how far away the train station was.

A bakery was the only shop open that early, and we bought two long baguettes that turned out to be breakfast and lunch that day. We headed inland down the main road because that *seemed* like the way we came. We walked about a mile and came to a railroad crossing. I suggested that the station had to be in one direction or the other, and we could walk the tracks to it if we were lucky. Jerry pointed out that being *un*lucky might mean walking for miles and miles.

We took a chance and left the direction to a coin toss. The coin was charmed, and we were soon sleeping like babies, with half-chewed baguette in our cheeks, flying through the countryside on the train to Spain.

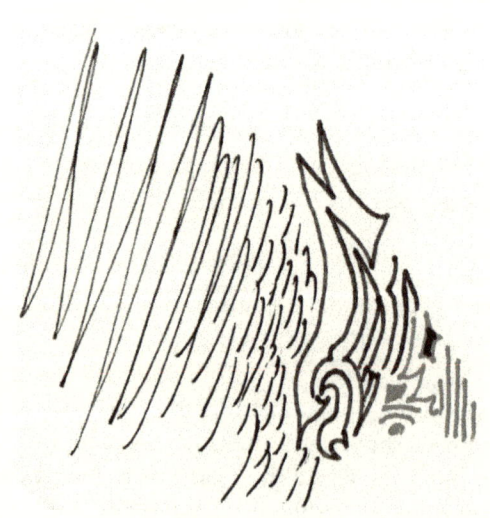

The Train in Spain

stays mainly in the plain

I've mentioned before that some of the French train cars were a brand-new design. They were quite nice with tall, comfy seats facing each other across from tables, in a big, open car.

We found ourselves on one of these, passing through wine country on June 21—the midsummer solstice. Back in Sweden, after a cold, dark winter they celebrated this longest day of the year. We hadn't experienced Midsommar, but had heard our Swedes talk about the celebration in the same reverent tones that we reserve for the Fourth of July. A pair of Swedish girls who happened to be on the same train overheard a snippet of our Swedish and sat down across from us. They had a bottle of wine, and we toasted "Skol" while they told us more about their favorite holiday.

We were heading for Madrid, and Jerry had another family friend there. When we planned the trip, I hadn't thought to ask who his friends were, or what accommodations we could expect from them. It was all just an adventure that we would take as it came along.

By the end of the month, we were both tired of not knowing if a bed would be there at the end of the day, or if the food there would be comforting or bizarrely unidentifiable, but at this point we were still content to meet adventure where we found it.

As we left Brittany I asked what our destination in Madrid was, and Jerry told me we were looking for the American Embassy. The "friend" in this case turned out to be the U.S. ambassador to Spain. Jerry's family had some juice!

We hopped off the train and found a grassy area where we could lay out our still-damp sleeping bags to finish drying. There was a payphone close by, and Jerry called the embassy.

Many pesos later, The Ambassador himself got on the line to tell us he was very sorry.

President Jimmy Carter was on his way to Madrid from the latest G7 Summit, and they had to get the place set up so he could give a speech at the embassy. The employees there needed some reassurance after Iranians had stormed the embassy in Iran last fall. They had taken embassy employees hostage, and the rescue attempt that spring—which had happened only a month or two prior—was a fiasco.

Security would be super tight, and the whole affair had the embassy on lockdown for the week. We would have to find a place to stay on our own.

Over the previous couple of weeks, we had developed a skill that many Eurail Pass-holders acquire: Spotting fellow travelers. Their age, their backpacks, and the wide-eyed stare at their train schedule made them easy to pick out of a crowd. As we were forming a plan, across the station we saw a group of three Japanese girls who also appeared to be at a loss for a place to stay. Their English was thin, so our year long experience with making ourselves understood without words helped yet again.

Our group found our way to an old hotel close to downtown with creaky wood floors and transoms over the doors. We thought of it as a "flop," but looking back, it was really a cool find. We hadn't seen the rest of our trip yet, and this was nice compared to some places we flopped. Our rooms were right next to each other, and we set up a date for the five of us to eat dinner together.

Hot dawg, they were cute!

A restaurant just downstairs specialized in Tapas, which is kind of "appetizers as dinner." The old guy at the desk told us it was a good way to try many different Spanish dishes at once. We ate a tasty dinner while pantomiming our intentions to the waiter and the girls.

I was dead set on something romantic happening after the meal and was trying my best to be suave, but the girls just were not having it. I told my ego that the problem lay with the language barrier and not my pickup skills. Jerry thought my efforts were hilariously lame, though.

The next morning, we weighed our options. We hadn't made any real plans for Madrid, thinking that Jerry's acquaintance could be our guide. As our next stop was exotic Africa, in the Arabian world of Morocco, we decided we'd sacrifice time in Spain to spend longer in Casablanca. We stopped by the Plaza Mayor and Royal Palace, and then headed down to the train station.

One of our treks through Spain was an overnighter. I don't remember which stretch it was—north or south, going or coming—but a full three cars of that train were crammed with Spanish soldiers on leave, and they had brought their sangria. We didn't get much sleep that night, as all of the compartments around us were in riotous celebration. At one point very late at night, or very early in the morning, the entire train was singing "Cielito Lindo."

Ay, ay, ay, ay canta no llores ...

Parts of Spain were a lot like West Texas, with hot weather, scrub, and hills in the distance. It was ungodly warm for most of that leg of the trip. Thank goodness you can ride with the train's windows down. We did, standing in the passageway that ran the length of each car and risking the conductor's wrath by leaning on the open window frame to get some wind in our sweaty hair.

Hours of standing, countering the constant sway, made our legs tired but the fatigue helped us sleep later. And since we had to sleep sitting up in a cramped compartment, we traded into the middle seat every few hours, so a fellow traveler could take a shift leaning against the wall.

As we got further south and approached Cadiz we passed through low, rolling hills and farmland that reminded me of San Antonio.

Our goal was to meander down to meet up with an old friend of Jerry's in Casablanca. Mustafa had worked with the Peace Corps in his younger days and stayed with Jerry's family on Saint Croix. The path took us through the port town of Algeciras on the southwest corner of Spain, where the Rock of Gibraltar dominates the bay. The Rock was an imposing landmark—a mountain rising up across the bay, and we wanted to go over and visit if we could.

There's only one way in or out of the Mediterranean, and it is through the narrow Strait of Gibraltar. The Rock overlooks all of that, so they built a fortress into it, and countries have been fighting over it for a thousand years. Control the Rock, and you control shipping for the lower half of Europe.

The Brits controlled it right then, and that was a real burn on the Spaniards (since it's, you know, *in Spain*) so Spanish dictator Francisco Franco had locked down all travel to and from the Rock. Franco's recent death meant that the two countries were just coming around to better terms and had signed the Lisbon Agreement that summer. However, the ink wasn't dry enough on it to allow us to go over and climb the famous Mediterranean Steps ourselves.

We loitered around the harbor waiting to board the ferry across the Straight. The ferry was an ocean-going vessel and easily the largest of our trip, even counting the one that the entire train boarded.

As we found a spot to stand on the deck, I spotted an odd-looking ship across the harbor flying a Soviet flag, with four enormous radar dishes on its deck. After I had returned to Oklahoma, I took my developed pictures to the Duncan Library reference section, and with a copy of *Jane's Fighting*

Ships identified it as the Soviet space-control monitoring ship Kosmonavt Yuriy Gagarin. At that time, *Jane's* also classified it as a possible spy satellite tracker.

The visit from the CIA that I expected from showing the librarian my photos has never materialized.

Learning to Bargain in Tangier

don't drink mint tea with strangers

According to a *New York Times* article from 1954, Ernest Hemmingway and his wife survived two plane crashes in the same day while on safari in Africa, emerging from the jungle after the second, carrying a bunch of bananas, and half a bottle of gin.

Anyway, here is one of *my* stories from Africa.

A couple hundred passengers, Jerry, and I boarded the ship to cross the Strait of Gibraltar to Tangier. We saw crew members loading freight as well as boarding passengers, so it was probably engaged in shipping also. Its size may have been necessary for the crossing, as the route ventured slightly out into the Atlantic.

We were off to the land of the Sahara!

We went up to the deck and found a bench close to the rail so we could watch as we crossed. A grinning boy—about two or three years old—kept running back and forth from a woman in an abaya to the "rail," which was only a couple of cables strung along the edge. The lowest was at his neck-level, and Jerry and I missed some of the view of the crossing, as this kid kept coming within inches of running off the deck and falling down twenty feet to the ocean speeding by below.

"Hey! Knock it off!" I shouted when I finally had enough of his nerve-wracking foolery.

The boy cried and his mom was mad at us, so she gathered him up and went inside to glare at us through a window. However, as Jerry said, it was worth it to save a life.

We leaned over the rail as Tangier came into view over the horizon. A guy about our age walked up and introduced himself. He was outgoing, and an interesting conversationalist and we were happy to find someone who knew Tangier.

After confirming that we were American, he asked if we had any plans for the night. We could eat dinner with him—he knew a good place, and even knew of a reasonably priced hotel close to the Medina. He told us that the Medina was the old, scenic part of town, where the good shops were.

What luck—imagine randomly running into someone our age so knowledgeable and hospitable!

Tangier was as exotic as we imagined it when we sat planning in Jerry's bedroom. The town is on a point of land with the Mediterranean Sea on its north beach, and the Atlantic on its west beach. It was the best natural harbor in North Africa—all the way back to ancient times.

The beach on the Mediterranean side is a big, crescent-shaped amphitheater with hills in the distance all around. The town's geometric hodgepodge of whitewashed houses and apartments rose away from our viewpoint. It looked like it was all one structure, with a thousand brightly painted doors.

Up the hill on the left, we could see the castle towers and dome of the *kasbah*. Pictures taken from the beach today show those same palm trees in front of modern hotels and high-rise apartments, but back then, we saw mostly one- or two-story buildings that looked like something from an Aladdin cartoon.

Our new friend and guide walked us to a modest little hotel of that same theme, with arched doorways and a medieval pattern carved in the cobalt blue, heavy, wooden door. Stucco walls, wicker furniture, and ceiling fans in the lobby made us feel like we were in a Humphry Bogart movie.

The hotel's eight or ten rooms were all on the second floor with a shared toilet. The breeze from the sea blew under the doorways and cooled our feet as we walked to the tiny room at the end of the dark hallway. Our room had a window at the foot of the bed that overlooked the road along the beach. There was barely enough room for a creaky dresser, with a pitcher and bowl atop.

We were glad to see it had a shower We hadn't washed in a few days, and the long, open-windowed trip through Spain had been gritty and grubby. The shower was only a low place in the corner of the room where the tile sloped slightly to a drain, with a curtain on a curved track. The corner of the bed pushed the curtain in a little as I washed off a long day of travel.

I had noted that the toilet-room door had no lock and held my foot against it while I was busy. As we got ready to leave, we noticed that the room didn't lock either. We were only slightly ruffled by this. We didn't really have any valuables, and we always kept our credentials and supply of traveler's checks in our travel pouches around our necks. We pushed our backpacks under the bed and went downstairs.

We met our new friend, who led us to the Medina through a grand arch, and then a labyrinth of streets and alleys. Some were narrow enough to reach out and touch both walls. A naked toddler ran out in front of us chasing a chicken. A fat man in a *thawb* and *fez* appeared in a doorway, then backed into the shadow as we passed.

The movie we seemed to be in had changed from *Arabian Nights* to a James Bond flick. The city of Tangier had been considered International Territory since the end of World War I, independent of any nation. It was the place to do business for real-life spies, and was full of foreign agents and diplomats, thieves, pickpockets, and shady dealers. All of those old movie clichés had been based on the reality of Tangier.

We three padded on, over bricks and cobblestones, under hanging laundry and around baskets, with a complex and unique scent growing stronger as we went. Cumin, turmeric, allspice, cloves, and ginger—Moroccan dinner time was a smell that was strange and new.

Our winding passage through the drastically different moods of the Medina brought us to a bistro where we crowded into a corner table and let our guide order for us.

We talked as we ate a spicy beef stew, and our friend asked us questions we had grown used to answering about where, how, and who we were. He kept concluding from our answers that we were rich, and that we were probably looking for good shops to spend all of that money. We assured him we were just poor students.

But he brushed that aside with a simple, "You're American!"

To him, all Americans were rich, and we were in luck. His very good friends owned a shop that sold only the highest-quality merchandise, and it was very close to where we were now.

"Sure! Yeah, we'd go see the shop, what could it hurt?" A couple of souvenirs to put in a pocket of our backpack. It'd be fun.

We didn't realize it until the next day, but our friend was a *tout*, an advance man paid to bring people to the shop.

The shop was closed when we arrived, but the man at the door said that they would open back up "just for us."

No need to go to all the trouble, we said.

"No, no! We make time for men with money to spend," the man said.

He let us in, locked the door behind us, and took us upstairs to a second shopkeeper who sat on a big rug. The air was dank with a sweet-smelling smoke. Our "friend" had disappeared at the doorway, and we never saw him again.

The first shopkeeper took the brass hookah they had been smoking into another room as the new guy told us to sit and engaged us in conversation. He told us that his partner was making mint tea for the group and offered us a bit of mint tea lore. It was a long three-step process, done slowly and deliberately.

As he poured the tea over sugar from one etched glass to another, he said, "The first glass is as gentle as life, the second is as strong as love, and the third glass," he stared directly at me as he spoke, "is as bitter as death."

We were told to sip loudly.

"Serving mint tea is a ritual in our world, meant for the best of friends, or men engaged in a business proposition. Maybe we will become both. I have been told that you are looking for a carpet of very high quality and have a great deal of money to spend."

"Oh man," Jerry said as he smiled nervously and chuckled. "No, no there's a little misunderstanding. We're just students."

"Yeah, we're poor as dirt." I added.

The other shopkeeper had busied himself bringing out, and unrolling big rugs, and our host remained undeterred.

"As you can see, these threads are dyed by hand. This one is pure silk, and all are hand-knotted. What would you think something of this quality would be worth?"

In the most literal sense of the term, we two high schoolers had *no idea*.

Our host leaned in, "Give me a number."

"I don't know, five hundred dollars?" I guessed.

So far, Jerry and I had lived and traveled mostly in Northern Europe. In

Sweden, all prices are clearly marked, and because there was no sales tax, you paid exactly what you saw on the sticker.

I knew nothing at all about "bargaining," and it came as a bit of a shock that in Morocco, from the dude selling hard boiled eggs one at a time, to this rug dealer, everyone expected you to lowball an offer then put up a fight. We were now engaged in a game that we didn't even know we were playing.

The merchant became very animated, "Five hundred dollars? You insult me! A rug of this quality is worth twice, three times that!"

"Well, maybe?" I said, "We don't know anything about rugs. If it's worth a thousand, okay then!"

"Your offer is still low," our host calmly countered. "A thousand is too little for this quality."

Jerry nearly spit out his tea. "No, you don't understand. We don't want a rug. We didn't come to buy a rug. We just want to buy a belt or a keychain or something."

The mood suddenly turned very dark. Our merchant stood and leveled a penetrating, red-rimmed stare down at us.

"Then I have been lied to," he said. "Which do you think would lie to me? My good friend? Or someone that I met an hour ago?" He turned to his friend. "What should we do with liars?" The other man moved over to the stairway to block our exit.

Jerry turned to me and switched to Swedish, "What can we do to make him understand? They're smoking pot, and I think they're dangerous. We don't have a thousand bucks!"

"Yeah, he's ... (I didn't know the Swedish word for crazy) ... dumb in the head," I said. "I mean, we *do* have a thousand bucks, if we put our money together, but—"

"Då är det vad du bör göra," said the shopkeeper.

Oh crap, he spoke Swedish!

Defensive babbling kicked in as I switched back to English. "We *can't* buy a rug and continue on our trip we *don't* have any way to carry a rug and we are five thousand miles from home we're sorry but we *didn't* understand that we were implying a deal you can beat us up or whatever but that won't change any of the facts..."

"What if we agree to buy something we *can* afford in your shop downstairs?" Jerry suggested while I caught my breath. "Just let us pay you for something small, everyone will save face, and we'll go away!"

After a few seconds thought, logic gave way and the men led us downstairs, to glower at us as we picked out a couple of doodads. I made a generous offer on a coin-purse, which was accepted.

"You have lied and treated us as fools," the shopkeeper said as they walked us out. "You drank tea with us, then did not behave as men. You have been as babies. I should be very careful if I were you. Men who behave as babies do not live long in our world."

He closed and locked the door, and we scampered back through the labyrinth to our hotel, scared to death.

We arrived after midnight. Our transaction had taken hours but seemed like minutes. The first thing we remembered as we turned the knob was that nothing in this place had locks. Our "guide" knew where we were staying and could lead those crazy shop-owners right to us.

A gentle breeze from the sea blew the curtains. The window wouldn't close. It was painted open, which was great on a hot summer night, if you weren't scared of being mugged in your sleep. We scooted the iron-framed bed over in front of the door and laid down fully dressed, our packs ready to go. If they pushed the door in, we'd just jump out the window ... or something.

We survived the night but didn't sleep at all and jumped at every noise or seagull squawk from the street below. The first rays of daylight brought new confidence, and we paid our bill and cleared out. The train to Casablanca didn't leave until that afternoon, so we made a project of riding across town to stick our feet in the Mediterranean and then in the Atlantic, both in one day.

When we revisited the story recently, Jerry reminded me that the temperature was about 103 degrees Fahrenheit.

"You were redder than a Maine lobster," he said. And he received his first skin-peeling sunburn. "I remember it vividly because I never thought black people could get sunburns—much less a black guy from the Caribbean."

We were the first customers that morning at a beachside deli and ordered a couple of sandwiches.

"What would you have on them?" said the guy running it.

The sage old advice from seasoned travelers is: Try it the way the locals make it.

"Make it the way you make it!" we told him

"With everything," he said.

We said sure, not realizing he meant literally everything. He put chicken, macaroni salad, peas, sauce, beans, and everything his glass-front deli cooler held on those two sandwiches. And our travel advice held true.

Like almost everything else that trip, it was strangely good.

NUMINOUS

Dine and Dash Casablanca

this evening's meal will include exercise

The trains in Morocco were air-conditioned—a luxury. It was something we had not yet seen, even on the long, hot haul through Spain. We skirted the Rif Mountains on our way south to Casablanca and cranked up the air as we passed through the Chaouia Plains. The heat reminded us that Morocco's south is part of the vast Sahara desert. What a change from the green forests where we lived in Sweden. We pulled in at *Gare Casa-Voyageurs* (Casablanca Station) and set out to find Jerry's family-friend.

A taxi dropped us off at the only address that Jerry had for him, and we found ourselves in front of a school. As would be the case in most countries, it was closed for the summer.

We sat down on the curb, out of ideas for what to do next. As we came to the realization that we had no idea how to even start to find a guy named Mustafa in an Arab city of two million, a kid happened by, just going about his day. He noticed us, told us his name was Boukrib, and asked what we were up to.

Our sad tale brightened his eyes. He knew Mustafa. He had been Boukrib's teacher last year.

Did he know where Mustafa lived?

He did!

We walked to an open-air café and had a coke. As we sat, we asked him about his good English. He said that with all of the western influence in the world it had been easy to learn.

"But isn't English the 'most difficult language in the world' to learn?" we asked.

That was a myth. Boukrib spoke several languages and English had been the easiest to pick up. Another old wives' tale busted.

Boukrib led us to Mustafa's apartment and bade us goodbye. I took his address, and later sent him a mixtape of music that I'd promised. Music was always a great place to start a conversation with someone you just met. For the last year, *everyone* had been someone that we'd just met.

Mustafa's wife said that he was out, but that she needed to go to the market. We could wait inside for him, but she would be happier if someone waited with us. Would we mind watching her kids while she shopped?

We encountered so many different levels of trust during this trip. We were young and learning where to put our faith, I suppose. This was a leap on her part, but I think she had heard Mustafa talk about Jerry's family. I have a mental snapshot of us sitting on one couch, opposite another couch where the three kids sat. We tried out different languages, trying to communicate.

"Prata ni Svenska?"

"Sprechen Sie Deutsch?"

Then, *"Parlez-vous français?"* brought a giggle and a nod from the eldest, a girl.

"Oh no," Jerry said under his breath. "My French is terrible."

Just then, the front door burst open, and in strode a big man, with a bigger grin. Mustafa was a force-of-nature. He was quite a character and got us into as much trouble as he kept us out of.

Years later when I saw the first *Indiana Jones* movie, Indie's friend Sallah, played by John Rhys-Davies, very much reminded me of this new friend.

Mustafa recommended a decent hotel between downtown and his place, (with a bathroom *in the room*—plus a lock on the door), and we settled in. The ground floor of the hotel's building had a French bakery, and every morning a heavenly smell drifted into our open window and commanded us to go down and buy two *religieuse*—a pair of filled eclairs, stacked, with a "hat" that made it look like a little nun, and the name refers to that appearance—one for each of us.

We spent the days walking the town or taking the train to visit one exotic *kasbah* or another. Like Tangier, Casablanca's Old Medina was a pre-twentieth century city that seemed frozen in time. Most of what the merchants in the bazaar sold was still handcrafted—leather goods, brass hookahs and bells, shoes and hats, oils and spices.

There, you can hear and smell the real personality of the town and truly feel transported. The shop owner in Tangier had said "in our world …," and we really did keep a sense that we were in another world.

In the Square of Muhammad V—which was nicknamed "pigeon square" for obvious reasons—we heard music played over speakers for the call to prayer and knew to be quiet and respect those times when we were out and about.

The local currency is the Dirham, and we later found we could not exchange it for any other currency once we'd left Morocco. A couple weeks later, we stepped into a bank in London to sell off the five denominations of pocket change that we'd collected.

"Get outta here with that," said a banker after taking one look at the Dirhams.

Having learned the hard way about bargaining at the rug shop, Jerry stood patiently for half an hour as I talked to a *fez* merchant in the Medina about a hat. The guy had to search around in the back of his booth and bring out a big, then a bigger, then a *huge fez*, trying to find one that would fit my noggin. We worked him down to a price that almost amounted to giving it to me. I think he wondered who else it would ever fit. As of 2020, I still have it—big as a bucket!

Our evenings were spent in the dives of Old Medina, eating bar food and meeting Mustafa's friends. We usually ate early, and vendors who walked in from the street, sometimes with their wares in a cardboard box, provided the food. No other packaging, just sitting in the box, soaking through the bottom. We'd pay our Dirhams and they'd grub-hand the food to us.

We ate roasted chickens, bought peeled hard-boiled eggs, and had one meal of large (bigger than butter beans) dark brown fava beans that we dipped in a hot sauce. We ate it all with our hands of course, on old newspapers that the bartender changed out with each patron. The bars also usually set out peanuts or other salty snacks.

One place we frequented, named after Paris' famous Moulin Rouge (but very much lower in standards) set out small bowls full of fish that were the size of minnows. They might have once been sardines but had been salted and dried to the point of being stiff little fish-jerky sticks that stood up in their bowl and staring with their little eyes. The locals popped them in and chewed 'em up whole. Jerry skipped them. I did too, after I tried a couple.

More than once during these pub-crawls I was flabbergasted to have a woman sit in my lap and ask if I would buy her a drink.

"You do know what she wants, don't you?" Jerry asked, when it happened the first time.

Mustafa filled us in on some rules:

- Don't buy a woman in a dive a drink … "She is a prostitute. Or seriously not your type, my friend."

- Don't give money to a beggar … "They'll tell their friends, who'll follow you around all day."

- Don't wear shorts in an Arab country … "Those are the mark of a gay prostitute."

- Don't keep your money in your pocket … "Pickpockets are everywhere."

"Well, this is all fine, but I think I'd like to let you experience some real Moroccan cuisine," Mustafa said one night, as we were finishing an improvised meal. "I know a fellow who has a nice restaurant. Let's meet tomorrow night and I will treat you with some real *Moroccan* food!"

The next evening, we met and walked to a very nice place. White linen, uniformed waiters, and bustling with nicely dressed people. Mustafa ordered everything he could think of. Jerry and I gave no thought to the bill—assuming it was Mustafa's "treat."

There was smoky *zaalouk* (slow cooked lamb), couscous, and pastilla. Strange mixes of spices that I had not tasted before nor since. There was soup, there was *khobs* (Moroccan flat bread), and every inch of our table was covered with a half-eaten dish. The three of us sampled, traded, and drank until we were full as ticks.

When the almond cookies came for dessert, Mustafa pushed back his chair and got the same thoughtful look he had gotten the night before.

"You know, I am a little disappointed." He paused as he thought. "I wanted to show you real Moroccan, but this wasn't as good as I expected. As I told you, I know the chef. This … this should have been better. I'm a little embarrassed. I think I'll just go back and have a word with him."

He stood up and disappeared into the kitchen.

To provide entertainment for the evening, the dining room had allowed a harmonica player with a hunchback to come in. He was amazing at his craft and somehow able to play a melody while simultaneously keeping a pulsing bass line going, all on the same instrument. He danced and spun from table to table while the music meandered in a strange time signature. Jerry and I were enthralled and only slowly realized that a commotion was building in the kitchen.

Kitchenware crashed, and some kind of argument in both French and Arabic was coming to a crescendo, when suddenly the kitchen's swinging doors exploded, and Mustafa bolted past our table.

"Well, boys, now we run!" he said as he barreled by on his way out of the front door.

Jerry and I sat in slack-jawed disbelief. When the chef hit the same kitchen doors, waving a meat cleaver, and yelling a *zaghrouta* (that yodely-thing they do with their tongue) we woke up and pounded out the door after Mustafa.

We were running full out, Mustafa twenty yards ahead, the chef just five yards behind, desperately sprinting down the narrow brick streets of the Medina. The chef chased us for what seemed like forever before he gave up, and two turns later, when we stopped to catch our breath, we were standing in front of the Moulin Rouge.

Years later, I asked Jerry if he remembered the story, and I was amazed when he confirmed that it had really happened.

"Of course, you know it was all a show," he said.

I said sure, I had figured out pretty quickly that Mustafa had planned to skip out on the bill. How could he have paid for all of that on a teacher's salary?

"No, I mean ALL of it," Jerry said. "The chef and everything."

Then it hit me. Of course! The yelling and banging, the meat cleaver, the chef never quite catching up to us. Mustafa and his friend must have planned the whole show, as a gag to pull on two American teenagers.

Years after they had both passed on, I was just getting their joke.

The Man in Black Goes to Ipanema

I

Smelled

Ten

of a churnin' wrinkled wire.

It turned brown, brown, brown

and the blame got fired.

And it churns, churns, churns

that wrinkled wire,

that wrinkled wire.

The Long, Long Road to London

three thousand kilometers on the train

The next planned leg of our trip was a long haul. We would travel from Casablanca all the way up through three countries, two sea channels, and three days of what turned out to be a long, hot, stinky ride. The summer of 1980 brought a heat wave to much of the world, and we felt its effects on our trip.

We took the same ferry back from Tangier to Algeciras, although customs on the *return* from Arabia was a lot more thorough than it had been going in. It was thorough enough that it caused a long, slow logjam, which kept us on the boat for a couple of extra hours. Authorities, checking bags for drugs, made us glad that our biggest transgression so far had been too many beers in Germany.

All of the couple hundred passengers were in one of the ship's cargo holds waiting for the line to filter through. We all looked longingly at one hatch thirty yards away—where fresh air and sunshine came from our only route off the ship.

As we stood packed tightly together, Jerry and I wore our backpacks to keep from having to move them every few seconds. Daydreaming to pass the time, I was yanked back to reality when I felt a hand slip into my wallet pocket.

A pickpocket!

I'd wondered when Mustafa's prediction would play out. My valuables were in my neck pouch, so they were safe. I was next to a bulkhead, so I slammed the poor fella between my pack frame and the wall and gave it all of my weight.

Wham!

"*Arrête!*" my pickpocket cried.

I eased up almost immediately, and all I saw of him was his dark head of hair, as he cut a path through the crowd in front of me.

We shared the long ride through Spain with a good many different people in our train compartment. The route between Tangier and Paris was very popular with Moroccans, as the country had been a French protectorate until the mid-'50s, and people at both ends of the route had relatives in either country.

There were times when our little six-person cabin had eight or ten people crammed in it, with kids up in the baggage rack, and four butts in three seats. Opportunities to shower did not exist at our travel class, so the air got thick. It didn't help that people brought their lunch and ate it almost in your lap.

One guy that came and went had a damned live chicken with him. The chicken was in a crate on the floor, and the guy used it as a foot prop. As seat occupancy shifted, a coalition slowly arose.

A twenty-something Belgian couple joined us and occupied two seats. Then a pale Swede with a wild red afro asked to join us, and hauled in a huge conga drum, which took up the remaining seat. We closed the cabin door, locked it, and pulled the shades. No Livestock Allowed!

The Swede was from Göteborg and was very protective of his conga. He confided to us that it was crammed full of hash. We didn't ask how he smuggled it out of Morocco, but he was a bit of a sketchy character, and acted very nervous whenever a conductor walked by. I gave him marks for being an Iggy Pop fan, but he would not shut up about Iggy for his whole time with us.

Train travel always involves many stops. Some are obvious, as every town of a certain size has a station along the way, but we also occasionally stopped in the middle of nowhere for reasons that were never disclosed. The conga-player freaked out after a conductor took a long look at his passport and took advantage of the next of these odd stops to jump off the train somewhere in Northern Spain. I have wondered since if he ever made it home to Sweden.

All in our little group were traveling back from Africa, and the Belgian couple kept referring to their "escape" from Morocco. I'm not sure what they had experienced, but it must have been worse than our night in Tangier.

Or maybe not.

They struck us as wieners when it came to travel or just life in general. They bitched about *everything*, and they were just amazed when we talked about the size of the United States. When I mentioned traveling two hundred miles to see grandparents every Christmas, the woman said that she hadn't been to see her grandfather in years because the other side of Belgium was too far—Belgium is only about ninety miles wide.

Them Belgians were frisky, though!

Our route took us up through the Pyrenees Mountains between Spain and France. The conga-player's sudden departure had left an empty bench for the Belgian couple to stretch out on, and as the elevation got higher, the temperature drop gave the two an excuse to cuddle.

We started encountering tunnels through the mountain. The first wasn't even long enough to have time to turn on the compartment light. As we approached the next tunnel, I reached for the light. The guy looked from me to his girlfriend and back, then gave me a little "no" gesture.

As we came out on the other side, they were caught in a full-grope lip-lock. Our presence didn't bother them much—it was actually having the opposite effect. They had a conversation in Dutch that made her look Jerry and me up and down, then giggle and blush.

We wound around the mountain, and as we approached another tunnel, the guy said, "Dis next iss a rather long one. I hope you don't mind if ve leaf de lights off again?"

So yeah, trains are always incredibly noisy through tunnels, but not noisy enough that we didn't hear those two going to town. They were already pulling clothes off before we hit the dark, and they didn't bother to get dressed until we broke daylight again.

Yeehaw, nekkid people!

The couple finally bailed out during the stop in Bordeaux, and we were glad to be rid of them for the leg into Paris.

We found that days and days of riding and sleeping on the train created an odd illusion when the train stopped, at a station or otherwise. You became used to the sound of the gaps in the rails and their constant rhythm: *Kachunk-kachunk, kachunk-kachunk*. We had also grown so used to the telephone poles passing by from front-to-back in the window, that during a stop the poles seemed to creep back-to-front in our peripheral vision.

We finally approached Paris early in the morning and expected the train to stop for lunch at one of the major stations. Instead, we found ourselves dropped off at a small station on the southwest edge of town and were informed that there was no rail or Metro service through Paris that day. The union was on strike.

Strikes are a common occurrence in France, especially during the spring and summer when the weather is *really* nice, and it's only a *coincidence* that a little difference of opinion would arise just when the weather is perfect for some time off.* Our departure point to continue by rail was in the far northeast corner of Paris, but really, how far could that be? Taxis were expensive, and we were healthy, so we decided to walk it. We had hiked a few legs of this journey before. Well, Paris is *big*, and this hike took us *six danged hours.*

We did see a lot of Paris that day, though, and we were completely beat by the time we hopped on the train out of town.

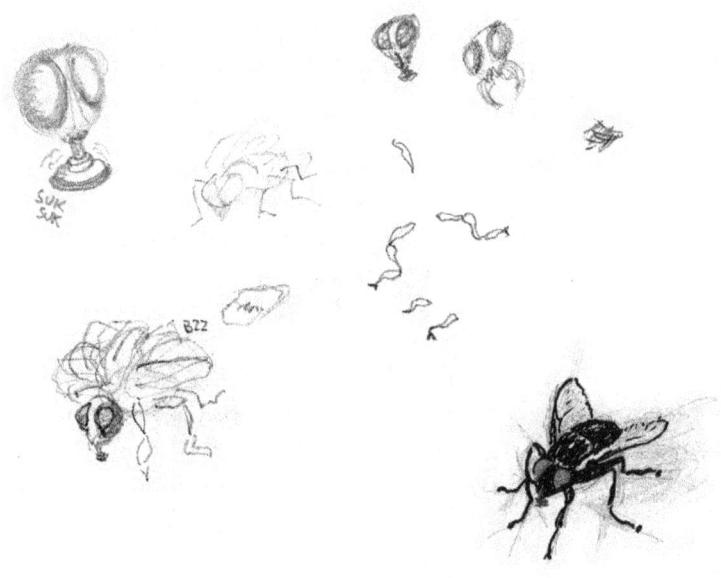

---
* When Kelly and I visited Paris a few years ago, she wanted to see the Catacombs. We took the Metro out and found them, only to be greeted at the door by a young lady with a disgusted expression who told us, in monotone English and a big sigh, that the Catacomb-workers union was on strike. Wasn't she also on strike, then, we asked?
"Noh." (Another long sigh) "Zey. Zey are on strike." She flicked her cigarette into the road and rolled her eyes. "Not me."

Mrs. Moorehead and the Tower of London

does scotch pair well with lo mein

We reached the coast of France at Calais and crossed on another large ferry. This was long before they'd built the "Chunnel" under the sea, making it possible to cross by car, and in those days, it was possible to take a hovercraft across! I was really into the idea, but it was out of our budget.

Jerry and I ordered hamburgers at the ferry's snack bar, and the waiter chastised us for requesting fries.

"They are called CHIPS, gentlemen."

He was also somehow able to make "ketchup" sound like a naughty word.

The famous White Cliffs of Dover loomed into view. It had been a long day, at the end of a long three days of travel. It was already getting dark as we walked down the ramp in Dover, and the famous crappy English weather turned cold and rainy.

Our home base for London would be Guildford Surrey, where we planned to stay at the home of a friend of Jerry's mom, a Scot named Mrs. Moorehead. To picture her, think of a Monty Python pepperpot. She was kind and generous and took us into her home.

Mrs. Moorehead loaded us up at Guildford station—chilled, tired, and soggy. I'd kept track of my *fez* by sticking it on the end of my bedroll, and it had gone completely limp. We had stopped at a roadside stand to get some Chinese "take away," and she plopped us down at her dining room table, set out three tumblers, and plunked down a bottle of scotch.

"Poor yoorselves ah drink, bois" she said, and ducked into the kitchen to plate the food.

"I'm not much of a scotch drinker," I whispered to Jerry.

He nodded his head in agreement.

We poured a half-inch in each glass and pretended to sip as she returned. She set the plates down and looked the scene over.

"Ach! Bois, poor yoorselves ah DRINK!" she said and filled the three tumblers up (*bloop-blip-bloop-bloop*).

We slept well.

She let us sleep in, telling us, "I'm gonty goa shoppin, an also stop at tha newsstand. A'm partial tae tha scandal rags, but mebbie ya like yoor news straight?"

We opted for scandal and marveled at the topless "page three girl" in a newspaper that she had just bought on the street.

"Oh yeh," she said. "They're *all* like thaht."

It had turned into a sunny day, and she drove us to the station. I sat up front, and being on the wrong side of the car, on the wrong side of the road was jarring. We waited with some tall-mohawked punks for the train into London.

On the train, we began to enjoy the benefits of our native language. We'd been nearly a year without English and suddenly it was everywhere. We could read the signs! We could tell where we were going! The names of the shops all meant something to us.

"Look Jerry! It says, 'Roast Beef!'"

Over several days, we did all the tourist things in London. Mrs. Moorehead turned us loose. She'd seen it all and was content to listen to our stories when we came home. We mastered riding the Tube (London's Metro, which is officially known as "The Underground") and found it an excellent way to get everywhere. Like the European trains, the cars of the Tube varied greatly, and one car we rode must have dated back to Prince Albert.

We went to Piccadilly and had tea at Harrods. We saw the Queen at Madame Tussauds (she wasn't very talkative). We spent an entire morning at the British War Museum, where I bored Jerry to death prattling on about the Hurricanes and Spitfires, the Messerschmitts and the tanks. We skipped the usual fish-and-chips—Jerry has an allergy that prevents eating any fish at all.*

We spent the afternoon at the Tower of London, getting icked-out by its gory history. One goal had been to catch a Broadway-style show in a theatre on the West End. We were naïve to think we could get tickets without planning and couldn't find a single show that wasn't sold out. With an evening to kill

---

* *Back in the little restaurant in Saint Malo, the menu negotiations kept moving over to seafood, and we'd relayed the problem of Jerry's allergy to our gracious hosts by drawing on napkins: A picture of a fish with an X through it and a badly-drawn chicken with a check mark next to it. The wife had smiled and brought forth the cheese-platter that we shared.*

and theater on our minds, we settled for a premier showing of Monty Python's *Life of Brian*.

One morning, as we rode quietly through the English countryside in a train car with an open floor plan, we heard a couple of guys talking on the bench behind us. What were they saying? It was thick, and it was lyrical, with a lot of rolled R's.

I turned to Jerry and said, "Man, I'm not sure, but I think they're speaking English!"

He cocked his head to listen for a minute, and then came back with, "Ha! Yeah. They're Irish."

Frank Zappa and the Mothers of Immigration

an illegal alien

During our second morning in Guildford, I realized that the calendar had finally ticked by to the day before the Frank Zappa concert. I had said that no matter where I was on July 2, I'd use my Eurail Pass to travel back to Munich and see the show. Jerry wasn't interested in Zappa, so I'd have to go it alone.

We checked the schedules, and it looked like I was in for about a twelve-hour trip through France, Belgium, and Germany. We spent the day in London doing our tourist bit, and I hopped the train at Guildford Station late that night, so I'd be able to sleep for a lot of the trip. Thinking ahead to the next day's ride, I paid a sleepy attendant to cook me a hamburger to take as a sack lunch to eat on the train.

The Channel was very choppy that night, and the ferry across made me ill. Someone told me to go to the front observation deck—that seeing where we were going would help.

It did not.

It was after midnight, and there was nothing to see except windshield wipers beating back the rain. The enclosed deck reminded me of the waiting area at an airport gate—if B2 at Newark was rocking slowly and jumping up and down by six feet.

I was very glad to see the lights of the dock at Calais.

I slept on the train until mid-morning and ate my hamburger for breakfast. I had a paperback that I'd bought at a newsstand in Casablanca and passed the time reading *Raise the Titanic* by Clive Cussler.*

I had my head in the book and missed lunch at Frankfurt, so by the time Nuremberg rolled by I was starving.

When I got to Munich, I bought a big pretzel in the Olympic Village, sat on a bench, and ate as I finished the book.

It was afternoon by then, and the show wasn't until eight o'clock. I chucked

---
* *I started the trip with* The World According to Garp *and finished that one somewhere around Algeciras.*

the paperback out with the pretzel trash and bummed around in the park. Zappa's show was to be in the Olympiahalle, somewhere in the park, and I had no map.

A steady migration of European-style hippies was flowing in only one direction in front of me, so I followed it to the huge tent-shaped venue next to a space-needle tower. We stood in line for an hour and a half, before an Italian fan told me I didn't have to, if I had a ticket already. I killed the rest of the time sitting on a berm with a bunch of German students, debating about which era of Zappa's music was best.

I got a great spot on the floor, not far from the stage, and the debaters who argued (as I did) that Frank's late-'70s lineup was best, wound up right next to me.

One of them was bugging everyone around us, in boozy German, for a cigarette. He had produced a napkin with an ochre lump in it and needed the cig to put this booger of hash in, so he could smoke it during the show. When his mission was finally accomplished, he offered me a toke.

I'm glad I turned him down, because halfway through the show, during "You Are What You Is," he turned green, stifled a heave, and ran off. We didn't see him again, but he'd been such a pest it didn't bother me much.

Frank came on, and the crowd went nuts in a dozen languages. They played a great show! The band included two members from the lineup that we'd argued was the best, so my little group (minus Mr. Pukey) was thrilled.* I had little time to waste after the concert. I had to get across town to the station and catch the overnighter back toward London. I hopped on an almost empty train, closed the door on a compartment all to myself, and drifted off to sleep with my ears ringing.

Sometime during the night, I found myself uncomfortable. I was lying on my stomach with my travel pouch between my chest and the cushion, so I pulled it from around my neck and stowed it under my seat. Later on, I pulled my pass booklet out of it to show the conductor, and then jammed the pass in my pocket.

I awoke groggy the next morning on the bumping, clacking train and walked down the corridor to the bathroom to wash my face and pee. I noticed that the door to my compartment had been opened but didn't think much of it. As I stood in the toilet, I thought of the evening's sleep.

My pouch!

I finished quickly and ran back to the compartment. It was gone. I startled the passengers in the cabins to the left and right, searching for my pouch and asking if they'd seen anything.

Back in my compartment, there was my show-program and t-shirt—the thief hadn't been interested in them. What they probably had been interested in was my passport.

Gone!

They also got my traveler's checks, which wouldn't be worth anything to them. Besides the dollars-worth of deutschmarks in my pocket, the checks were all of the money I had. I had no money, no passport, and I was alone—and 4,829 miles from home.

I spent a good bit of the morning in the police station next to the railyard in Ostend, Belgium, in the office of the *rechercheur*. He spoke little English, but he was very sympathetic, and we filled out a police report to help my effort to get back into England. He was portly and had longish grey hair and

---

* *While checking facts for this story I discovered that the show had been simulcast as a radio program on the King Biscuit Flour Hour. They archived the tapes and later released a CD, and it documents Frank and a stripped-down touring band that played a lot of new material, and slicked-up versions of a few oldies. Just as I remembered, he burns through half a dozen ten-minute solos of glorious screamin' treble. I left the place with a stinker of a headache.*

a mustache. That, along with his uniform made him look like Bob Keeshan, the guy who played Captain Kangaroo, which was somewhat comforting.

Because I hadn't put it back in the bag the night before, I still had my Eurail Pass booklet, the only ace in my otherwise crappy hand. In the line for the ferry back across the channel I showed the English Customs guy my police report and the pass book, turning it to the stamp that showed I had been in England just two days before.

"No passport, then?" he said. "Aye, ah can let ye on tha boat, but ah shouldn't. Tha boys on tha other side won't be as chipper about it. They're liable ta throw ya into tha Channel."

Yeah, he was right, they weren't so "chipper."

When the immigration officers heard that I had no passport and no money, they grabbed my arm and led me to a tiny room with just a table and a couple of chairs. It was stuffy and dimly lit, and they took the police report and my train pass from me and left me for what seemed like hours.

I had shown them the phone number for Mrs. Moorehead, the lady that Jerry and I were staying with, written inside the cover of my pass, and now I sat there with no ID or papers to show I was legitimate.

Two uniformed men returned and turned the lights up to a blinding level. Officer Bad Cop sat down opposite me and started the interrogation. He told me that the Dover Immigration Removal Centre was right down the block, that it was a prison for visa violators, and that *no passport* meant that I had *no proof* of a visa.

He leaned in and told me that the United Kingdom didn't put up with vagabonds (this was becoming my least favorite word), and that it looked very much to him like I was one. He paused for effect, and then let Officer Good Cop continue.

"We rang up this woman on your train pass, and she vouched for you," Good Cop said. "So, with her endorsement, we're going to put you on the train to Guildford. The U.S. embassy is at this address in London, and it opens Monday at eight o'clock."

Bad Cop stood up and bent over just inches from my face. "We will call them, and if you're not there at eight-o-one, we will find you and arrest you."

They put my pass in my hand, walked me to the train, and a couple of hours later I was standing in front of an astonished Jerry and Mrs. Moorehead. I have often wondered how my family spent *their* Fourth of July that year.

I was waiting on the steps of the embassy when the Marine guards unlocked the doors that Monday morning. They were able to get me a new passport with the visa and signatures that same day while I waited.

I wasn't amazed (just relieved) then, but I am now. This was in the age before desk-top computers, and they would have had to make a dozen overseas phone calls and hustle to verify everything. Nevertheless, they got it done. They sent me down the block to a shop that specialized in passport photos. The shop had a huge bulletin board in the waiting room with little two-by-two-inch photos of every celebrity who had been there to get a visa. I saw Gregory Peck, Marty Feldman, and at least three of the Monty Python guys.

The shiny new passport didn't solve the problem of being flat broke, though, so Jerry offered to front me the money I'd need for the remainder of our trip home.

Luckily, we were coming down to the last few days of our epic.

Back to Sweden

our adventure winds down

We finished out our list of London tourist spots. As we'd done with our other hosts, we wanted to give Mrs. Morehead something for having us. We remembered that first night with her, and I knew that my dad thought highly of Johnnie Walker Scotch. So, we sought out a shop that had a bottle of Black Label and presented it to her. We bade her goodbye and hit the tracks one last time.

On the boat across the Channel, I happened by a kid wearing a golf shirt with a logo on it that read: *Fellowship of Christian Athletes, Marlow, Oklahoma.*

I couldn't let *that* go unbothered.

I walked up and said, "Hey, how ya doin'? From Oklahoma? Me too! Although I've never heard of Marlow."

He was surprised to meet us, and asked, "Where are you from?"

We got a good laugh when I told him "Duncan"—Marlow is five miles north, basically a suburb.

He was only one of several homey coincidences. I also ran into a classmate from Sweden named Kristina in a crowded train station in Paris. It really is a small world.

The only thing that stood between us and our adopted home country of Sweden was one last haul through Northern Europe. Though some countries were only ninety miles wide, we'd still log a full day of travel.

This leg of the trip was fairly uneventful, and my memories of it are clouded by the anxiety of my last few weeks in Sweden. The train station in Cologne was close enough to see the famous cathedral, so we checked off one last tourist box. We'd been avid collectors of stamps in our passports and tried to get as many different countries as we could, but I lost all that when my passport was stolen.

I was ready to be "home," where my days didn't include scouting for food and shelter, being thrown out of places and off of trains, and eating chicken in bars.

Photo by Jerry Garcia

We vowed that when we came back, we'd only travel first class. Our social status during our journey had highs and lows. Authorities were only interested in us when they saw us as vagrants. Jerry encountered racism in Munich, and we got caught up in a bit of a scam in Tangier. Most of the glitches were just us being goofy teenagers.

In countless places we were taken in, indulged, and treated like kings by people I barely knew. Jerry's friends and acquaintances made a fuss over us like we were prodigal sons. Our fellow "vagabonds" shared their wine, train seats, advice, and stories. Even the annoying dude with the crate of chickens offered us an egg.

The hospitality we received from friends, strangers, and fellow travelers showed us that the goodness in people really is universal.

There have been times in the recent past when I've seen news stories about American students who were hiking on the border of North Vietnam, or in the Afghan mountains who were picked up, imprisoned, even tried as spies. I've yelled at the TV about how dumb these kids are, just la-la-la camping out in a place where tensions are hot and ready to snap. Then I think back to parts of *our* trip and wonder what we were thinking as well.

The hostage crisis in Iran had erupted that November, making half the Arab world mad at Americans. Just two months before, the U.S. had attempted to rescue the hostages at the embassy in Iran, making things there worse. What were two American kids doing going into Morocco?

At the time, we had no qualms about the trip. We had spent that news cycle in Sweden, where we were somewhat insulated from the politics at home (and in the Middle East.) We hadn't encountered much anti-American sentiment in our year—kind of the opposite. Americans still enjoyed some esteem back then, and I was a B-list celebrity in my little town in Sweden.

More than once in Casablanca though, when Jerry's friend introduced us to someone, I would see them bow and greet him warmly, but scowl at or ignore *me*. I suppose I was a pale white, skinny teenager in the wrong corner of the world, but we did just fine. We had an amazing adventure and came back with stories to tell.

When you face adversity with a friend and have as much fun as Jerry and I did, those memories stay vivid forever. As a small-town kid from Oklahoma and Kansas, the trip changed the way I viewed people, it changed the way I smelled food and what I looked for in a beer. It changed my view of authority and what I thought I was capable of.

I think it was all for the better.

Snow Day at Home

In a sausage, in a case

ohm resistor heat sink paste.

Archimedes' tooth decayed

while Marcelino was delayed.

Tollhouse guacamole bin

amplifiers set on ten

and Philomena can't get in

her driveway.

An Academician

A Scholarship for College Track

at least Dad thought it was funny

Karl and I ran track together for years—first in high school and then at Southwest Oklahoma State University (SWOSU). After participating at the collegiate level for a year, we realized that scholastically, it wasn't such a good idea to stay in sports.

High school sports are fun extracurricular activities, but if you are a college athlete, there's nothing extracurricular about it. The coaches act like that is the only reason you are on campus—if anything, coursework is an "extra-athletic activity." So the next year, Karl and I elected to be on campus to actually go to a few classes.

Before all of that, Karl and I ran cross-country in the fall, and track in the spring. We were both distance runners, long and lean, and anything under a few miles seemed like a power sprint to us. College cross-country is a five-mile race, and the workouts were typically divided between days of consecutive one-mile sprints and days where we did a ten- or twelve-mile run (I sure can't do that anymore).

During track season, my event was a two-mile race on the oval—eight laps around and around the track. I lost track of my lap-count once and had no idea how far I'd gone. They fire a gun when the leader starts his last lap, so I waited for the bang and ran like hell.

At one track meet, I think it was at Southern Methodist, Karl and I were hanging out waiting for our event when the coach came by.

"There's a steeplechase today, do you two want to run it?"

Karl and I figured ourselves to be as manly (or crazy) as anybody on the field, so we lined up, they shot a gun, and off we went.

Have you ever seen a steeplechase? My god. It is three thousand meters (about two miles) and there are twenty-eight barriers and seven water jumps. They named the "barriers" correctly—although they look a bit like hurdles, they are a four-by-four beam held up by poles (each around three-feet high), cemented in place. They don't fall over if you hit them, and after slamming into a couple, we figured out that the best move is to try to step on top and launch yourself.

The water hazard is sloped on the far side of the barrier, so the farther you can push off, the shallower the water is where you land. You are going to get wet. You are going to fall face first in the water and have someone jump on you with spiked track shoes. It's just going to happen. What'd I say, seven times? I'm surprised they didn't make us fistfight a wino at the finish line.

But I digress. I think we were talking about my scholarship offer.

I came home for Christmas during my year in track and walked in to find Dad with a huge grin, holding an opened envelope addressed to me from the University of Kansas. My grandpa Herb went to KU on a scholarship for track before he had to return home and take over the family farm when his dad died. Kansas was still one of the powerhouse track schools even in my day, so I didn't mind that Dad had opened my mail—he and I both would have been very interested in what they had to say.

He read the letter to me, and it was full of flowery prose about how they were interested in me and that they had a lot to offer. Full-ride scholarships available, blah-blah—standard recruitment jazz you would expect to hear if you were a sought-after competitor.

But, umm ... my times were *okay*. I mean, they were competitive. I was always up in the front group, but I wasn't winning any races. What were they going on about? The letter talked about a scholarship possibility, and they sounded serious! "A tradition of excellence," and "We feel you would be a fine addition," okay, okay, I was getting really excited!

I should have known from the sideways grin on Dad's face that something was up. It was a real letter, really from KU, really a scholarship feeler, but when he read on down to the closing "... so in conclusion, MISS Randle ..."

My first name had struck again: I was offered a fat scholarship for *women's* track. Well at least Dad thought it was funny.* Oh, and the next time our coach came looking for volunteers for a steeplechase, Karl and I hid behind the bus.

---

* *The scholarship offer might also have had roots in a gag that Karl and our friend Dom pulled on me at the OU Invitational meet. They'd entered me in the Women's Mile, and then snarfed and giggled when the officials announced over the public address speakers that I was late to the starting line.*

The Karl and Andy Totem Pole

and collectable barware

Man, could we drink beer. You may attribute it to our young and speedy metabolism, our extensive training in the art, or (mostly) the low alcohol content of the beer available to nineteen-year-olds at that time.

Our quick metabolisms were even more accelerated by cross-country season, when we could "slam" a Coors tallboy immediately after a twelve-mile work out and get an intense buzz that only lasted for as long as it took to shower. The alcohol came and went, and we'd be sober by the time we walked over to dinner.

Our bladders must have been exceptional, also. There are tales, too loutish to relate here, of riding with Walt, our friend Rosser, and others in Walt's orange jeep on Highway 81, each of us looking through the handle-holes of our own twelve-pack beer box. To earn a "Beer Helmet" you had to drink the twelve beers within.

The dive bars in college towns of that era can also be blamed for promoting many schemes that involved over-consumption of weak beer. They'd have you pay five bucks at the door, then let you drink as many watered-down tap beers as you could wait in line for. "Pitcher Night," "Bucket Night," I don't know how joints got away with some of the things they did in the '80s.

One school night we went to The Kendall House (*the* popular place in Weatherford, home to SWOSU, for throwing up in the parking lot) for their "Drown Night." We drank about ten thousand beers and came home to the dorms drunk as skunks.

I flopped on my bed and put in Candy-O, and then from down at Karl and Andy's room I heard "TURN IT UP!"

After a bunch of giggling and some kind of struggle outside the hallway, Andy came into the room with Karl sitting on his shoulders. As low as Andy ducked to get through the door, he still nearly brushed Karl all the way off his perch. This configuration put Karl's shoulders at about seven-foot, eleven-inches off the ground, so the eight-foot ceiling made Karl's head completely superfluous.

The joyous rag doll-dance of the Karl-and-Andy totem pole had Karl hanging on to Andy's nose with one hand with the other across his eyes. There was nothing left showing of Andy's face but a big goofy grin as he painted the ceiling with a floppy Karl, knocking in tiles as they went.

We also used to steal barware from The Kendall House. The place had an emergency exit with a broken alarm at the back of the dance floor, and we'd slip out and down the fire escape with a glass pitcher or a Coors-branded bar glass to add to our set in the dorm room.

A big, blonde mook of a bouncer whose nickname was "Bamm-Bamm" (rumored to be an Olympic alternate in judo) caught Karl by the neck one night, on the stairs of that fire-exit, but solved the transgression by walking Karl back in to return the pitcher to the bartender. For Karl, this embarrassment constituted a challenge (cue the famous Bug Bunny quote: "Of course you realize, this means war!").

So, we made it a game: Grab something and be seen leaving with it, then try to outrun Bamm-Bamm.

We *could* do it, but not in a short race. We had to make sure he was all the way across the bar, which gave us enough lead that we could get our pace up and simply outlast him. A couple of motivated, college-level cross country runners can keep loping along for hours, and we would just run the couple of miles back to campus and leave Andy to drive home.

I kept one of those glass pitchers and used it for years. When I dropped and broke it, the wife wondered why I was so sentimental about the ugly old thing.

McCabe's Lectern

Huckyulla Buckyulla Bargatta Poot

Oskiwallablottaskaktabrazoot

A Degree in Mischief

don't make us call the police

In high school, I was a perpetual C-student, and it was mostly because of my work ethic. I had a few teachers tell my parents I was smart enough to rule the world but that it would never happen, because they couldn't get me to do any work.

My folks oversaw my enrollment every semester and made sure that I took every single college prep class I could while I was in high school, so I was only one credit short of graduating at the end of my junior year. The plan was for me to take college courses during my senior year and to be able to get into whatever school I wanted to. I did well on placement tests, which made my mediocre grades frustrate them even more.

Such a rebel.

Then, I was selected to be an exchange student to Sweden. Since Swedish would be a new language, they told me they wouldn't grade me very strictly. This fit nicely with my scholastic philosophy. When I returned, my parents decided that I'd go to a small college for a semester or two to get my head in the game, and then aim higher.

My high school buddies and I were fans of the movie *Animal House*, which was a blueprint of how *not* to succeed in college. Unfortunately, I took it as a bible of how *to* behave. I went to Southwestern Oklahoma State out in the scrubby little town of Weatherford and set to work drinking beer. My friends Andy and Karl had been beer-drinking buddies back home, and they stayed in close proximity, although *they* actually made their grades.

My Dad's stories of growing up always featured a cast of several friends. There was Max, Joe Bob, and one he called Jake the Snake. A few of his stories were about getting into trouble, and it seemed like all of those stories had Don Fincham in there somewhere. As I heard more stories, I came to the realization that Don was a bit of a catalyst for trouble, at least for my dad. Not trouble himself (I knew him, he was a great guy), but Dad might have not gotten into as much trouble, had the two not cooked it up *together*.

I had a theory that everyone has their own Don Fincham. I definitely thought of Karl as mine, and you'll hear his name a lot when I reminisce. Many years later, at Karl's funeral, those of us who knew him well were asked to each tell a story they remembered about him. Everyone took their turn, and as they did, it slowly dawned on me that everyone, even his parents, thought of *me* as *Karl's* Don Fincham (a little bit of self-discovery, that).

I hit the ground running at SWOSU and took eighteen hours my first semester. Chemistry, botany, honors English, a 7:30 a.m. zoology lab, go dog go. Just beat my brains out, right off the bat. Well, I turned in my usual C average for the semester, and The Folks *freaked* completely *out*. They were paying my way and threatened that if I couldn't do better than Cs, they would cut me off and cut me loose.

And so, bolstered by that motivational speech, next semester I didn't do much better. I had hit my stride partying, and it didn't help that I was competing in track. I knew I was stinkin' up the gradebook, so I changed my official correspondence address to my dorm room and had my grades sent there instead of home.

When they asked, I told my parents I was now paying my own way and would make whatever grades I wanted. *Hahaha, ha! Ho, ho.* They liked that one.

Oh, and I went and got a job. I made a hash of summer school, and I had determined to be a bad influence on Andy, too.

The next fall, in an effort to improve my GPA, I quit the track team and changed my major. It took that semester and a couple of weeks of spring before the trouble I was getting into caused Southwestern to decide that I and they should, uhm, *part ways*.

But gosh, Jode! What kind of trouble could a nice guy like you have gotten into that was that bad?

Well, it started low-key. I mean I wasn't walking around looking for trouble. Not at first, anyway. That came later.

You could call it youthful frivolity. You could call it small rebellions that went sideways. Whatever it was, it slowly added up.

Like when Karl and I were told that pets were not allowed in the dorms, so we went out and bought two mice. We named them Bill and George (after our dads, of course) and kept them in an aquarium in Karl's room. That is, until an inspection discovered them, and we were told to, and I quote, "let them go." We let them go, in the cafeteria during lunch. The authorities *kinda* knew who did it but *kinda* couldn't prove it.

Barrington was another freshman from Duncan. Together we wrote and illustrated a sheet of instructions for how to make a bong out of parts that could be swiped from the chemistry labs, which was xeroxed many times.

Barrington and I were out on the prairie that surrounds Weatherford one night drinking beer, when a tumbleweed crossed in front of his firebird that was *as big as his car*. We pulled up alongside, I grabbed the stem, and we drug it back to the dorm. We stuffed (and crammed and shoved) it into the dorm's elevator and left it there. Again, people had their suspicions, but no one specifically *saw* us do it.

One morning the resident assistant swung by and said that someone told him that we had been using the hot part of a popcorn popper to cook grilled cheese sandwiches in our room, and cooking *in the room* was against the rules. So, during a really nice day, Karl, Andy, and I crawled *out of our room* window onto the ledge that ran around the outside on each floor. Up three floors on the two feet of ledge with our legs dangling off, we grilled hamburgers on a little charcoal hibachi that we'd brought out with us. We snickered at the people coming and going below who couldn't figure out where that wonderful smell was coming from. Someone did finally look up, and the *outside*-versus-*inside* technicality went over like a turd in a punchbowl with the school's dean of men. I was beginning to be a blip on his radar.

Karl and I liked to hang out and talk late into the night there in Weatherford. One of our favorite places was at the base of a radio tower a few miles out of town. We'd sit in the car and ramble on and hoist a few beers, while we watched the red beacon on top of the tower slowly, silently cycle on and off in the black sky. More than once, we wondered aloud how big the beacon was, and talked about someday climbing up and unscrewing it. We made some kind of bet about which of us would be crazy enough to beat the other to it.

We lived on the third floor of Jefferson Hall, and we "thirds" had our pride. I mean, we weren't going to take any guff from fourth if it came to it. And it did. Someone had a friend on fourth that they pranked, and after a few more pranks, it just kind of escalated to entire floors being *at war*. Now, all of the following aren't things I specifically did by myself. But many are ones I saw, or happened to me:

- Go in the bathroom while your victim is taking a nice warm shower and fill a large cup up with cold water. Splash! That's an easy one.

- If you push hard on the bottom of a closed dorm door (they open inward) and push pennies up in between the door and its jam, it will create pressure on the door that can't be overcome by turning the knob. This locks the victim in his room and makes him miss class. That's a little meaner.

- Take all of the drawers out of someone's dresser. Turn his dresser upside-down and put all of the right-side-up drawers back in their slots. Turn the whole thing back right side up. Now, when he opens a drawer, he dumps his socks and underwear all over the floor (and he has to dump out every drawer to fix it.).

- Pushing in on the corners of an old-school record album cover makes it easy to fill it with shaving cream. Quickly put the mouth of the album cover under the victim's door and stomp: BLOOF! The foam continues to expand as it floats down and covers a good bit of their room with suds.

- Take a travel-sized tube of toothpaste and squeeze an inch out of it. Push a firecracker into the tube, light it, and slide it under the victim's door. Pop! There are now tiny grey dots of sticky toothpaste on EVERYTHING in ~~my~~ their room. Every. Thing.

- The bottom of a dorm door is plenty high enough off the floor to just slide a long string of lit firecrackers under, too, Dude. How 'bout them apples?

- This one was extremely evil and was reserved for a guy who had pissed the entire floor off. Someone bought a pound of hamburger, left it in its plastic package and put it up in his ceiling, then replaced the tiles. The undiscovered ground beef stayed sealed up tight while it decayed, with the plastic slowly expanding, until it rotted so much that the packaging exploded and released an ungodly, inescapable smell of death in his room. This was enough to make the poor asshole transfer to another school.

- The telephones in the dorm were all on their own local extension system and were numbered by floor, sequentially. Karl and I came home from a track meet very late one night/early one morning and decided to stay up until class began. At about four o'clock in the morning we called every phone number from the top of the building to the bottom, and woke everyone up, one at a time.

- One floor visited another floor in the dead of night, bringing thirty-gallon plastic trash cans that they'd borrowed from around campus. They disabled the alarm on the emergency fire hose and used it to fill the cans with water. They leaned the cans against a few selected victims' doors, and in the morning when the victims opened their doors, the cans fell inward and flooded their rooms.

- The "trash can" victims retaliated by running the aforementioned firehose up the stairs and into the offenders' hallway at three o'clock in the morning, and just turned the damned thing on full, to blast, bash around, and spray. When word of this one got back to the dean, a great many people were in trouble.

As I said, at a certain point I got a job and had all university correspondence sent to my campus address, so I was also getting bills for the dorm rent. They were just exorbitant, especially for a twelve-by-twelve shared room. I began to get a crappy attitude, born of the idea that I was forced by the rules to live there, when I could be living in an apartment for less, and of not following all their damned stupid rules about having mice and beer and girls in *my* room.

One of the small things that bugged me about that dorm was that there were no markers on the doorframes of the floors when the elevator stopped. Every floor looked the same, and the floor number lights inside the elevator didn't work, so you frequently got out on the wrong floor. I flexed my art student muscles and set about remedying the problem by painting a carefully rendered "3rd Floor" on the metal frame you could see right as the door opened. Guys from other floors liked it, so they asked, and I did a few more.

A while later, over a holiday weekend some moron took a can of black spray paint and tagged the walls all up and down the stairwell. The stairwells were visible all over campus, as they had glass windows from top to bottom, and this thoughtless vandalism made our dorm look horrible. During the next break, it disappeared, and I was glad to see it gone.

Each floor plan of our dorm had rooms around the perimeter, and then the middle had a laundry room, a bathroom/showers area, and a common area. Our floor's common area was empty—only bare tile and a big spot of water-damage on the wall from a bathroom leak upstairs. The women's dorm across the courtyard from us was a mirror of ours except, to maximize the number of available rooms they had turned the common areas into an extra-large dorm room on each floor. Discovering this on a (forbidden) visit to the girls' side inspired an idea.

I asked around and was told that the dean of men was in charge of granting permission for what I wanted to do. I got an audience with him and proposed that if I were to repair the wall and paint it at my own expense, could I move in and use it as my own dorm room?

By this time in my career, Dean Ash recognized me by sight and knew my name (I learned later that this was absolutely not a good thing). On that day, he was a merciful deity and accepted my offer. I fixed the leak and the wall, primed it, and painted a big blue graphic I had designed for an art class. To make the design pop, I shelled out for some expensive custom-color enamel paint.

I moved in and all was fine. At least now, I was paying too much for a private, bigger room, and it was painted snazzy, too!

Behind some stuff in the tiny laundry room, Andy found a telephone (Kids: In *those* days, a telephone was a plastic device the size of your head with a separate piece you held up to listen to, just like in the old movies!) The phone had survived some kind of fire, and was a strange, two-piece black blob that still functioned perfectly. I took it, since my manufactured room didn't have one, and we dubbed it the "Melt-O-Phone." It was always stinky and just slightly sticky because of its terrible past.

Well, there was *some* dumbassed tomfoolery involved in my eventual expulsion.

Karl and I were horsing around in the lobby, shoving each other, and I was pushed backward into a window that was a decorative piece of the front of the dorm. Like one of the stairwell pieces, it was four feet wide and ten feet tall. One big, $300 piece of glass, very expensive for the time.

Dean Ash called me to his office and told me that I owed the school the three hundred clams to have it repaired. I told him that I'd only broken the bottom third of it and that the maintenance guys had cut the glass there and installed a plywood panel. It looked to me like I owed him for ten bucks worth of plywood. He said that a bill for three hundred would be in the mail.

I told him, "Yeah, so will the check."

That conversation led the dean to decide to pay a visit, in person, to look at the job I'd done on the wall in "my" room while I was away at class—maybe I was in class. More likely I was in a cornfield with a hangover. Who can say?

The wall of my ~~doom~~ dorm.

I got a phone call summoning me to come to his office at once.

"Sit down Mister Randle. I saw the wall in your room," he said. "That is not what I meant when I said you could paint it. Go back and paint it over, and I want it plain white this time. You. Are. Dismissed."

What the hell? The wall wasn't obscene or rebellious. It was a nice tasteful abstract design. What was up his butt? I went back to my dorm and promptly ignored his "order." That is, until he called again and demanded to know why it wasn't done.

I told him I couldn't afford more paint, so he had the dufus maintenance guys come slop over it with crappy thin white paint, which my design showed right through—it was just kinda faded now. That his paint didn't work was Dean Ash's proverbial last straw.

The dean was waiting in his office for me with a long list of offences that he'd had typed up, most of them already chronicled in this story. He told me that my name had been brought up in a department meeting, and it was decided that "it was no longer financially feasible to keep me on as a student."

I had not only ignored the rules, but I had also ignored all of my bills from them and owed the school a good deal of money. I was to clear out of my room, and if I were seen on campus the next day or thereafter, they would have me arrested on the spot for vandalism.

I asked if he really thought of my wall as an act of vandalism. He said no, but the graffiti in the stairwell (*someone else's*) had cost them a lot of money to sandblast off, and that my "compulsion to paint other parts of the dormitory" was enough for anyone who cared to, to connect that criminal act to me.

I saw that I was screwed, so I packed my undershorts and fled the scene.

All these years later, what are my thoughts on my time at college? Man, I wish I'd bucked up and finished. It certainly would have been less expensive in terms of money and my time if I had. The amount of money that I owed Southwestern then (I got it all paid back around a year after I left, by the way) is about as much as *one stinking class* costs me now.

It's easy to see from this distance what a waste my fun, or rebellion, or whatever you'd call it, was.

The Mike Rowes of the world prattle on about how a degree shouldn't matter in a world where working people are essential to society. While I completely agree with the *theory*, the *reality* is that it is tough to get a job even doing manual labor when you are competing with other manual laborers with an MBA. And the people who tend to talk like that do it from the viewpoint of having a degree.

Everyone in my immediate family has a degree, and I'm very proud of all of them. I've gone back to school to work on a business degree myself, and I've completed twenty-four hours to add to my SWOSU credits. But it has its lumps. One of them is that abandoning my classes dumped my grade average to an F, and to be able to apply my usable credits from back then, I have to incorporate the F into my total academic score. I'm on eternal probation.

I was motivated to go back a couple of years ago by fear when yet another boss came by my desk and said, "Ah, ya know, uhm, your position requires a degree. I mean, you wound up where you are. But if you want to go any higher, you might want to go back to school."

I took my now-grownup work ethic and dug into some classes. I've made straight As but found that one thing hasn't changed—I still hate schoolwork. I mean, like, *really hate* it. Bummer.

After Karl's funeral, while I was talking to his mom, Ann, I told her I had a guitar I had agreed to buy from him, but that he had never asked for the hundred bucks. Could I pay her? She told me no, no just hang on to it for him.

A few years later, a bunch of us were in town for a class reunion and got together over at Karl's house. Ann asked if I still had the guitar, and I told her "Of course!" and that we'd even used it on our last album.

While the gang talked with Ann and George, I wandered back to Karl's room. Ann had kept it just as he'd left it, with his souvenirs and sports memorabilia still there. On a shelf above his dresser, in between a couple of track trophies, sat a cylinder of heavy, dark red glass, as big as a gallon bucket. It had a thick aluminum flange around the bottom marked "WESTINGHOUSE AUXILIARY BEACON."

I guess I lost the bet.*

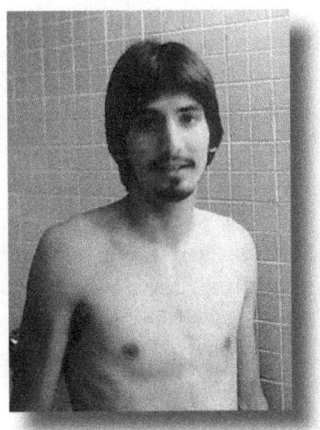

Karl Hazelbaker

---

* UNDER NO CIRCUMSTANCES should you attempt to climb, or even go near a radio tower. Most are powered with high voltage, and the entire structure and support wires are electrified. Karl had been very lucky.

A Rat Race in the Subaru

stay off of the putting green

Karl wasn't the first of us to "roof-ride." I believe it was Trip who crawled out of the open window of Karl's Malibu on a back road southwest of Duncan, laid down flat on the roof of the car, held on to the trim and sang at the top of his lungs while Karl maintained a bumpy sixty miles an hour. We all tried it at least once, on the Malibu or Andy's Grand Torino. I think you feel like you can live forever at that age.

I'm not sure what happened to Karl's Malibu, but when I got home from Sweden, he was driving a poop-colored early-'70s Subaru. Karl had been a dirtbike racer before getting his license and was a daredevil behind the wheel. He spent a lot of time driving the streets of Duncan, and with the tight handling of this overpowered tiny car, he was actually a decent street racer.

He was one of those "I paid full price for that tachometer, and I'm going to use all of it" kind of guys. He talked about installing a roll bar but figured his mom and dad would be onto him if he did. He *did* have a custom license plate that said "KARL." He once told me he was taking accounting classes only so he could handle the money from his future racing career. That might have been the beer talking, though.

Karl liked to "troll" people, before that was a thing, and long before the internet made it easy to do without real danger. Karl *liked* the real danger of bugging someone to the point of them being fighting mad, then outrunning them, physically or in his car.

One summer evening, he told me he had been doing what he called "Rat-Racing."

He described cruising up and down Highway 81 (as you did in Duncan) until he found some redneck types with a big pickup, then road-rage pestering them until they were so mad that they gave chase. He'd then use his driving skill and knowledge of Duncan's streets to give them the slip, but not before leading them on an angry chase all over town. The cops were often a random third player in this game.

He offered to get a six-pack and take me along for one.

We did just as he described, finding a Cummins Diesel full of cowboy hats, and giving them the finger as we passed in front of Taco Tico. We heard the Cummins engine roar, and the chase was on!

Karl's little tan box tore up Bois D' Arc (that's "Boe-Dark Street," y'all, like the fence post), then we fishtailed north on Fifteenth Street, with the huge white pickup belching smoke and bellowing like a bull behind us. Down to the park, both vehicles around the loop twice, up to Tenth and tearing along with houses flying by. We just couldn't shake them! We blew through the stop sign at Elder Street as Karl floored it.

"I've got a plan!" he shouted over the whining engine.

When we hooked a left at the golf course entrance, my heart rate shot up. The road was a dead-end. We'd be trapped behind the clubhouse! We had gained a three or four block lead when our foes stopped at Elder, and as we followed the road down and around, Karl turned off his lights to make us harder to see. At the end of the road, Karl turned down a gravel path that led to the golf cart shed. From there we were suddenly cruising along down the side of a fairway. His Subaru's wheelbase was narrow enough to fit on the golf cart path.

"Bill home?" Karl asked casually.

My family's backyard was on the edge of the sixteenth hole of the golf course, a wide-open green field with ponds and trees for blocks in three directions.

I told him yeah, Bill (my dad) was home, and probably in bed.

He turned the Subaru off, and we quietly coasted to a stop in the backyard. We sat on my family's deck and drank our beers, and Karl told me about a previous Rat Race that had inspired tonight's move.

He had oopsed a tire-squealing turn right in front of a cop car, and they came after him down Tenth Street. He knew what to do. The gravel path to the cart shed went all the way across the golf course and up to the back side of the Chisholm Trail Hotel. He had followed this route, and then gone around the hotel and back out onto Highway 81, evading Duncan's finest that night. When he tried the same trick to evade the police on another night, they were on to him and had a Highway Patrol car waiting at the hotel for him. Our friend Ace McCown told him to go home and not be caught pulling that stunt again.

I was done with my beer. "Do you think the rednecks have gone to bed yet?" I asked.

We figured they had, so we set out to see what was happenin' on the loop. The guys in the Diesel were what was happenin', and suddenly we were zigzagging for our lives again, at break-neck speed.

There is a narrow alleyway between Twelfth Street and Grand in Duncan, and Karl flew down it at no less speed than he would on a regular street, with utility poles and bushes whizzing by close enough to touch, and the high-beams of the big white pickup burning the back of our necks.

At the far end of the alley was a city water department manhole. That manhole rose up like a fortress, right on the centerline of the alley, and when I saw it from two blocks away my life flashed before my eyes for the second time that night. I remembered Walt telling me that when garbage trucks picked up from houses there, they'd have to back all the way out in reverse because they couldn't get around it.

Karl turned to me and grinned. He'd done this before.

He downshifted and we slowed to a crawl, just barely passing to the left of the concrete obstacle. Karl floored it and threw gravel everywhere.

The Headlights of Doom got so close they became a single light. Their screaming diesel engine was the only thing we could hear. They were two car-lengths from us and closing when a single, terrible, crunching, smashing *wham* split the night, at the same instant that their headlights suddenly ceased. They thought they could clear it. They'd gambled and lost.

There was nothing but the whirr of Karl's motor to cover his whispered "Holy shit."

The next day we sneaked by and checked out the scene. There was the truck, high-centered on the manhole, bleeding oil everywhere, its frame bent and engine ruined.* Karl went to the tag agency and got a nondescript, generic license plate the same day.

---

* *In June of 2021 I went and looked, and there is a big rectangular patch where the manhole once stood, with a pair of more carefully considered utility-access-covers on either side.*

Crossington

Down the Cambridge long and trippy

trod a hawthorn-smoking hippy

of sofette hair and gilded sky.

The hawthorn turned into a pie.

A mighty thong of sandalwood

flipped and flopped right where they stood.

Hawthorn abraded as well as could

then tasted it, and found it good.

Was it named to match my eye?

Or could this festival be why

the cane-bridge long

and sandaled hippy

found the guilty sofa trippy.

Booze and Bobsledding

and toasted buns

When Dean Ash at Southwestern asked me to relocate, I called my old friend Roy and asked if he had an extra bed. His group took me in, and I moved to Edmond, where he was going to school. Roy and I were the straight males in a gang of eight of us that occupied two apartments across the courtyard from each other. Four guys, four girls: straight, gay, bi, and our parties were *outrageous*.

Each of the apartments was four stories tall, with the four rooms stacked one on the other. We ran up and down the stairs from room to room with the music booming—dancing on this floor, mixing drinks on that one. And if a door was closed? *Well, that's where those two disappeared to ...*

A fire broke out one weekend while I was away, and Roy had to jump from a third-story window to escape with his life. I lost very little, as I was living light, but Jim and Clyde lost everything they owned. That marked the end of our little hippie commune.

The next fall, Roy and I found a tiny apartment that we were able to afford on our minimum wage salaries. I continued my career (so to speak) in restaurants, and Roy plugged away at his degree while working in the paste-up department of the local newspaper. It was a fine life for a couple of young bachelors, but rather quiet compared to our party days, and once in a while we'd get an itch to get out of town.

We'd drive an hour up to the other big college town and spend the weekend bar hopping, and we'd land wherever the bouncer threw us.

Amy and Tricia were friends from long before high school, and one of our trips to visit them in Stillwater produced a favorite story that they still like to tease us with.

We had a few beers in a bar with a great band, and at one point Roy was so into the music that we saw him with his hands on one of the speakers, rocking out like it was his dance partner, though his affection for the PA may have been entirely platonic. When the girls remind Roy of it, we remind them that they were seen dancing on our table later that night.

I've read that to enjoy life you should "dance like no one's watching." We certainly did on those road trips, and always looked forward to them, and when our friends visited us in turn.

Amy stayed over on the couch at our place one cold weekend, and the three of us hung out, watching the snow through our living room window. We put a B-52's record on the turntable and debated late into the night about guitars, philosophy, and foreign travel.

During breakfast the next morning, we decided we'd join a big group that was sledding and making a happy roar over at the campus.

We bundled up, fortified ourselves against the cold with schnapps in our hot chocolate, and walked a couple of blocks over to the stadium. There were about a hundred other people there, sliding from ground level down into the amphitheater around the football field. We all bumped and coasted on inner tubes and big pieces of cardboard, turning slowly backward, or crashing upside down, and we laughed and yelled and beat ourselves silly skidding into each other and onto the field. I think, actually, there might have been a *lot* of schnapps in our hot chocolates.

On the walk home we saw a short, wide hill that was a giant sparkly strip of pristine, untouched snow. The married student housing apartments sat above it, and our discovery was like a huge billboard that faced the stadium. We stood there marveling at its potential, and then all had the same idea at once. We jumped in, tromping up and down the hill, writing in HUGE letters:

F ...   U ...   C ...

A "Karen" opened a window in the apartment above us and stuck her head out, yelling down at us, "If you write the *K*, I'm gonna call the cops!"

Roy thought a minute, and hollered back up, "What are they going to do, make us mess it up?"

She stared blankly at us for a second or two, then slammed the window closed. We wrote the K and tromped off giggling, back to our apartment.

The little floor heaters in that place were lame, so when we got back we turned on the oven to help warm the place up. Amy was chilled to the bone, and to warm up she stuck her ski-panted rear as far in the oven as it would go.

When her seat started smoking, she jumped and yelped, "I'm burning!"

She couldn't see back there, so we offered to check her booty for her.

Not burned, just medium rare.

Shot At and Missed

sometimes you just know when it's time to leave

Since the small apartments that Roy and I lived in were next to the campus, they were always full of students. We lived there for several years, and there were quite a few times that a pair of girls would move in across the way, stay a semester or two, and then move on.

One particularly cute set was a dark-haired gal with exotic eyes, and a blonde who liked short skirts and had a thick booty, who we nicknamed "Cheerleader." Both were hot stuff!

Roy liked Cheerleader, so I worked at getting Exotic's attention ... and worked and worked and worked. We just really didn't get anywhere, not even friendly interaction. That's the way it goes sometimes, so we moved on.

A while before this, I had been working for Hardee's as an employee (not quite manager yet) with a tall, jacked, white guy named Sam. We had gone to a couple of parties, smoked and drank, and rode around together a few times. He was an intelligent guy but was always using it to scheme up something distasteful—and he was a racist, so it didn't take long before it wore me slick. I stopped hanging out with him but still had to work with him every night.

We had a new manager who was a smallish black guy named Morey with a really dark complexion, hard features, and a gnarly scar right across the front of his face that made him look just mean as hell. Get to know him, and you figured out that he was a nice, kind of easy-going guy (the scar was actually from a car wreck).

Sam and I were working one Saturday night and the new manager asked him to do something ordinary, like mop or sweep, and Sam bowed up.

"You?," he said. "*You* people do not tell *me* what to do."

It escalated into a verbal altercation pretty quickly, and Sam quit right there. Just took off his apron, stomped out, and left. We closed late on Saturdays, and when I finished up, I left Morey and went home for the night.

I went in for my shift the next day knowing that Sam had quit, but a new manager had replaced Morey! When I asked what happened I was told "Oh man! Somebody jumped Morey in the parking lot and put him in the hospital!"

I was never questioned about having any part in it, and I didn't want to be. I would have had to tell them I was sure it was Sam, and I didn't want anything more to do with him.

One afternoon, Roy and I were derping around the apartment when we heard a quiet tap on the door. I opened it and there stood Exotic and Cheerleader. Exotic said that they had been invited to a party but didn't have a way to get there.

"Would you guys like to be our ride?"

"Um, yeah!"

"Do you want to check with your friend?"

I looked back, and Roy was doing that OhBoyOhBoyOhBoy nod.

"Nah," I said. "He's in."

A party! This should be fun!

Roy and I brushed our teeth, put on clean undershorts, and loaded the girls up in the car. They directed us to an older house on the edge of Edmond, and when we walked in, I started recognizing people right away. I worked with that guy, this guy was at some party I vaguely remember, that guy is a friend of *Sam*, and the back bedroom had a huge Nazi flag on the wall.

Aha! We were at Sam's house.

Sure enough, Sam appeared, and right away things got uncomfortable. It was the middle of winter, and suddenly, the house was very stuffy and excessively warm. Sam was being really stiff toward me and getting spookier by the minute. Surely, he didn't associate me with the Morey thing (I hope). I had forgotten about it myself, but seeing Sam brought it all back.

This was the early '80s, and due to the recent Dirty Harry movies, Smith and Wesson .44 Magnum revolvers had become very popular. Sam had just bought one—a huge shiny bastard that he waved around and told the guys at the party all about.

He invited the gathering to go out back and take a look at it.

I balked, thinking I'd go see if Roy was getting anywhere. I wanted a minute to figure out what I wanted, exactly, from this party. Even without the redneck racist gunplay element, I was not digging the scene. But I wasn't uneasy enough to bail on a hot date. On the other hand, my "hot date" stopped showing any interest in me the second we got there. Where the hell was Roy, anyway?

When it looked like I wasn't going outside with his little group, Sam pivoted, leveled a glare at me, and said, "Come. On. Out."

I went.

Five or six guys gathered around, anticipating what everyone would expect at a beer party in Oklahoma: He was going to show them how loud that Smith and Wesson was and how much it bucked. I stood in a shadow about fifteen feet away. I couldn't really hear what they were saying, but suddenly the crowd parted on my side. I looked up, and the barrel of that .44 was pointed right straight at me.

Zip - BOOM!

I swear to gawd I heard that slug whiz right by my ear.

He had missed on purpose and was immediately up in my face, yelling at me about *his* girlfriend.

What? Who? Aha—Exotic. She had only invited me to make him jealous.

I don't think she knew anything about Sam and me working together, or about Morey's beating. It was just a dumb coincidence.

I let Sam shout out his anger, then told him (jeezus, as calmly as I could, I'm sure I was shaking) that I was just a stooge and that I was *leaving right now*.

I went back inside, found Roy, and told him, also, "We're leaving. *Now*. RIGHT NOW, get up!"

"What? No! I'm getting somewhere."

I told him to give me the keys, he was not getting anywhere, we are going now, seriously, get in the damned car. If you don't get up right now, I'm gonna walk the hell home. LET'S *GO*!"

I never saw Sam again, but through mutual acquaintances, I kept a low-key track of his whereabouts, where he was working, and whom he was running around with.

Looking back, I'm just glad I didn't wet my pants.

Short Tales, Fun Facts

that you might not want to know

Kelly and I visited New York City a few years ago and checked as many of the tourist boxes as we could manage in a three-day weekend.

To get our Broadway merit badge, we bought tickets online and saw *Newsies* at the Nederlander on West Forty-first. The lobby was packed before the show, and Kelly waited in the corner as I went to stand in the will call line to get our tickets. The crowd parted slightly in front of me to let a man through, so I stepped back a couple of feet to help. As I did, I backed into someone, almost knocking them down, and heard a yelp. I turned and apologized to a small, cute lady who seemed to be in my age range. She asked if this was the will call line.

"Boy, I hope so!" I said.

We shared a chuckle, I was next to get my tickets, and I returned to Kelly.

"Do you know who you ran over?" she asked.

I didn't.

"That was Lea Thompson!"

I looked across the crowd as Lea turned from the ticket window. She smiled at me and disappeared into the sea of people.

●

While I was a student at Southwestern, a friend on the student council approached me and asked if I wanted to play the role of the team mascot. I asked what they might expect of me, and Clay told me they hadn't had anyone wear the Bulldog suit for several years and were looking for someone who could make it their own.

"I told them you were a nut," he said. "Just do that."

I gave the home games my all for a couple of semesters—worked all the football games, some wrestling matches, and got my own corvette in the homecoming parade. Basketball season was tough, though. The suit was comfortable on a cold night during a football game, but inside the gym, it was almost unbearably hot. The cheerleaders knew my secret identity, and hanging around with them made it worth the work and sweat, for a while.

For the sake of comedy, I'd make a real nuisance of myself during the games. The fans and a lot of the players liked my antics, but the band's drum majors were worn slick by me running around, weaving in and out through their formations. And the football coach was done with me: I had cracked up a huddle of players by miming him while he was chewing them out, in the middle of a crucial game (he was also the track coach that entered Karl and me in the steeplechase, so he can bite my furry bulldog butt).

People were starting to figure out who I was, so the anonymity that let me pull some crazy stunts was drying up, and I can't count the number of times a little kid ran up to me, yelled "Hey Bulldog!," then punched me in the crotch.

I let the next guy take over.

A few years later, when sister Jen attended the same school, she took over the role and was better at it than I was.

•

There is a spot on my head that may be a buried piece of glass. One night at closing time at the restaurant I managed for several years, I yanked upward on a piece of a bathroom stall that had come loose, to check if it was sound. My pull met with no resistance, and the piece rammed into a fluorescent light fixture on the ceiling, cutting one of the long bulbs in half. One of the halves fell and spiked me in the head, so I put my hand tight over it and went out to the lobby to ask my girlfriend at the time (a real hottie named Kelly) if she could see any damage to my head.

By then it was a moot point, as I was trailing blood. I probably could have used a stitch or two, but we had a can of blood clotting aerosol spray in the first aid kit.

Kell sprayed my head down and it lived up to the name. But though that was thirty-five years ago, my noggin still gets a strange, intense itch in that one spot every once in a great while. Jeez, I have so many scars on my head I hope I never go *completely* bald.

I've had a few stitches ...

•

My Dad, being a veterinarian, stitched me up a few times. The first one made the scar that's on my forehead. At thirteen years old, I hit a steel beam at a full-out run and knocked myself out, so he drove me to his clinic and sat me on the operating table.

He told me it looked like about seven stitches worth. He also told me he had two kinds of anesthetic: One that produced numbness in an area so small that I'd need one or two shots per stitch, and the other put dogs all the way out, but he wasn't licensed to use *that* on *people*. Did I want to go ahead with eight-or-ten shots? Alternatively, we could just do it without.

I chose without. It hurt. I could definitely feel the needle, and the suture material being pulled through. He did a first-rate job, and by the fourth or fifth stitch I kind of got used to it, enough so that other times I let him sew up a slash to my arm, and a finger stab the same way. With that experience, I think I could manage to sew myself up in a survival situation ... *ha, maybe*.

•

I have good teeth. I've only had one cavity and didn't wear braces as a teen. I have a cracked molar, though. It has been drilled, ground, filled, and capped, and it's had root canals.

All this began one day when we were playing sandlot baseball on Lakewood. I hit a line drive for a homer, and it really burned the catcher. So, as I came back around to home, he picked up the bat I'd used and smacked me in the head with it. He broke one of my molars and it's been a bother ever since. Poor kid was a skinny little guy that I towered over, and I beat the soup out of him a couple of times after that.

•

I wore hard contact lenses when I was a kid. They were the old-school ones that were tiny discs of inflexible, hard plastic (this was 1974, long before gas permeable ones were introduced). They had to make molds of my corneas to fit them, and they had a sharp edge that made your eyes unbearably itchy after seven or eight hours.

One day, the big brother of the guy with the baseball bat got tired of me beating up his little brother and punched me in the eye. It scooted the contact over, which cut a neatly shaped little semicircle in the white of my eye that seeped one tiny little spot of blood.

That is yet another *unique pain* that you will remember forever. It healed quickly, as kids and eye wounds usually do, and I only had to wear a pirate-patch for a couple of days.

•

Speaking of contacts, for a while I used a type of hobby glue that came in the same exact bottle as my contact lens goop. Yep.

One morning I was late for the bus and filled my contact with glue, then popped it in. The glue was designed to melt plastic, so I watched as my vision went *"BEEE-ROARP"* when the lens shriveled up and stuck to my eyeball.

I peeled it off, then waited until after school to tell my parents, and then only told them because in those days you were only given one set of lenses. They were *pissed*. Them old ones were a couple hundred bucks a set.

•

Dad was a tickler. He'd tickle us kids until we screamed, then keep on going. The only thing that would stop him was when Mom would yell for him to quit. I hated it. I wasn't having fun, even though my involuntary laughing made it look like I was. I suppose I can be accused of abusing tickling too, having done it to my girls and wife. I've apologized since then.

One day when I was a kid, I just turned my ticklish off, permanently.

I was sitting on my bed thinking about it, and poked around on my own ribs, thinking, *Why doesn't it tickle when I do it? It must be all in my mind.*

It worked, I stopped being ticklish (for the most part) that day. I've told people this, and they thought I was making it up. A friend of mine recently told me she was able to do it herself, too, so I don't think I'm crazy.

Try tickling me. It ain't a big thing.

•

I wrestled for six years in grade school. I wasn't quick enough (or killer enough) to be very good, but I stuck with it until I got too tall.

I was in Flint Pruitt's weight class for the first couple of years and came home with many bloody noses. Then, as I got taller but not bigger around I wound up in a weight class with a guy who was a foot shorter than I was. Gourney went on to be a state champion, and I like to think he wouldn't have made it that far without having me as a guinea pig for every damned new pin-hold he'd learned. In sixth grade, he lost weight just before the annual citywide tournament, and I finally got a chance to wrestle someone else.

My first match forfeited, so I went on to the next round. I beat the next guy, but that's as far as I got, and it was my last year. It was good for a bronze medal, though!

I beat that one guy so thoroughly (my first win ever!) that I felt bad about it and made sure to tell him, "Hope you're okay," and that he wrestled really well, and good luck next year.

As I said, I wasn't really a killer.

•

I bought a book at the Scholastic Book Fair about ways to fake movie-monster makeup with supplies that are available to kids. One entry used toilet paper and watered-down Elmer's glue to make reasonably creepy mummy skin. I tried the recipe and showed Barry, and he was impressed.

We three kids were probably eleven, six, and five. Left on our own while Mom was at the grocery store, Barry and I hatched a plan. We made some small talk in front of Jen about how Barry "just wasn't doing too good today" and how he "felt kind of *monstrous*" (snicker, giggle). Then, we tiptoed over and closed the bathroom door behind us.

I applied the mummification to Barry's face and hands, and we suddenly burst out of the bathroom—Barry roaring his best monster imitation, and me chasing behind firing a cap pistol at him.

"The monster is loose!" (*pow!*) "Oh my god!" (*pow! pow!*) "RUN!"

The screen door on the back porch was notoriously easy to pop out of its track, so Barry smacked it down and just kept going, through the yard and off over the hill with me in hot pursuit (*pow, pow!*)

A glance at Jen as we ran by showed her to be in wide-eyed terror.

We came back over the hill laughing and backslapping but pulled up short. We'd taken longer than we thought to apply the makeup, and Mom drove into the driveway just as we pulled our gag. She was waiting for us where the door lay on the porch, and we were in *big* trouble. Not just about the screen, either: Sis had been so scared she wet her pants.

•

Ten-O-Six is the magic number, in all of its forms. The root of it was an acne treatment that our mom bought that was called "10.0.6 Lotion." We *hated* the stuff. Why? Probably only because she wanted us to use it. You know how kids make up songs and folklore about stuff they hate. We avoided that stinky stuff like we avoided broccoli, so it was already on our minds on one October sixth morning when she *yelled* at us about it.

Barry noticed that the date was 10/06.

We were getting dressed to go to a football game in Norman, and somewhere during the game, all of the 1006 chips cashed at once.

Score 10 to 6.

Ball on the 10 with 6 yards for a first.

10:06 left in the quarter.

Then we started making stuff up, "Yeah, the Quarterback has ten toes, and six teeth."

Ten-O-Six is always a good omen, if you see one in the wild. But it can also be invoked by telling the story, when you're in a jam and need some luck.

•

Like many in my family, my mom was a teacher. When we settled into our new town of Duncan in '67, she taught drafting and Spanish at Empire High School southwest of town. But her master's degree was in art education, and she soon found work in her specialty, teaching seventh grade art at Duncan Junior High.

I avoided the horror of having her as a teacher by taking marching band that year. Both the band and art classes were held in what they called the "Annex." She was friends with her fellow art teachers, and I got to know them well, taking art every year, and through college.

The Annex had originally been the New Duncan Hotel. Built in the 1920s, across from what was then the high school, it had been purchased in the early '60s by the city for additional classroom space. Mom's room was in the corner of the building and may have been the hotel's former lobby. Behind a wide, locked door in her room was a grand staircase that only a few people knew about. Since it was in her room, she was given the key that led up to an entire second floor of hotel rooms that had sat abandoned for all those many years. One summer, when we went to set up her room, she let me go up and explore.

A long hallway ran the length of the upper story, lined with doors and light fixtures that hadn't worked for twenty years. A heating duct that had been added during the renovation ran down the middle of the hall like a giant gray serpent, disappearing back into the black. The only light strained through cracks in room windows painted over from the outside.

Dust floated in the air and sat thick on top of bed frames and old mattresses in the still partially furnished, deserted rooms. A broken water basin and peeled wallpaper lay on the floor. In some places, you could see from one room to the next through big holes in the plaster-and lath walls.

Something was scratching around in the dark at the far end of the hall, and it convinced me that helping Mom move desks wasn't so boring after all.

•

The Science Fair was coming up and I needed something, anything, for an entry, as my eighth-grade science teacher made it mandatory for a grade. As was my usual operating method, I put off doing anything about it until it was almost a crisis. Picking around at a garage sale with Mom, I happened upon a pair of fifteen-inch-diameter Plexiglass domes, the kind a restaurant would use to display food. A half-assed idea came to me all at once, and I could use the domes to make a model that would demonstrate what I had just "invented."

Mom had a greenhouse and had to put dark screens on it in the summer, to keep her plants from cooking in the heat it could generate. For insulation in the winter, the greenhouse was constructed of double-walled plastic panels. Liquid Crystal Displays were new technology at the time, and I postulated that the space between the panels could be filled with whatever LCD stuff was (I had no idea), which could be clear in the winter, then electrified in a pattern to block light in summer.

I epoxied one dome over the next and filled the gap between them with water that I'd colored with blue food coloring. Under this, I set a houseplant. I wrote up a flimsy proposal on the first page of an otherwise empty spiral notebook and borrowed an already painted display board from an older neighbor kid's previous project. I don't remember what my project was titled, but it *should* have been: "Can Liquid Crystal Panels be Used to Regulate a Greenhouse? F*ck if I Know!"

The Science Fair was at the County Fair building, and everyone else had very impressive research on display. One kid had raised a mouse in an aquarium, underwater in a self-sustaining habitat fashioned from a big pickle jar. My friend Kyle and his engineer Dad had painstakingly welded together a device that successfully distilled methane.

When the judges came by, I explained my concept, and when they asked if it worked, I bullshat my way through a couple of hypotheticals. They oohed and aahed about my "very original idea," and awarded me the Blue Ribbon.

Kyle was, quite understandably, mad at me for months.

That next Monday, my science teacher gave out the grades for our projects and made a point of announcing my grade to the class.

"Mr. Randle's little *art project* won the science fair this weekend. However, since he proposed no procedures, conducted no testing, and made no observations, He will get a C-minus for his 'work.' And that forms the basis of today's lesson: *Flim-Flam* is no substitute for scientific method."

I deserved it.

•

A driver who worked at the feed store with Roy and me always marked the beginning of his lunch break with, "I'm gonna go have me a pork and beeeean sandwich!"

We puzzled over his daily announcement. Was he serious? If a pork and bean sandwich was *possible*, would it be any *good*? After hearing it many times, we decided we would just have to try one ourselves. Roy's grandmother, Ma, lived close to the shop, and we called and told her we were coming over at noon, but we wanted to fix our own lunch.

Ma stood in the kitchen door with a look of resigned disbelief as we discovered that pork and beans between two slices of white bread is an almost inedibly-sloppy proposition. As far as flavor goes, let's say that it stands as the only time we ever attempted one.

•

Our album (I've played in a few rock and roll bands—but we'll get to that later) has one song that has a driving, *Bonanza*-style beat. It starts with bass (that's me), and when the guitar player, Tony, brought it to us, he told me he also wanted a bass-solo in it. I usually resist bass solos. Anything you do on stage is lost in the rumble of live music, so no matter how simple or complicated one is, to the audience it just sounds like a pissed-off rhinoceros.

We worked it up to play live and he kept buggin' but didn't sucker me into a solo.

We played a place called the Boar's Head for a while and got comfortable with acting goofy—it even became an expected part of our show. One night, we set up there, and I made sure that my mic stand was shortened down to about chest level.

I told Tony, "I've worked up a bass solo for your song! Gimmie about eight measures."

He was pleased as punch, and when the time came, I stepped up to the mic, stuck my hand up under my shirt, and gave him eight measures of sweaty armpit farts. He stopped buggin' me, although I did record a nice solo for the album.

•

There is always a song in my head. Always. Sometimes it's one you've heard, sometimes it's just a meandering tune with lyrics that follow whatever I'm doing right then:

This tool-box is rus-ty, an' I'm gonna clean it up, yeaaaaah, I'm a gonna clean it up!

My friend Turk says that I'm not alone—he usually has one playing in his head, also. When we talked about it, he wanted to know if I also ever had two at the same time, fighting each other. That only rarely happens to me, but it does.

To say I know the lyrics to a million songs is not exactly accurate. I can sing a million, but it's not as if I *know* them. They just kind of build themselves as I go. One word leads to the next, sort of.

As for the song that is currently in my head, I can usually hear the full instrumentation, and can tell you a little about the production, just from what I'm hearing in there. Ask me, I'll tell you what's playing.

•

Pastor John announced one Sunday that next week we'd have a barbeque contest. Church members could enter, and we'd have a picnic out back to give everyone a chance to judge the efforts.

I signed up and immediately forgot about it. We spent the last part of the next week in Kansas, and Saturday night, on the way back, I realized that I'd need to cook the next morning.

We stopped by the grocery on the way home.

On Sunday morning, I loaded the grill into my pickup, and we went to church. After the service, I laid out a big slab of salmon and lemon-peppered it liberally. Then I coated two pounds of shrimp with barbeque sauce and threw it in a basket.

There were about six other entries in the contest. Some had spent all week ageing and smoking ribs. Others had lovingly hand-rubbed their own special spices into their ribs. Still others banked on their original sauce recipe to make their ribs special. Untold hours spent on those ribs. Ribs, ribs, ribs. And I only spent about fifteen minutes laying my salmon on the grill, then picking it back off.

Since "the guys" had all entered the contest, it wound up being judged by "the gals." And the gals were, by the end of the "tasting," tired of ribs. So, the guys were all mad when the one guy who *hadn't* made ribs won the contest, just by the power of being different. Perhaps flim-flam is no substitute for scientific method, but it may be a substitute for ribs.

My prize was a nice set of nice BBQ tools, by the way.

Momentary Hooligans

*In a tavern in the town
a cannon-hatted monkey brown
with gravy-Guinness pool to drown
watched a football game.*

*In a canyon in a cavern
excavated for that tavern
sat a penguin, name of Davern
who thought to do the same.*

*Arsenal and Chelsea battle
Gooner sweats and bar flies prattle
flightless bird and simian rattle,
their loyalties aflame.*

*Fur and feather, tooth and nail
the raging rivals swung and fell
on cigar ash and peanut shell,
bandwagoners took aim.*

*But, alas, a tie was staged
upon the pitch where havoc raged, so
chimp and chicken disengaged
their dignity to reclaim.*

*And as in uffish thought they stood,
the Jabberwock with legs of wood
bought a pint for all who could
say it was "just a game."*

Rock and Roll Bedtime Stories

"I'm Not a Musician; I'm an Entertainer"

~ *Johnny Ramone*

A drummer friend who knew me in high school, asked me recently what path I took to become a musician, since he didn't recall me playing back then. Here's how it happened:

First off, I'm more of an "entertainer" than a musician. Real musicians study their craft. Many can even read music. I never took guitar lessons, just whacked away at it, mostly to amuse myself. That I can talk people into giving me money for it is mighty amusing, also.

I have always liked the sound of bass (I played baritone horn for a few years in school) and thought that Gene Simmons, Phil Lynott, and Paul McCartney were the coolest members of their bands. My friend Turk had a bass, and I dinked around in Roy's garage while the two of them actually played songs, but I couldn't really produce any tone.

In college, I bought a Fender bass (still have it) from a guy that lived on our floor. Karl had his Rickenbacker guitar (I have that, now, also), but they were more-or-less props. It wasn't until I roomed with Roy that he and I learned a few songs. We liked The Cars, The Pretenders, Devo and other '80s rockers.

I made a friend out of a serious violin player on her way to a music degree. She taught me many things (some of them are musical). I wound up marrying her, and soon after, a guy I knew rang me up and asked if I could play the bass he saw at a party at our place. He'd been rehearsing with some guys who were forming a punky three-chord band and wondered if I'd like to try out for them on bass. It wouldn't matter much that I was not a great player.

We practiced up a few sets of scratchy punk songs and started gigging. A couple of years later, Roy stepped in when the guitar player quit. He had to learn a lot of Iggy Pop real quick. We did a couple of albums, hung out with Jonathan Richman, and called it quits having never made much more than gas money.

I knew Tony and our drummer, Mark, from those days, as they were in a really good band that played the same joints we did (and my wife knew Tony as The-Guy-With-the-Mohawk from her music composition class.)

When their band sputtered out, Tony and I got together and decided we were ready to give up on art and try to make some money. We did pretty well—worked with a promoter and made some great cash on the frat-party circuit. But it was a serious grind. We had to put up with lying promoters and scheming bar owners and sleeping on the floor of an empty space above the bar (and we weren't kids anymore).

It didn't matter how far we got from home or how bigtime a show it was, we parked the van by the dumpster and came in through the back like any other servant.

After a thousand gigs, the barflies in Austin and Little Rock look just like the ones in Oklahoma City. By the time we talked Mark into playing with us, the pendulum had swung back, and we decided that we would just play what we wanted to hear. And if the crowd was the same everywhere, we could just as well play for the ones close enough to sleep in our own beds.

There have been many times when I was just done with it. Driving home from Dallas after playing outside in freezing rain to a "crowd" of three can do that.

The times when you feel like the king of the world keep you coming back. You stand on top of a huge stack of speakers and look out on a bar full of heads that are bobbing in time to what you are beating. It's so loud that every time you hit the strings it compresses your chest a little, and you're sweating and they're sweating with you, and all of the faces turned up at you are smiling.

That's their favorite song, man.

Even on a good night, no matter how much they loved you at 11:30 p.m., by 2 a.m. you're just another bum in the alley, trying to lift that big ol' speaker by yourself.

But I'm a member of a musical family.

My daughter Amanda is a strings teacher with her own orchestra. The band called her down one night to help us learn a song with a strange rhythm. She figured out the count right away, and then drilled us on it by having us clap with her. Kelly walked in to hear her dressing us down:

"If you're not gonna pay attention, I'm done here."

She got us through it!

Daughter Abby played the sax for a jazz band for a short while. And that girlfriend that I married? She was so good at violin she was on a full scholarship to play for her college.

I'd have a hard time getting away from music, even if I tried.

The Bull Pen

know your audience

The first band I played with started in the mid-'80s: Scot singing and picking the songs, Aaron on guitar, James on drums, and me on bass. Scot was its muse—inspired by the pre-punk rock and roll of bands like The Velvet Underground and Iggy Pop. He was one of those guys who just didn't think the same way that everyone else did, which can be a form of genius. Dealing with that can also get tedious after a while.

I knew James by association with Roy, and Aaron worked with James. Aaron called, telling me that my lack of experience musically was an asset, as we were to be a Punk band. Unsaid, was that it would be an asset democratically, because none of us knew anything, at first.

Scot had a name picked out and had practiced with several previous members who didn't work out, before bringing us together. Our band name was to be Fear of Rejection, and that was amusing, at first.

One of our early gigs (and our first road trip) was a scene right out of the movie *The Blues Brothers*.

Scot got us booked at a dive in Watonga, Oklahoma, called The Bull Pen. It was, as the name implies, a country and western bar but the owner told Scot he wanted to expand a little, bring new business in besides his bar-fly regulars, and that he thought having rock bands perform might do that. We knew going in, that we were an experiment.

The place was big by dive-bar standards. It had a real stage, and a big screen projector—TV that rolled The Playboy Channel for the entire short time we were there.

In our early practice sessions, we decided that our show would be a mix of songs we wrote, with our versions of obscure songs by bands that no one had ever heard. This is a tough sell in small markets like ours, and in the short time we had been playing, we learned to bash on regardless of a negative response from the audience.

Scot in particular was all about "artistic integrity." Hailing from Atlanta, he thought of Oklahoma as a small-time setting that needed to be educated.

We were booked for four forty-five-minute sets, and we hit 'em with an original song right off the starting block. It went over pretty well. It was one that James wrote that had a '50s feel to it, so it wasn't too foreign to their ears.

Our second song put them on alert. "Joe the Waiter" by Gary Numan has a great melody, and an obvious homosexual theme. You could see the hair on the back of their crusty cowboy necks stand up. During the last chorus a red plastic ashtray, the kind with a beer brand printed on it, sailed past my head and bounced off the wall behind me. The song ended to dead silence, which was eventually broken by the screech of bar stool legs scooting on the floor as a roustabout stood up and turned to stare us down. I knew what song was next.

Scot liked the *live* version of Velvet Underground's song "Waiting for the Man," where Lou sang, "I'm waiting for *MY* man."

"Why don't you sing it like the album tonight?" I said to Scot. "No reason to rile these boys up any further."

"I sing it how I sing it," he said.

Time seemed to slow down. The change in lyrics turned the song from being about waiting to buy drugs to possibly waiting to buy a man. That was just too much for the good ol' boys in Watonga. The roughneck walked over and pulled the fire extinguisher off the wall, set it off as he moved toward the stage, then hosed us down with white fog.

We couldn't see anything of the bar through the haze but heard the background noise of patrons clearing out.

The owner materialized at the edge of the stage and said, "Well, boys. I kinda think you're done for the night."

While Scot negotiated for twenty-five of the hundred bucks we were supposed to be paid, to cover our gas money, I packed the projectile-ashtray in my guitar case as a trophy. It was not the last time we were an "experiment," nor the last time we heard "I think you're done" long before we were.

Welcome to the road!

Many years and two or three bands later, we did play a few successful gigs at that same building. The bar was named something new of course, and the later act went over just fine. It was still an Oklahoma dive.

One of the times we played, a fight broke out over at the pool tables that busted out through the big front window. As the brawl raged on, we improvised circus music until the cops showed up and shut it all down.

Another time, a gal whose ex was the bartender rode her horse right in the front door and up to the bar to yell at him from her saddle before galloping off. What do you play during that?

After the load-out of yet another show, the current owner came out to the parking lot to pay us, and after we'd chatted a while, said, "Oh ooh, hold on, I got something for ya!"

He hotfooted back around behind the bushes, and for a few long minutes, we heard digging sounds (*What the heck?*) while we stood looking at each other. He came back grinning and produced a dirty metal box he opened to reveal a bag of pot and some papers.

"Smoke?"

We declined. It was three o'clock in the morning, after all.

Rumble at Club Nitro

how to not get paid for a gig

Tulsa has always had a happening music scene. There are many young bands with great names playing stuff you've never heard and doing it loud.

Back when Fear of Rejection was trying to get some traction, there was a place around Sixth Street and Peoria that has kind of passed into legend, called Club Nitro. The owner was a Persian guy named Kay, and he became famous for digging up new talent, and also famous for not paying them.

The club was in an industrial area (all the good artsy clubs are) and in a frowzy old two-story building. Kay owned the whole building and let Mark and Tony's band sleep on the wood floors of the abandoned offices upstairs after they played a show there.* We always enjoyed the trip and playing in that hyped atmosphere, but for the distance we had to drive, we were tired of being stiffed on the cash.

We hadn't played Nitro for almost a year when Scot announced during practice that he'd booked a gig there. It was met with an immediate uproar. We finally all agreed that we'd go and we'd play, but we would demand our money after the first set. If we weren't paid in full, we'd walk out in the middle of the show. That would effectively shut them down for the night, as his crowd would disperse if he had no entertainment for them. If he was going to stiff us, we'd cost him some cash as well. Scot was a little uneasy about that part, but the rest of us held firm.

The place was packed when we arrived, and the longhaired body-builder/bouncer/doorman (who had a Fabio vibe to him) was collecting five bucks a head at the door. Our deal was to play two sets and we'd get the entire take from the door, so with a full house we should have been set to make a good haul. We're not sure what the band that opened for us was supposed to be paid—we presumed it was *squat*.

The bar provided the sound system, so all we had to load was our amps, which we did, then a couple of us sought refuge outside from the first band's crashing blast. The opening band was local and called Slugwrench. Their stage-presence showed their inexperience, but the music was great. They were young enough we wondered if they really ought to be playing in a bar where grownups went.

---

* *If you want to hear the story of the sleeping bag, the groupie, and the rat, go read "Tony's book"—when he writes it.*

Scot and his wife stayed inside and listened from the bar. She was working up a buzz after having a run-in with Fabio. She took a shine to him and tried to flirt (Scot said he didn't care; whatever kept her happy). When that went nowhere, she'd taken a different tack, insisting she was cool and should be let in without paying because she was "with the band." She kinda put herself on his shit list.

We went on and *rocked* 'em. The crowd had come to see their friends in the first band, but we kept them glued. They were as young as their band, and hungry for new music. It was a fun first set, but we kept to our plan. We left the stage and went over to the bar to check on our payout.

"So, Kay! How're we doing tonight?" Scot said.

"We fine. Look around."

"No," I said. "He means, how much money are we getting?"

"Oh, no money tonight," Kay said. "Bad night. You not selling my beer."

"Aw come off it," I said. "Looks to me like every under-age kid in Tulsa is walking around this joint with a beer in his hand."

Photo by Mark Hancock

This was a little below the belt. Owners are sensitive to that accusation—however true it might have been in this situation.

Kay puffed up, "You call me a liar?"

"No," Scot said. "We'd just really like to be paid for our work."

Scot's wife, now pretty drunk, added from the end of the bar, "Yeah, mufugger! Pays upper getta rargh!"

Roy and Derek saw that the negotiations were dwindling down to zilch and began loading our equipment into the vehicles while we talked to Kay.

Kay had been standing near his cash register and opened its drawer. He started wadding up $1 bills and threw them, bouncing them off us as he yelled, "You want to get paid, even though I'm not making anything? You want to rob me, go ahead then, and rob me! Take it, take my money!"

You may note, at this juncture, that Kay's command of English suddenly revealed itself to be much better than he had originally portrayed it as being. Everyone started hollering at once. Scot's wife joined in, waving her arms as she yelled, and hit the edge of the bar with her beer, accidentally breaking her mug, while Fabio stood right behind her.

As I'd learned in Sweden, bar-fight etiquette dictates that breaking off a bottle on the bar (or a mug in this case) means that things have moved beyond the negotiating stage.

Things got ugly real fast.

The soundman got involved, and there was a kind of Keystone Cops chase scene around the bar. When the fracas spilled outside, I wound up standing on the sidewalk waving a mic stand over my head at Fabio and Kay, protecting Roy while he finished throwing the last amp into the Bronco.

"Back up, man, back up! I know how to use this!"

Roy jumped in the driver's seat and started the motor, I jumped in, and we squealed the tires off down Sixth Street with the Club Nitro personnel shaking their fists and shouting behind us.

We had planned to stay in town with our friend Tricia and her husband, but we called them in the morning and told them we had just kept drivin'.

We were temporary heroes with our little circle of band-friends for having stood up to Kay.

A couple of years later Kelly and I were in Tulsa visiting Andy, and we all decided to mosey by Nitro, just to see what was happenin'.

Kay was there and stopped us at the door, barking, "Hey! Five bucks each!"

"Yeah?" I said. "How much of that is the band getting?"

His eyes got squinty, then got wide, then he threatened to call the cops if I didn't get off his sidewalk. "AND DON'T COME BACK!"

Don't worry, dude. Not much chance of that.

Swanson's Lament
stuck at your desk for lunch

Frosty aluminum hockey-puck slop:

microwaved lunch and a bottle of pop.

Shoe-tongue in gravy,

potatoes: once dust,

keep up your blood sugar! Do what you must!

Noon-hour Face book; the Boss walks by.

Hold up your spork as you explain why,

and at least it's not porn! It sure could be worse!

You could be wasting his time writing verse.

Tales From The Sip

short takes from a stereotypical dive

We have played for many years, and if you made a list of the names of places we played, it would be a lot longer than the number of physical bars to play in. They change hands so often that one of them has had at least six different names.

Many aspiring entrepreneurs dream of owning a bar, so that your only job is to throw a party every night. But it's a tough game, and we've watched several times as the hottest place in town flashed, and then went belly-up in the space of just a few months.

One place that has kept the same name through my whole career is on N. Western Avenue in Oklahoma City. It was called SipanGo (get it? "sip, and go") for most of its existence, but it is all hipster now, and has morphed into "The Sip."

I played my first ever paying gig there—Tony and Mark had given my band their number. Back in those days, the boys were in a legend of a band called Video Fish, with a legend of a bass player named Brett. He's a great, huge man—tall enough that he used two straps spliced together for his bass.

For some reason The Sip has always been a place to go if you want to get into a fight. That makes it a great place to practice dealing with hecklers, too. Must be something they add to the beer that turns an ordinary citizen into a jackass. Or maybe it's just the beer. You'll see an example in "An After-Gig Photo" (a story later in this section), which started inside The Sip and ended in front of us at the bar caddy-corner to it.

Fear of Rejection also played our *last* gig there before we went our separate ways. The Monkees song "Steppin' Stone" had been one of the first ones that Fear learned, and we had always played a fast, punky version of it. The chorus was a mess. We played it too fast for it to be musical, so we just punked-out and beat on our guitars while we jumped around.

Usually, our flailing would crack the singer up, and he'd have a hard time getting the words out. It got to be a *bit* that we did: What can we do to get him this time?

For this last gig Scot said, "You know guys, I don't think there's anything you haven't done. You won't be able to break me this time, I'm not gonna crack up."

I told him he was right. I wouldn't even try. Then, I leaned into Roy and told him to follow my lead. We hung back for the first and second choruses, playing it straight and staying out of his field of view. In the buildup to the last chorus, I undid my belt and pulled down the back of my pants. I stepped up into Scot's field of view, then swung my bass around behind me and played the chorus with my naked butt. Scot could not breathe for laughing, let alone finish out the song.

Turk's band played a double bill with us there one night. He had been an early influence on my musical tastes, and it was great to get to finally play with him.

We had a bunch of friends show up, and a couple of the cuter girls in our gang parked on the sofa over by the jukebox. A local ne'er-do-well wandered in and took a seat next to them (I hadn't seen him come in).

I wanted to impress the girls, so I came down off the stage while I was playing (we always used wireless packs, so we could roam). I plopped down on the sofa, and then saw the guy jump up. Next thing I knew an ashtray hit me in the chest! I had spilled the guy's beer and embarrassed him without realizing it.

The music stopped suddenly, kind of like when the bad guy walks into the bar in an old western. He stood over me and yelled in my face that I was going to go up on stage and apologize right now.

By the time he balled up his fists, I'd had about enough.

I stood up holding my bass by its neck, waving it over my head like a baseball bat. We locked eyes, and I informed him this was my show and not his and that he could "beat it or get a beatin'."

He chose to run, and on the way out, he dumped what was left of his beer into our soundboard. I'm still a little embarrassed that it all went down in front of friends

The Sip had no stage for the first eight or ten years we played there. The band just played on the floor in one corner. The crowd was right up against us, and sometimes among us, dancing on our cords and equipment.

Back when Roy was with us, we played a long night to a houseful of frat boys and their dates. Our first sign of trouble: Some guys that were standing right in front of our speakers turned them inward because they were hurting their dates' ears. That caused a honking squall of feedback, and we went back and forth with them about where they should be standing if they didn't like noise.

It got busier, and the crowd got thicker, until it was shoulder to shoulder and we in the band were just part of the crowd.

During "Jumpin' Jack Flash" a couple of the guys who had given us trouble with our speakers wound up on our side of the microphones and started shouting into mine. I pushed the offender aside and wagged my finger at him. He gave me a smirk, turned, and returned to his Mick Jagger impersonation.

That fried my fritters, so I put the head of my bass in the middle of his sternum and gave it a mighty shove, which moved him back about five feet.

His face changed from "merry frivolity" to "murder." He crouched into a wrestler stance and pushed back his sleeves. So ... I hadn't paid attention, or noticed yet, just how much younger and bigger than me, this kid was.

I'm sure my face changed, too—probably to "Oh sh*t!"—just as this guy lunged, a hand came out of the crowd. A hand with fingers the size of corn dogs. It was the big brown hand of Big Bad Brett. It closed around his neck, and *shaboop!* he disappeared backward into the crowd.

Aw, praise Jesus, Triple-B had saved my skin. I hunted him down after the set to thank him.

"I just told him he might want to find somewhere else to drink his beer," Brett said.

This *wasn't* at The Sip, but I gotta throw it in somewhere.

One night, we played at the Blue Note on Robinson, and I went back to the men's room. A true sign of a classy place—they had a machine that dispensed prophylactics on the bathroom wall. Plain white metal, put in a quarter, turn the knob. Someone took a sharpie and wrote across the front of it, "This gum tastes terrible!"

Still one of my favorite gags.

Another *not-Sip* story: We got the closing spot at the Arts Festival one year. We think it's the best slot of the week—you're given a longer time to play, and it's well attended.

We usually do something extra for the festival—an artsy or nutty stunt—and for this closing gig, we came up with a new one when we remembered that dinnertime is right in the middle of that set. Around six o'clock that evening, a pizza guy came all the way down the arena stairs and onto the stage to deliver us four big pies. We tipped him handsomely and invited the audience onstage to get a slice. Stage-manager Dave said it was a first.

We were on the road doing a two-nighter in some backwater town, staying in the cheapest flop we could find—a fleabite motel* with stained sheets, glass-brick windows, and a bare yellow bug-bulb in the socket over our doorway.

We slept until we were thrown out at checkout time, and then piled into the van with nowhere to go until the bar opened at three o'clock in the afternoon. We pulled into a Sonic and hoped that a cheap corndog lunch would fix our headaches. The radio DJ said that Frank Zappa had died that morning, and we sat there the rest of the afternoon, listening to their all-day Zappa tribute, and ordering one small bag of French fries at a time so they'd let us stay.

It was lucky that we got a motel on that trip—it didn't always happen. At one small-college-town gig, we couldn't nail down anything prior, but at the end of the show we heard some kids talking about continuing the party over at a friend's place.

We packed up quickly and showed up at the house party, and since we'd been seen at the bar, we blended right in. When everyone had left or gone to bed, we racked out on their couches and the carpet.

We were rudely awakened the next morning by the occupant, who kicked Tony in the ribs and shouted, "Who the hell are you?"

It was okay, I suppose. We didn't recognize him either.

When we were called Boneyard, we played a New Year's Eve gig at Sipan-Go, and the entire street corner was mobbed with people.

The promoter put on a show across the street from us with several bands, and the Latest Local Phenom as the headliner. They oversold their tickets, so the fire marshal raided it and shut their show down for being over capacity.

---

* *On the subject of fleas, we played a gig in a bar in downtown OKC that'd brought in and dumped an entire truckload of sand, and then decorated the place with surfboards and beach umbrellas. We called each other the next morning complaining of sand flea bites all over our legs. I would assume the bar patrons suffered the same fate, as that joint only lasted a couple of months.*

We, and the other surrounding bars, benefited greatly from their misfortune and made scads of dough that night.

One pair of college girls was wearing holiday dresses that were cut exactly alike, but one was Christmas red and the other Christmas green. They looked like they were having a great time bar hopping and came and went a couple of times as the crowd ebbed and flowed. By late in the evening, they were in their cups and came up on stage to ~~grind~~ dance ~~on~~ with us.

Kelly was in the audience and was *not impressed*. She nicknamed them "the Doublemint Twins," not meant as a compliment.

While they were putting on their show, two cowboys showed up and stood right in front of the stage with their arms folded across their chests. They were both about five-foot-six and had their big ol' cowboy hats pulled all the way down to their eyebrows. They glared at us until the girls got down off the stage and left with them.

We made a public service announcement as they were leaving: "Remember, fellas, if you don't stay with your gal, she might not stay with you!"

At load-out, we discovered that the band van and my truck had been pummeled with eggs. We figured the Doublemint Twins' goat-ropin' boyfriends did it. We got the last laugh: Sometime before the egging, a freezing mist had coated our vehicles with ice, so their handiwork just melted right off in the morning.

We had discussed this gag a few times before, but finally pulled it one night at SipanGo.

It was a snoozer of a night. We were getting bored, and the crowd was getting thin. It came down to the last song, and after we'd played the majority of it, I just nonchalantly unplugged and packed up while the boys kept playing. I rolled my gear out to the truck and came back in.

I started packing Tony's stuff, and when I had almost everything put up, he unplugged, and we rolled his stuff out. This left Mark whomping away at the song by himself, and we took his drum set apart while he soloed on an ever-diminishing kit.

We got him down to his bass drum, and he finished the song with, *thumpthumpthump-thumpthumpthump ... thump.* "Thank you very much, and goodnight."

I Believe That

Fingers fing, alligators alligate.

Scissors sciz, motors motate.

One slat is a fent, one leg is a pant.

Monsignors monsign,

Consignors can't.

Dead Raccoon

now what do we do with it

We played a show in Ada, which is a college town and good for gigs, and I took a back way down to the show. It was an hour and a half drive, and Tony was probably three hours ahead of me, as he always likes to get there early, get comfortable, and scope the place out.

Ten or fifteen minutes from the bar, I passed a raccoon that looked like it was just taking a nap in the middle of the road. I was ahead of schedule, so I pulled over and backed the Bronco up to the critter. I got out to check on him and found him dead with no signs of violence. Oh well, died of old age, perhaps. On a whim, I lowered the back window of the Bronco, picked the coon up by his tail, and carefully placed him where he'd be the first thing you saw if you opened the tailgate.

When I walked in the front door, Tony was sitting on a stool at the bar and chatting with the bartender. As I passed by, I tossed my keys at him.

"I gotta pee. Go get my stuff out of the truck!" I said, rather assertively.

Tony looked a little puzzled by my jerkiness, but I saw him get off the stool as I went into the men's room. I stood there taking care of business for about forty-five seconds before I heard, outside in the parking lot and loud enough to hear all the way inside the bar, a blood-curdling yell.

I laughed so hard that I almost made a mess of my business. I washed my hands, walked back out in the bar, and there stood Tony, backlit in the doorway, huffing and puffing with his fists clenched at his sides.

"I THOUGHT IT WAS A HAT!"

Of course, then we were left with the task of trying to figure out what to do with poor ol' Rocky.

Rolling Ant Farm

they like Kool-Aid

Tony called me one Sunday morning, and seemed quite different than usual. He is typically fairly easygoing, a diplomatic type, more interested in getting on with whatever needs done than starting an argument. So, his adamant tone during this phone call was uncharacteristic.

A couple of weekends prior, we had a road gig in Dallas, or some such, that required bringing all of our equipment. Some bars provide a house speaker system, some don't. For this one, we loaded up in the band van and hit the highway on a hot summer afternoon.

Tony owned the former delivery vehicle we used and kept it in his driveway with the equipment in it. Those were our "big speaker" days, so speakers, amps, and mic stands filled the vehicle. It was one of those rattletraps without air-conditioning where the engine was housed in a covered bump between the driver and passenger. This made for a very hot, sweat-dripping trip through South Oklahoma on a summer afternoon, with the windows down and our hair whipping the whole way.

About two thirds of the way to our destination we stopped at a convenience store to pee and get gas. This joint had a reach-in cooler by the cash register full of popsicles. You know the kind: A plastic bag an inch wide and a foot long, full of frozen Kool-Aid.

What glory did my eyes behold but a giant popsicle, three times as big as normal, and my favorite flavor—green lime-ish.

Sold!

It was a great relief in the 110-degree van. I held it against my forehead for a good bit of the way. I had bought more popsicle than I could chew and was only half done with it when we pulled into the bar parking lot. Always ready to rock and roll, I shoved the plastic sleeve of remaining juice under the seat, and we jumped out and got to work.

Tony called me some weeks later, and said, "Hey man, you're gonna come down and help me unload the van this afternoon."

He was not asking. He was informing me. And when I arrived, I found out that when he said, "The van has ants," he didn't mean they were coming and going from the van in a neat little ant-train (as they do.) No, they had moved in and set up a full-on ant colony under the carpet, with workers, soldiers, eggs, and a queen.

We had to empty out the van (with ants on the walls, ceiling, and equipment), completely strip the interior, spray down all of the equipment (it's makin' my hair itch just typing this), and set off a fogger inside the van shell to chase them out. All because I left about a pint of lime sugar-water under the seat. For two weeks. In the summer.

Don't do this.

Like a Rolling Stone

not quite the cover

In 1993, Tony and I were winding down one band and just breathing some life into the next one when we got a call from our friend Thomas Anderson. Thomas is a songwriter who started in our area, and now makes his living in the music mecca that Austin has become.

I met Thomas when he interviewed my first band for the *Daily Oklahoman* and found him to be friendly and very knowledgeable about music. This last attribute is one not often found in music writers. Just sayin'.

The band (that was Fear of Rejection) went to see him perform a solo acoustic guitar gig and had a great time. His songs were catchy and smart. Later, we played a couple of double-bills with him before he moved to Austin with a record deal in his pocket.

When he called, Thomas said that he had been asked to come up with a single for his record company. He had a song written, and what he had in mind for the guitars was just a big bunch of noise, so he had immediately thought of us.

He sent us a demo of the song a few weeks prior to our arranged studio time and advised us a little on what to work up for him. We met at Mike McCarty's studio to begin laying down tracks. Besides being our sound engineer, Mike was our drummer for the session. He had played with The Holy Modal Rounders, an influential '60s band with a song on the soundtrack of the movie *Easy Rider*. For a time, actor Sam Shepard had been a member of the Rounders, too.

We unpacked, put on our headphones, and recorded through a rhythm section take of just bass and drums.

Thomas listened through it, then turned to me and said, "Hmmm. Too many notes."

I had worked up a complicated little counter to his melody, and he thought it was a bit much (Tony finds his assessment amusing to this day). So, I pared it down, we did another run, and that was that for me.

They let me hang around while Tony put on guitar after guitar, building up a wall of squalling noise. Titled "Uranium Road," Thomas' song describes a post-apocalyptic world and the truckers who drive through the wasteland to deliver their goods. Thomas wanted the guitars to add a desperate edge, and Tony delivered the goods (you can Google the song and find it on YouTube or Spotify, if you'd like to hear it).

As a sort of payment, Thomas sent us some promo copies of the single. Unclean Records had released it on a red-vinyl 45.

Neato!

My name is misspelled on the sleeve, but whattaya gonna do?

Later, Thomas also sent us a couple of copies of the CD it was released on. We hoped that Thomas could put the word in at the record label for us, but we heard nothing from them.

We thought that was pretty much the end of it, but some months later Thomas called and told us that that week's *Rolling Stone* magazine had a small write up about "Uranium Road" in it! As soon as I hung up, I got in the truck, went down to the corner, and bought three copies.

Mom was not super impressed. Thomas was mentioned but it didn't have my personal name in the blip—and it *was* just a blip. But one favorable sentence by Anthony DeCurtis in his "Raves" column in *Rolling Stone* number RS662 is more than a lot of guys can say. It's on page twenty-four of the magazine.

Here, I'll hold your drink for you while you look.

I Stared Down David Allen Coe's Posse

well, kind of

Lawton, Oklahoma, is a military town, and bands looking for a gig have always had many bars to choose from. One joint that we liked to play, The Asylum, was a huge place that was a dance club in the front, and a concert venue in the back.

The concert side could probably hold five hundred or so people, and the kid who booked bands was sometimes able to bring in some major acts. We got the opportunity to play with names like Bad Company and Big Mike Griffin. We also opened for The Kiss Army—a tribute band that did Kiss' whole shtick, with makeup, fake blood, fire, and the works. That was a strange night!

Brandon (the guy who booked the place) decided that he liked us because we got the place a good write-up in the local newspaper when a music critic saw us being nutty on a slow night. It has long been part of the act that, if Tony thinks he spots a guitar player in the crowd, he'll walk over while we're playing something everybody knows, hand the guitar to him, and go get a beer (we usually play through wireless transmitters).

Sometimes the "guest guitarist" is better than we are! It always gets applause, especially if the player is a regular at the bar.

The night the writer was there we were bangin' away, and a group of cute college-age girls sat down at a table right in front of the stage. I wish I still had the newspaper article, the writer said something like, "... the band talked three blondes who obviously had no musical talent into taking over the stage and sat in the audience cheering them on as they made horrendous noises for two minutes! I hope I stay as cool as these guys when I'm their age."

Ouch!

Some weeks later, we got a call from Brandon asking if we were interested in being the opening act for David Allen Coe. It would be unpaid, but we would get to play in front of a big crowd. Even though DAC is a country-rock act, Brandon thought we'd go over just fine.

"He's old. You're old. It'll be groovy," he said.

We agreed, drove down, and walked in to see a packed house. The venue put up barriers, the kind they use at Mardi Gras in New Orleans that look like bicycle racks, in front of the stage to keep the crowd at bay.

We gave 'em both barrels—played a great set, very rock and roll. When we did our call-and-respond bit with the audience, they yelled loud enough that it vibrated the stage!

DAC liked us enough that he bought us a case of beer at the bar (we can drink us some beer, but we still had a long drive back that night, so we had to leave most of it there). He also asked for us, to play with him again when he came back through on his next tour.

Both times that we played with David Allen Coe and his band, they arrived before us, and set up their gear all over the stage. It was their show, after all. The first time around, we were told to leave our amps in the van and just plug our guitars into their amps. We were warned that Coe and his crew were pretty gnarly and that we were not to fool with the knobs or move things around. We had no trouble and were happy to just run off the stage after we were done.

In fact, Coe and his guys were pretty friendly. The second time we played was a little different story.

We were pumped to get to play such a big show again and saw an even bigger setup than last time already on stage when we got there. Coe had expanded his lineup with a couple more guitar players between our first gig and our second. The place was packed to the gills with fans. There must have been six hundred people there, and all eyeballs were on the stage.

Yipes!

We expected the same load-in routine but were told to hurry and set up our *own* stuff this time.

Where? The stage was nearly covered with *theirs*!

We found places, and I set up right in front of the new guitar player's rig. He was a little bit big-for-his-britches and hovered around watching me get too close to his stuff. He had a nice rig: An expensive computer-modeling amp set on top of a speaker cabinet with two guitar hangers bolted to the top—a Telecaster in one and a Stratocaster in the other.

I had my *big* rig with me, which meant a speaker the size of a refrigerator with an amp box set on top of that, so I had to squeeze to get it only an inch or two in front of Grumpy Guitar's amp. We plugged in, flipped the switches, and with only a cursory sound-check we were introduced.

Get to blastin', boys!

The set itself was another rock and roll experience to add to the list of highs. We played well and worked the crowd like old pros.

During his first guitar solo, Tony took a flying run and jumped over the top of the barrier onto the crowd with his wireless. That looked fun, so I took a jump also. We walked around taking our back-pats and wound up in the back of the mob looking at the stage.

"How are we gonna get back up there?" I yelled to Tony.

We knew the bouncers pretty well by then, and the two that heard us turned around and pushed a path through to the stage for us. We were as big as the Beatles for fifteen seconds.

On the way up front, a gomer stepped out in front of me with a pint bottle of Jack Daniels with only about a half-inch left in it and shouted, "DUDE! YOU, TOO!" while he poured it at my mouth and down the front of me.

Ptht-thpp—thanks, buddy?

We climbed back up on stage and crashed and banged for another forty minutes.

As we progressed, I noticed ... a *change* in Tony. His normally brilliant guitar work was, uhm, *slipping* a bit toward the end of our set. I had seen this before, maybe at the Ramada Inn in Enid where an older patron in a little black dress had taken a shine to Mark and had sent shot after shot of tequila up to the three of us on stage.

That night at the Ramada, when Tony asked me what I thought, I'd told him, "Well, we have a free room. Drink up and we can just crawl to bed from here." And crawl we did.

But tonight, Mr. Dude with the Jack Daniels bottle, had only half an inch of hooch left, because he'd found Tony first, and Tony had taken a four-gulp pull (insert face palm). He had a sledgehammer buzz and was feeling heroic.

When we were done with our set, Tony was not—*twangity-twangity*, "I don't want it to be over yet!"

We slowed him down for a big finish though, and our orders were to take a bow then get the hell off the stage so DAC's crew could take over. They were already onstage and among us when I grabbed my big speaker rig and spun it around on its casters to pull the wires out.

Wham. CRASH!

The corner of my rig caught on one of the guitars behind it and pulled the new guy's whole rig face down on top of both of his guitars.

Coe travels with a posse of huge, gnarly bikers. The previous time we played with them, we saw a drunk climb up on the stage and try to rush Coe, only to be grabbed by one arm and one leg and get spun out over the crowd's heads like a Frisbee. They were mean, they were nasty, and they obviously were not there for moral support. They were the Muscle if things went to shit. And in their opinion, Things. Just. Had.

Grumpy Guitar's yelp set them in motion. Two of the goons grabbed me, one arm each, while Goon Two grabbed my neck and slammed me up against the wall, stage left.

He got right in my face and hissed, "If they can't go on because you f**ked up their stuff, we'll take our pay out of your skin."

He meant it too. He had hold of my throat tight enough that my voice came out as a hoarse squeak.

"Gentlemen, I am certain that if you will just let go of my neck, we can reach some sort of an agreement that is mutually—"

Just then the guitar player's amp interrupted with a pleasing *whaang*. While the posse and I were wrasslin' he had stood the amp up and plugged in, and his test had been successful.

The goons looked back and forth from me to Grumpy, and he gave them the high sign. Goon Two eased off my neck but kept hold of my arm.

I looked over at Grumpy and said, "Look, I can stay right there at the edge of the stage where you can see me, until the end of your set. If anything is wrong, I'll make good. I swear. Is your rig okay?"

He nodded to the goons.

"Alright then!" Goon One said. He let go of my arm, then pointed at Tony.

"And get that drunk Mutherf**ker OFF THE STAGE!"

Tony was three sheets now and on his knees on the front edge of the stage, trying to help a fan get over the barrier, "Heck yeah, I'll introduce you to David Allen Coe!"

We packed his stuff, led him out to his car, and sat him down in it. Mark and I finished getting our stuff, and when we went back out found Tony wandering around the parking lot. We led him back to the car, put his seat back, put his keys in his pocket, and locked him in. I slunk back in to take my place in the goons' line-of-sight.

As the band got going, I discovered why the DAC crew was testy that second night. Turns out they'd had a rough gig just the night before. Coe himself was in a foul temper, and not three songs in he got out a barstool, sat down, and went on a rant while the band vamped behind him.

He'd been booed, and he didn't appreciate Tulsa trying to tell him how to live his life. All he had done was use the N-word in polite conversation!

His rant just went downhill from there, and I stood by hoping to heaven that if anything was wrong with their equipment, Ron at the guitar shop would repair it and let me work it off in payments.

At least Lawton was much more receptive to racist rants.* When Coe's band finished, I slunk my way back up on the stage and stood by while Grumpy packed.

"How'd it go?"

Silence.

"Is your rig okay?"

He was putting the bright yellow Stratocaster into its case and flipped it over to show me there was a fresh inch-long chunk out of the back, probably from the metal corner of his amp.

---

* For a while, Kelly and I had a deal where I could stay out as late as I wanted on Saturday if I got up on Sunday to go to church with the girls. I showed up at church one morning after a gig night, with my hair on sideways and my eyes bloodshot. I ran into Preacher John before Worship, and he remarked, "You look rough! Did you play last night?" I told him I had, and in Lawton. He laughed, "Ha! Don't you have to win a fistfight just to get into Lawton?"

"Look, if something needs fixed, I've got a guy that does repair work for big names. What do you say?"

He turned the guitar over, closed the case and said, "Let's just call it 'shit happens.'"

I was tempted to ask for that in writing but was happy to get what I could.

"If I find something wrong with it later, does the bar know how to get hold of you?" he asked.

"Oh, yeah," I said. "They do. They sure do. Always." I was lying through my teeth.

About noon the next day, I got a call from Tony.

"Hey, I just woke up in the parking lot," he said. "In Lawton!"

I told him I was glad to hear that he was okay. I also told him the harrowing tale of the night before.

"Well, the bar has MY number," he said. "What if they call?"

I told him to take down their information, and I would make good on any claim they forwarded, but *do not*, under any circumstance, give them my home address. I was done with Coe, and his entourage.

A coda to my night: While I was waiting for Coe's band to finish, a guy came up to me in the crowd with a puppy dog look on his face and excitedly said, "You were in that band that just played, weren't you!"

Recognition!

I tenuously answered, "*Uhm* ... yeah?"

He busted out, "You guys were great! I never ... Wow! You gotta. We gotta. I mean, my girlfriend's got to meet you!"

Fame!

He disappeared into the crowd.

At last. I am a Star.

In a minute or two, he came back up, dragging a poor girl behind him.

"This is him. This is the guy! This is the best drummer I think I've ever seen in my life!"

Yeah. I'm the bass player.

"Welp, thank ya very much then," I said. "Glad ya liked the show."

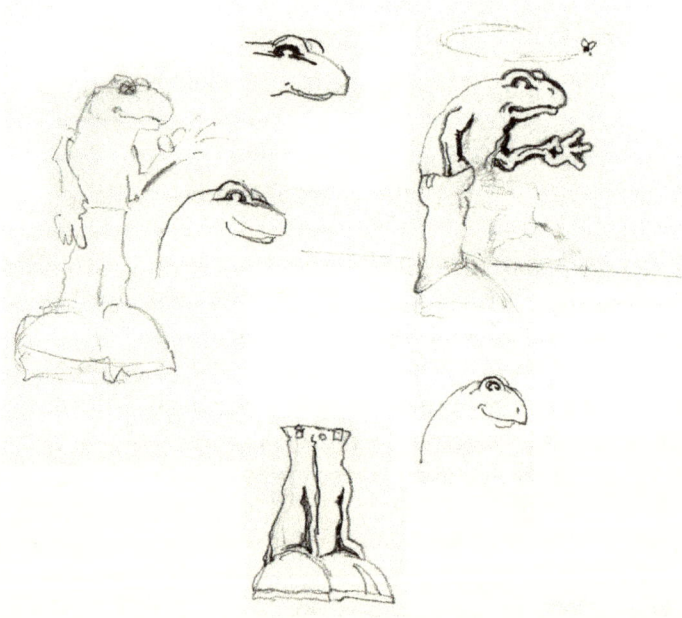

Lucas

In the darkness

In the black

A grey-haired green-eyed cat looks back

Rollins Meets Ong

and leaves his mark

Our band Ong is named for its guitar player, Tony Ong. After Tony proposed that name, Mark said we might as well name the band Pumping Tony's Ego, but Tony wasn't as into that as we were.

We used to play at a bar called The Boar's Head in North Oklahoma City a lot. We liked playing there. Fritz managed the place, and treated us well, and he booked big names, so occasionally we rubbed elbows with someone famous. The joint was a former twin-screen theater and they had removed the middle wall, so it was a big place with a huge stage. If you played with a Name-band, or on the night after one, you got to play through the *giant* sound system he used for the big acts. It had six bass cabinets with two 18-inch speakers in each and a 500-watt amp driving each box!

There was a sweet spot on stage where a low E-note would rattle my liver. The downside was if you played a stinker-note they heard it all the way to Cleveland.

Fritz liked us, so we became their short notice fill-in when another band cancelled.

One week, we played a regular Friday night gig there, and I picked up some needed duct tape on the way. All the store had was shiny-chrome tape—it was kind of odd. So, while we were setting up, Tony got to he-hawing and making fun of my "Las Vegas" duct tape and used it to write "ONG" in huge letters on the carpeted stage.

We banged out a couple of fun sets, got paid, drank beer, and went home. At the entrance, we saw posters for the next night—famous punk-rocker (and movie and TV star) Henry Rollins from Black Flag would be there Saturday!

That Sunday afternoon we got a call from Fritz, "Guys, could you play tonight? The band I booked cancelled!"

We were happy to, and when we showed up there was the usual fifty-jillion-watt gigantic PA that had been used for Rollins the night before. We got up on the stage to set up, and the huge ONG was still there, but now it said:

DONG

The boys and I were standing there marveling at the new handiwork, when the soundman walked by.

"Yeah, Rollins did that," he said. "He looked at it all night and decided he just couldn't leave it alone."

Years later, I told that story to a guy at work, and he said that he was at the Rollins show and saw him do it. Ha!

The High-Concept-Art Band

named after a dog toy

My friend Kevin is a multi-discipline artist and makes a good living at a variety of visual arts, from oil portraits to painting the logos on basketball gym floors.

One of his favorite jobs is a recurring gig designing action figures for toy companies. It's possible you've seen his work, as Stretch Armstrong or some of the Teenage Mutant Ninja Turtle figurines. He is a genius "idea man" with an art gallery downtown, an interest in a fine-dining restaurant, and the Toy and Action Figure Museum in Pauls Valley, Oklahoma. His projects are a recurring special-interest feature on the local television stations, appearing on *Discover Oklahoma* and the like.

Kevin is also a musician, and I rehearsed and played in a high-concept rock band with him for a year or two. It was a good group of musicians, and we wrote original tunes that were challenging to play. Kevin's constant flow of ideas led him to bring us new and sometimes weird concepts, two or three times every rehearsal. His big personality and raw enthusiasm could sell us on the craziest ideas.

On one of his larks, we played a gig in the middle of a skate-park with skaters zooming all around, and through the middle of us.

We also recorded a song for the town of Ardmore that their chamber of commerce used in a tourism commercial. For a while, he tossed around the idea of all of us dressing like different versions of Gene Simmons from KISS, makeup and all, and calling ourselves The Gene Pool.*

One night, Kevin announced that our current band had run its course, and that he had an idea for something new. Those of us who wanted to, would re-group for a band that would "never play the same song twice"—not at a show, not at rehearsal. We would write every song right then, and never revisit it. It would be *all improvised, all of the time*. And as a perfectly Kevin-esque non sequitur, we'd call it Squeaky Burger.

I stayed on, and it was one of the toughest gigs I've had. Each of us in turn would start a song by coming up with a brand-new riff, and then after hearing it through one time, the others would improvise over it. The first player

---

* *Kevin was able to pull off his The Gene Pool idea off, albeit with a different group of musicians. They played a whole set of nothing but Gene Simmons songs. I would have liked to have seen it.*

guided the others through as he made up chord changes, using eyebrows and body language.

The group was pretty clunky in the beginning, with the four (sometimes five) of us lost a lot of the time. After some practice, we learned to read each other's signals, and we gained a pretty good feel for where that guy's ideas would go next.

We had a middle period where we were really enjoying it and played a nerve-wracking live show, making up tunes on the spot for a bar full of college kids. We went over very well with that crowd. As you might expect, there were a couple of stinkers, but most of it was that strange kind of magic that happens when musicians are all in the same groove.

Eventually, we learned one another's chops *too* well, and it became hard to come up with completely new ideas. The guitar-player would start something, and it would remind us of one we did recently. We'd fall right into a previously explored groove, with Kevin admonishing us for playing one that was too close to the other.

When I said aloud that it might be that we knew each other too well musically, he had another brainstorm: The band would rotate musicians often, to keep that from happening. I had talked my way out of a job.

Squeaky Burger lives on, changing its format periodically and its musicians often.

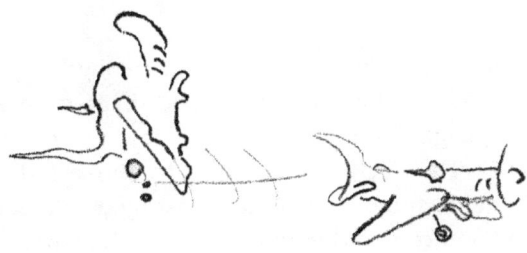

Meet My Friend Scooter

a fellow musician recaptures that feeling

It was the second of a two-nighter in a dive somewhere on the south side of Oklahoma City, and we were doing great. Our crowd that night was dancing and happy.

At the end of the previous night, the owner wouldn't pay us until we let her tell us that we needed to change our show. We played our songs "too fast for the crowd to dance to," and we needed to "cut it out with all those TV songs" (our set had a rock and roll cover of the *Beverly Hillbillies* theme, and we'd slipped in a mashup of "Ice Ice Baby" and the theme to *Gilligan's Island*).

"That was a problem?" Tony asked her.

"You guys didn't sell any beer," she said.

Yeah, that's a thing. You forget sometimes, with your silly chords and rhythm and months of rehearsal, that you are just beer salesmen.

So, the next night, not having had a lot of time to rehearse up forty new songs, we just played the *exact same thing*. But beer sales were spectacular, and the owner loved us.

Among the crowd that second night was a gnarly-looking *real* biker (as opposed to doctors who buy a Harley and call themselves bikers). He certainly looked the part, with a leather vest, a scar on his face, and a long beard, but there were also a couple of clues that he was the real deal.* He was a rough-enough character that he was totally comfortable with his biker name: Scooter.

Scooter talked to me a couple of times between songs and told me he had been a drummer, that it had been a while, and that we were really making him miss being on stage. I'd experienced that itch when I had been a long time between bands. The smell of stale cigarette smoke and cleaned-up barf, of sweat, of women's perfume, and of dust roasting on a vacuum tube, it gets in your blood, and you can miss being the life of the party. I could see that longing in his eyes.

---

* *You may meet a rider someday that has three patches that take up most of the back of his leather jacket. He'll have a top rocker with his club name, a middle patch with their "colors" (a logo for their club) and a bottom rocker with a location. They may also have a square patch with MC on it. The location patch isn't just, "Hey, I'm from L.A. how 'bout you?" It's a statement that they will defend that territory. All of this adds up to: leave this guy alone.*

I talked to Mark and asked if we could start the next set by letting Scooter play one with us. Mark asked if he was any good.

Oops—I didn't know!

So, Scooter saddled up, and with a look of sudden panic, he asked what we knew how to play.

"Just give us a beat," I said.

He started in on something steady and rockin'. Tony and I improvised a dancy R&B thing and the dance floor packed up tight led by five or six girls-night-outers having a really good time (*have mercy!*)

Well, Scooter was grinning ear-to-ear, and after the song, he thanked us profusely.

After that set, I headed out to the van to get some fresh air and Gatorade (bar owners don't like you to bring outside drinks in, even if it's not beer).

I thought I was alone in the big old parking lot, but while I was leaning against the van, I heard what we all dread: The sloppy holler of a mean drunk looking for somebody, anybody, to provoke. His bellow came from all the way across the parking lot.

"AAY YOO! MUHFUGGA! WHADDER YOO LOOKIN AT?!"

Ugh. I started a path to the front door, keeping an eye on him as he stumbled over to intercept me.

"YOU WANT SOME TROUBLE, DON'T YA?"

The bar had a glass front door, and just inside I could see a three-piece patch on the back of a leather vest.

"WHERE YOU GOIN, SMARTASS?"

He followed me in the door.

"YA SCARED UH ME, CHICKENSHIT?"

As we walked in, I said, "Nope, just wanted to introduce you to my friend Scooter here."

Scooter slowly swiveled around on his barstool and calmly said, "Yeah, I got this."

It's nice to have friends.

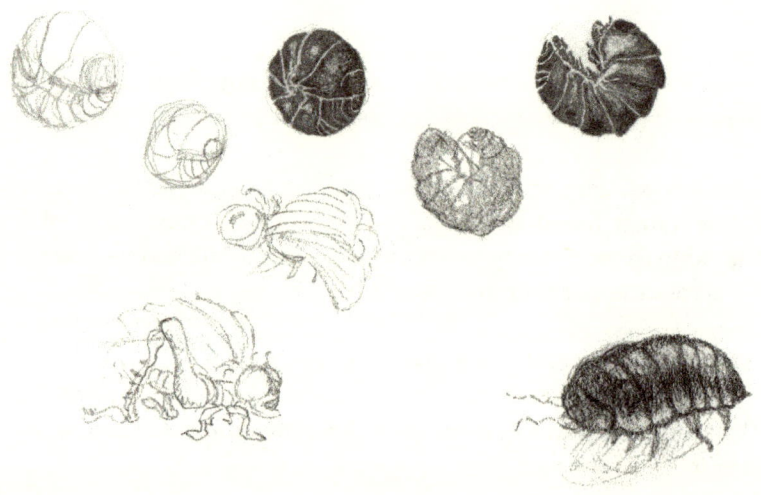

An After-Gig Photo

the difference between a Harley and a Hoover

There was a street corner in Oklahoma City on N. Western Avenue with a couple of popular bars and a small theater that always made it a hot place to play.

The theater is a sushi place now, and the bars have changed hands, but it's still a great corner for a gig. We played a night there in July of 2018 to a crowd of people about our age.

"Our age" means that the show was really cookin' until about midnight, then the crowd pooped out and the joint emptied. The bar manager didn't mind us quitting early. They'd made enough to call it and wanted to go home.

So, we packed it up and hauled it out.

It looked as though the bar down the street and the restaurant next to it were still having a good night, and the sounds of their partying carried over to us. Neither our bar nor the other is right on the corner. The one to the north has a parking lot south of it, and our bar has parking on both sides.

I rolled my big speaker cabinet out to my truck, and as I rounded the corner, I walked up on a pretty twenty-something in a little black dress standing in the middle of the parking lot. She yanked down her bloomers, copped a squat, and started to pee right in front of me, looking me right in the eye the entire time. Her steady gaze unnerved me, and I left my speaker sitting right there in the parking lot and fled back inside.

Soon, the boys and I were finished loading and our crowd had dispersed, so Mark asked if we wanted to continue our recent tradition of taking a band-photo at the end of a show. The front of the bar seemed like a good location, and Mark got out his camera.

The dives north of us must have finally reached closing time, and their crowds spilled out onto the sidewalk and street. Some sort of argument was brewing up over there. We could hear a man's voice, then a woman's, and neither was happy.

We helped Mark set up his tripod, then we were turned back toward the other bar by the sound of a motorcycle doing a burnout (when the driver holds the bike's front brakes while leaning forward and gunning it, so the back tire squeals and smokes against the asphalt) out front. The roaring engine and screaming tire stopped our photo session, momentarily.

The beer signs lit a thick cloud of neon-colored smoke, and in it stood the woman from the argument, in front of the howling motorcycle. She waved her arms in the air, in a stop-it-right-now-you-idiot gesture. He dropped it in gear, and she moved just in time, as he roared off out of sight to the south leaving a disgusted group of friends in his wake.

Glad that the little spectacle was over, we posed and took a few shots. Mark set his timer for one more, and as he joined us, we heard Motorcycle Man coming back this way. The camera went off as the bike screamed by. I guessed his speed at about ninety miles an hour, and later found out that I wasn't too far off.

He disappeared into the dark, off to the north this time. He apparently thought he hadn't expressed his unhappiness enough with his first little demonstration.

Mark unhooked his camera and brought it over for us to choose a shot. As we scrolled through the pictures, we could hear the motorcycle coming back south toward us, his motor at an even higher pitch than before.

"That dumbass is going to keep it up until someone gets hurt," I said to Tony.

The sound of two vehicles colliding is a loud but short "crump." Not really a "crash." The sound is surprisingly brief, followed by a clatter from flying debris.

When I heard that sound, my quick thought was that Motorcycle Man had run into the back of a parked car. I looked up to see worse. A bar patron had stepped unexpectedly into the crosswalk in front of the bar, and the motorcycle hit him head-on. I watched the bike as it continued south toward us. The motorcycle was riderless, kept upright by its speed.

The driver skidded down the street behind it, on his back, feet-first, rolling slowly over to his front, and then over again. He lost a shoe, and then a glove as he went by. The motorcycle slammed into the side of a pickup truck parked on the street right in front of us and bounced off, having caved in the side of the truck.

The rider came to a violent stop at the pickup also, wedged under it below the driver's side door up to his shoulders. The motorcycle wobbled a few feet then fell over. Mark ran over to help the rider. I yanked my phone out and dialed 911. Tony had taken his hat off and stood stock-still, staring at the mess that used to be a pedestrian, and began to feel ill.

The rider's helmet was so scuffed that it was difficult to tell whether he was facing up or down. Mark gingerly pulled it off, found him facing up.

"Hey buddy. Hey. Can you hear me?"

The guy's answer was a hiss of bubbled blood.

It seemed like 911 was taking forever to answer my damned call.

Pick up the phone!

Several people ran down the street to help, and one of them told Mark he was an EMT.

A woman said "ohmygod-ohmygod" over and over.

The 911 operator finally answered. There was a fire station just down the street, and it only took a few minutes from when I hung up for the emergency vehicles to arrive. Mark held the rider's hand as the EMT did a quick assessment. The woman picked up a black sock from the middle of the road.

Photo by Mark Hancock

The police told us to stay to answer questions. They never asked us any, but we were trapped where we were because they blocked the streets in every direction.

They packed the pedestrian up and into an ambulance, and a fire truck cleaned the crosswalk. It took a good while longer to get the rider out from under the truck. As I waited, I used a map app to measure the distance from the crosswalk to the truck's parking spot. The rider had skidded two hundred thirty feet.

I read later that the pedestrian died immediately. A friend at work knew the rider's family and told me he was in the hospital for months. He was eventually charged with manslaughter, but by then I had stopped wanting to know anything more about it.

Q. What's the difference between a Harley and a Hoover?

A. The position of the dirt bag.

Pareto Improvement

Being right does not require anyone else to be wrong.

Being smart does not require anyone else to be stupid.

And going to Heaven does not require anyone else to go to Hell.

You Get Bored, Ya Know?

four sets make a long night

We played at a restaurant on Eighteenth and Boston in Tulsa one night, one of those places with a brass rail running all through the joint. The "stage" was an area right in the middle of the tables marked off by the rail, and it was small enough there wasn't any room to jump around or even move much.

A couple came in and sat down at a table right against the rail on my side, about four inches from my guitar as I stood playing. They ordered burgers and beers, and their order came out pretty quickly. Our blasting music didn't seem to bother them much, nor that I was banging away right next to them while they ate.

I watched the woman meticulously pick the vegetables off her burger one by one and lay them on her plate. I got fascinated watching her neatly arrange the lettuce, then pickles, then tomatoes, in rows. The guy probably spent fifteen bucks on this burger, and she had reduced it to meat and bun.

Yeah, I was bored. I've probably played "Rockin' in the Free World" ten thousand times.

After they paid and left, my boredom turned mischievous, and I started flicking the leftover produce at Tony while we played. Between notes, I grabbed a pickle off the plate and whipped it at him, all in a single motion (*zing*).

I missed, and it disappeared into the dark. The other pickle (*zip*).

Nothing.

I picked up a tomato slice and sailed it Frisbee-style across the stage. It hit flat on the front of his guitar (*PLAP*).

It didn't bounce, didn't slide down, just stuck there like a tattoo.

Did he see it? Yeah he saw it, and HE. WAS. PISSED. Ready-to-stop-the-show-right-there pissed. I didn't immediately get why it fried him so badly. I was just kidding around.

Well, he thought someone in the audience had thrown it. We took an early break and I bought him a beer and apologized about twelve times.

Then, as they say, on with the show.

A guitar player who had become a bit of a local hero for touring as part of a Monty Python stage show was in our audience that night. We'd known Scotty for a long time, but we were still pretty flattered when he asked if he could sit in with us on a few songs. We sounded good, and he and our drummer got on well. A couple of days later the drummer called us and told us Scotty had made him an offer, and he was leaving to go play with his band.

We weren't quite so flattered, after that.

Jackson's Last Fight

the wife lays down the law

During a time when we were between bands, Tony and I hung out and did some pickup shows as a two-man act that played tunes, did jokes, and interacted with the crowd a lot. A bass and a guitar—sort of a Smothers Brothers thing.

During one show, Tony introduced me by saying, "Here he is, Jackson Stinkhammer, ladies and gentlemen!"

He said he was looking for something that sounded like a character in a soap opera. He liked to try out different nicknames on band members, and if he hit on one you *really hated*, he'd use it relentlessly. I didn't mind the "Jackson" moniker, so I acted as if I hated it. Another thing that locked it in was that my mom told him she didn't like it. And everybody knows that pissing off your parents is a primary requirement of rock and roll.

Different performers have their ways to deal with the fright of getting up on stage and screwing up in front of a crowd. I found that my persona changed a bit at show time. I put on a tough-guy armor that helped me deal, and it could be kind of intense. You don't question Jackson. He has to be right, or he wouldn't be up there in the first place.

There have been more than one or two dustups when someone yelled something at the stage and was taken to task for it. I have also been up there playing and had Jackson walk off and leave me, though. It makes for an odd what-the-hell-am-I-doing-here feeling. But he always comes back in a few minutes.

My wife, Kelly, doesn't much like Jackson. She says he's an asshole. I'm sure she's right, but it's nice to be able to blame leaving your undershorts on the bathroom floor on a split personality.

We played a show at a restaurant in a nicer part of OKC that had a microbrewery, and the show was just a stinker. That night, the PA was on the fritz, which made us cranky, and that made us play crappy. As they say: Some days chicken, some days feathers.

To make things worse, we had some backward-ballcap-wearin' college boys playing pool right in front of the stage, who were low-level heckling us.

"Ya suck."

"Get off."

Not too loud, just enough for us to hear them, and they kept it up. All. Stinkin'. Night.

When it gets close to closing time, bars usually run everyone out except for employees. For some reason, they didn't run off the college boys that night, who stayed and played pool while we loaded out.

The stage was elevated, and I put one of the dishwasher-sized bass cabinets on a dolly and carefully inched it down the three steps. On the last step, one douche backed into my path, leaving me balancing the big speaker while he lined up his shot—and he lined up his shot, and he lined up his shot, and then he turned to grin at me as he made it.

Grrr!

I *rolled* that speaker out to the van, *threw* it in the back, *stomped* back in, and picked up the other speaker, with steam coming out of my ears. When my dolly and I came down the stairs again, Mr. Douche backed up in my way again, so Jackson ran right over him with the speaker cabinet.

WHAM!

He was back up in a flash and knocked me flat with a shot to the eye.

I popped back up and we grabbed each other by the collars, standing on either side of the cabinet. We were nose-to-nose, arms straining, huffing and puffing while his friends talked him down.

"Let him go, Chad!"

"He's not worth it, man!"

"He's wrong, and he knows it!"

Just then, I had a moment of clarity—if the owner didn't run these guys off, they must be his friends. If they are his friends and I continue being an asshole, we will probably not play here again.

Through gritted teeth, I hissed, "Yes. They. Are. Correct. I. Am. Wrong. I. Apologize."

Chad let go of my shirt, and it was done.

I'm always happy to get home after a gig. Kell is there, asleep in the dark in our big comfy bed, and when I crawl in, she greets me with a hug. She lets me sleep late, and I have a nice quiet Sunday to recover.*

That particular morning, I opened my eyes and there was Kell on the edge of the bed with her jaw set.

"So. Tell me about your black eye."

Before I go any further, here is a piece of advice for the men and boys reading this: There is no way to tell a woman the story of a bar fight, no possible spin you can put on it, that will not make you sound like an idiot.

But no, I pressed on and related the tale of our rough night.

"Yeah, and?" she said.

I told her about the heckling.

"What were they saying?"

"They said we sucked."

"You just *told* me you sucked."

"Uhm..."

"What did Tony do?"

Well, she knew what Tony did before she asked. Tony is a pacifist and has some sense (sometimes). He had stayed out of it.

"And that was too hard for you?" she said. "I think I'm going to get you one of those WWJD bracelets, but instead of Jesus it'll say, 'What Would Tony Do?' *Ugh!*"

She got up and left me to shower and get myself together.

After a *very* quiet lunch, she leveled her gaze at me across the table and cleared her throat.

---

* *I get to sleep in on Sundays now that our girls are grown.*

"Look. I let you play. I let you go do your thing. You go out of town, to places I don't know and don't want to know. I trust you. You play your show, you come home. I put up with all of it, and I don't say a word."

—*Long pause*—

"If you come home with another black eye, you are done. Do you understand me?"

And so it has been. Jackson has found a new Zen, and the band plays on.

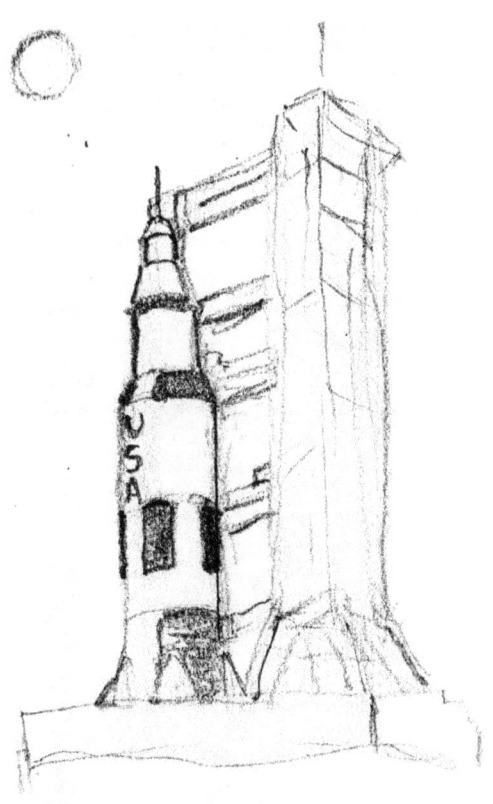

Apology

I'm not too bad at plumbing

and I can work on cars

fix the brakes, change a starter

wire a guitar.

I can tile up a bathroom

and take a lamp apart.

But sometimes, when I've been a jerk,

it's hard to fix your heart.

Adulting

Kell and Jode

just two crazy kids

I met Kelly while I was working as a line supervisor at Hardee's, during the time while I was rooming with Roy. Our manager hired a college girl, and my coworker Mike told me that "the new girl" was engaged to a manager at another of our stores, so I'd better be careful around her.

We worked together for most of Kelly's first shift, and I found her to be quiet and mature, very no-nonsense. She was pretty, and had that twinkle in her eye that said there's more to her than you saw at first. If I wanted to get her to talk to me, I'd better up my game.

At the end of that first shift, she set a piece of extremely hot equipment on the counter, and I misunderstood what she told me and grabbed it, burning my hand. Our mutual embarrassment broke the ice, and we ended the night gabbing about music. After a couple of months of handing each other hamburgers at work, I asked Kelly out on a whim. She surprised me by accepting.

Kelly is a violin player, and told me to pick her up for our date at the college performance hall. When I arrived, she came out carrying her violin case and wearing what musicians call "concert black": a little black dress, black hose, and black heels. My goodness, she was stunning.

After our movie, we sat in the car and talked. She surprised me with a question.

"Why would you ask me out?" she asked.

"I guess I want to get to know you. Why did you accept?"

"Same reason, I suppose."

She reminded me that she was spoken for, but the rest of our conversation convinced me that I liked her. If we couldn't be anything more than friends, I was fine with working on that.

Mike, who always wore his motives on his sleeve, asked me the same question Kelly had, although in a little bit different form, "Why'd you ask her out? You'll never get in her pants." I told Mark that I was kind of ready for someone who wouldn't let me kiss her right away.

Kelly came over to the apartment once in a while, to listen to records with Roy and me, and talk about life, politics, and music. We were as much of a music education to her as she was to us. Her strict upbringing only had room for classical or gospel and we introduced her to prog-rock and punk. For her part, she started us off easy with John Williams before easing us into Copeland and Stravinsky.

After half a year of hanging out with Roy and me, Kelly's engagement fell through rather abruptly. During that time we had become good friends, kidding each other and conspiring at work: leaving little notes in each other's locker. She didn't mind my strange sense of humor, and I found her (sometimes brutal) honesty refreshing. We trusted each other, and when the opportunity came, we fell easily into dating.

We saw each other steadily for several months and by then had known each other for almost a year. We were enjoying our time together so much that I hadn't reflected on how very close we'd become. Our relationship had developed into something larger than we'd realized for ourselves.

One evening in early spring, we were laying on our stomachs in the loft of her apartment, talking and watching the sunset through the big back window. We hadn't bothered to get up and turn on a light, and the room had slowly gone completely dark, as we gabbed on. A lull in the conversation got to be a little long, and I heard her start to cry very softly, there next to me. When I asked what was wrong, she sniffed and said, "Don't you think it's time?" Still clueless, I said,

"Time for what?"

Always the adult in the room, she had realized what I had not.

"For us to get married."

An odd way to propose, but of course she was right. Over the next week, we talked, made plans, and decided to set a date for late July to give us time to set everything up. She would tell her parents, and I would tell mine. I called Mom and told her that I would be home for the weekend. I planned to spring it on them in a big surprise.

I arrived at their house Friday night before dinner, and when Dad got home, tired from work, I sat them down and gave them the speech that I had practiced the entire trip down. I knew that they liked Kelly, and was expecting a warm reception. Dad didn't let me get all the way through before he stood up and backed me into the wall, red-faced with anger.

"WHAT THE HELL DO YOU THINK YOU'RE DOING?" he shouted in my face. "I AM NOT GOING TO LET YOU RUIN THAT SWEET LITTLE GIRL'S LIFE!" He huffed and puffed a couple of breaths, then stomped off into their bedroom and slammed the door. Mom followed him, stepping softly.

I stood in the kitchen, not moving. The unexpected explosion stunned me. I had no idea what to do next. For ten minutes, I stood in the same spot, trying to decide what to do. Do I wait it out? Do I pack up and leave? Do I go knock on their... Mom rounded the corner and motioned for me to sit back down at the kitchen table.

"He's upset, yes. And it's a combination of several things. He's still mad that you were thrown out of school, and that you haven't done much about returning to it. To that end, he and I are worried about Kelly. She is still in school, and we just don't know how a guy from a hamburger stand will be able to support a family, let alone pay for her tuition. We do not want her to have to drop out. We've seen good friends do sillier things for love."

I told her that Kelly and I had talked about those very things. I had promised Kelly that she would finish school, come what may. We had both been on our own for a while by then, and we were used to living on a shoestring. Besides that, she was a good enough violinist that her orchestra had awarded her a full-ride scholarship. That would pay for school, and we would make her degree our primary task.

"That makes me feel better. Give your dad some time, maybe a few days. He'll come around. Besides, think a minute about our story, then consider who's doing the yelling."

Mom and Dad had eloped, driving all the way to Mexico, because she was too young to get married in Kansas. They only told their parents when they got back. Reminding me of their adventure reassured me.

I didn't stay over, and headed back home that night. Kelly was not pleased by my dad's reaction, but accepted what Mom had to say.

As Mom predicted, Dad calmed down and even embraced the news. He called me that Tuesday and invited us up to our cabin in Kansas for the weekend. His friends would all be there attending a party, and we could come and announce our engagement to the group.

Kell and I got out a map. I had only driven to the cabin once by myself prior to that, and never from Edmond. We traced a line straight west out of Edmond, on a road marked on the map that appeared to run all the way out to highway 3, where we could turn north. I wasn't familiar with that road, but since it was marked right there on the map it seemed legit. Shouldn't be any problem.

After our shift on Friday, we loaded up the car and headed west. It had rained a gully-washer the night before, and the road was still wet. Our city road turned into asphalt at the edge of town, and then after another ten miles of countryside, the asphalt turned to gravel. The gravel was sloppy: steering was rather like driving a boat. But it was still navigable, if you kept a good speed up.

When we topped a hill, the gravel road (and our luck) ran out. The rainstorm had turned the remaining dirt road into thick, gooey, red mud, and we launched off into it doing sixty miles an hour. I reacted by braking, causing a sideways skid that ended in the ditch, with my little hatchback leaning far enough that a small push could have toppled it all the way over. We climbed carefully out of the driver's-side door to survey our situation.

We were stuck fast, in mud up to the floor pan. In our skid, the front passenger tire had struck a craggy tree stump and was mortally wounded. There was no way to get a jack under any part of the car to fix it. We saw what looked like a house in the distance, and decided to ask them to use their phone, and get someone to come out from town to help us.

We slogged a quarter mile west down the road, sticking to the high spots to avoid sinking up to our ankles. As we got closer, the appearance of the "house" made us start to worry about what kind of 80's horror movie situation we were getting ourselves into.

The little farmhouse had fallen into ruins, but somehow seemed to still be occupied. It may have once had a second story, but whatever had been there had been hastily replaced with a roof of corrugated tin. The walls were a hodgepodge of ancient clapboard, chipboard sheeting, and tarpaper. It was surrounded and partly obscured by waist-high grass and brambly bushes, and chickens bawked and scattered when we stepped onto the porch.

A wild-haired woman in a shawl answered my knock on the door and squinted at us from behind the rusty screen. She answered my question,

"Telephone? Naaw, aint no telephone here. Wouldn't be much use, it's just me an muh burds."

She wished us luck, then asked that we move on, as she "aint too enamored o' company."

With no better idea of what to do, we headed back to the car. As we slogged along the muddy road, we saw a man driving an open-cab tractor along the road that crossed ours, heading in our direction. He turned away from us at the intersection, having not acknowledged our frantic waving. But he was headed toward my car.

We saw the tractor turn around and back up, then the farmer disappeared behind it for a few minutes. He climbed onto the tractor seat and dropped it in gear with a black burp of diesel smoke from the exhaust stack. He dragged my car to just past us then slowed to a stop. He said dryly in our direction, "Git in" and we did, puzzled but happy to be rescued.

My car sloshed and slid on the end of the chain as he pulled us along. We rounded the corner south, and then after another half-mile bumped up onto sweet civilized asphalt. A quarter-mile further and we pulled into a pretty little farmyard with a white house and trimmed lawn. When we emerged from our muddy car, our rescuer gestured silently toward the house where his wife was on the step outside the kitchen door.

The farmer's wife sat us down and poured some lemonade. She asked us all about ourselves and seemed delighted by our engagement. Through the kitchen window, we watched her husband out in the driveway changing our ruined tire for the spare. We talked about our plans, for the weekend and for the rest of our lives.

The farmer came in, took off his boots and washed his hands, and joined us at the table. He had not spoken a word to us yet, except to tell us to jump into the car, and was all grim business until his wife asked him how the tire change went.

His face lit up, "Oh mighty fine, it was an easy fix. It should get you two where you're going."

He sat and drank half a lemonade with us, and laughed out loud when I got to the part about my dad's reaction to our engagement.

When we thanked them sincerely for their help, he told us,

"We were helped out of a couple of pickles when we were young. Sometimes by people we'd never met. Time'll come. Just remember to help them kids out."

We hit the road (a little less literally this time) with much better directions than we'd arrived with.

We made it to the cabin a couple of hours later than we said we would. It was after dark, and we found a note on the door.

My parents maintained friendships with old friends from their school days, and several of them had cabins near ours in Kansas. That bunch loved a party. Dad had been asked by his buddy Don Fincham to come up that weekend and help castrate some calves.* They took the opportunity to invite a bunch of the guys and their wives to the Fincham cabin for a get together. The note on the door instructed us to wash up and come down for drinks and finger food.

When we arrived at the Fincham's, the party was in full swing. The gals were inside, talking and listening to Tom Jones on the stereo, and the guys were out on the screened-in porch finishing their second or third drink.

Dad and Don's morning veterinary activity had provided the main ingredient for "calf fries". For the uninitiated, to make Calf Fries you cut the removed testicles into strips or nuggets, and brine them in beer for an hour or so. Then you batter them in cornmeal and fry them in oil like chicken. The meat does not add a lot of taste. Like many things, the quality of the hors d'oeuvre depends a lot on how the chef spices the batter, and what sauce you dip them in. The gals had supervised while the guys cooked a couple of batches, and when we arrived, they were passing around a platter.

When we knocked on the screen door Dad interrupted their revelry to announce our arrival. His attitude toward the idea of us getting married had experienced a complete turnaround, and he proudly introduced Kelly to everyone there as his "Future Daughter". He saved his good friend Don for last. Don was holding the big platter of fries, and after greeting her warmly, made a big deal out of offering her some:

"Aw it's great to meet you, little lady! How about a couple of... shrimp?"

He grinned broadly, and held out the platter. The men all held their breath,

---

* *Dad liked to barter his veterinary services. It was a great way to build up good will, for his business and around town. I once went with him to an older lady's house just south of town, where he took a fishhook out of her cat's cheek. A bunch of howling and meowing later, the lady thanked us and sent us on our way with a warm peach cobbler. I think Dad also liked that none of the bartering was taxed. Everyone has to have their own little bit of "stickin' it to the man".*

anticipating her reaction to his prank. Kelly looked Don right in the eye as she plucked a "shrimp" off the tray and popped it into her mouth.

"My daddy grew up on a farm," she said, chewing in the silence, "and I've been around a few cows." Munch, munch. "I knew when you offered it to me," munch, swallow "that it wasn't a shrimp."

A couple of seconds more of silence, then the room erupted in a cheer. She passed the test! I was congratulated on my fine choice, backslapped, and told by all how I was marrying "above my grade".

From that night on, she has been one of the family. I have to agree with the guys on the porch that night: I chose well, and in June of 1985 we were married.

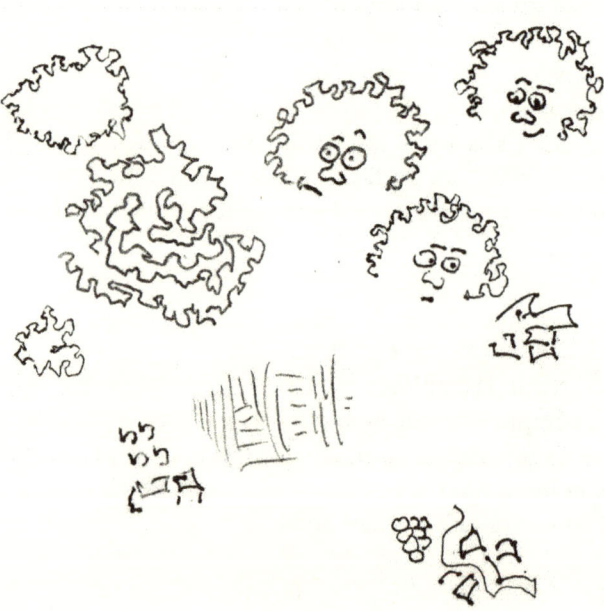

We Had Abby at Home

the Original Gang's first adventure

Kelly was pregnant, and the due date was December 20. This would be our second kid, and Amanda (our first) was so late they induced labor to get on with it. We went to all of the baby classes when she had Amanda, and when I was asked if I wanted to be in the room for the birth, I told them I wasn't skeered, I had helped my veterinarian dad operate on animals.

My band wanted to book a gig across town for the twentieth and Kelly said she'd be fine. Nothing had happened to make her think this baby wouldn't be late also, so I got the go-ahead to play.

It wound up being a good gig: A bunch of varsity cheerleaders had followed the rugby team to the bar (as they do), and they made a riot of the place.

As the gig wound down, the drummer bugged the fool out of me to show up at his house—there was to be a post-gig party, and all of the cheerleaders would be there. I told him: Married, kid due yesterday, I'm heading home. I got home at about 3 a.m., in bed at 3:30, and all was quiet.

By seven o'clock, things were no longer quiet. Kelly woke me up yelling and hitting me on the chest.

"I think something is happening!"

I was dead sleepy, and tried to orient myself with the world. Kelly's water had broken.

I called the number we were given for the hospital where we were planning to go, and the nurse asked me a few questions: Had the water broken? Was she dilating?

The nurse advised me to run a bathtub of warm water and have Kell get in. I told her *I* thought things were happening a lot faster than *she* did.

She said, "Have her walk around a bit and—"

Suddenly Kelly yelled from the bedroom. I hung up on the nurse and ran in to find Kelly on the bed.

A sidebar here: This was a brand-new king-sized bed we got each other as a Christmas gift. It was maybe a week old.

I got on the bed with Kell. She screamed, I yelled, and Ka-bam! Out came Abby. Just about that fast. Kell pitched, I caught.

What I caught was a little scrunchy pinkish-bluish person with her eyes closed, and not breathing.

A Her? It's a girl! We hadn't let the doctor tell us. We wanted a surprise and picked both boy and girl names.

She had some goo in her nose. I wiped it clear, and she took a huge gasp of air and let out a howl!

We had talked with Amanda, who was four at the time, and prepared her for the big arrival.

"You have a new friend coming, it's in Mommy's tummy right now, it's gonna come out..."

All those things you tell a kid, so I figured that she would want to be right there when it happened, to meet the new sister. I yelled for little Mo* to come see, but I hadn't looked at the scene around us. When she saw the blood and goo, she yelped, ran back into her bedroom, and slammed the door.

Oops!

She got over it quickly and came back out to help me with towels. It was cold, so we wrapped Abby up in a towel, put her on Kell's tummy, and pulled the comforter up over them. I went back to the phone to call the nurse and apologize for hanging up on her. She started with a scolding.

"Well, you told me that her contractions were fifteen minutes apart," she said.

"Yeah, I know, I'm sorry, but we're done. We had the baby. What do we do now?"

She congratulated me and told me to call 911 to dispatch an ambulance to bring them in. I called, and then paced around the bedroom relaying their questions to Kelly, while in my undershorts and covered with blood and baby-goo.

---

* *We gave Amanda the same middle name as Kelly—Marie. It became shortened to "Mo" when she was barely old enough to talk and has been a pet name ever since.*

I started to shiver, from both the cold and the excitement.

Kell and I fielded their questions while they were on their way (it sounded like they were just trying to keep me on the line), and they eventually got around to asking if I wanted to cut the umbilical cord.

"Yeah, let's do it!"

Next question was, did we have a package of new shoelaces? We did. They said new laces were something we could be sure was clean to use to tie the cord in two places.

Done!

I had the scissors in my hand when I heard the ambulance coming. Kell and I heard them go past the house, slow down and pull in somewhere down the street, and go quiet.

Well, we had moved just a couple of years earlier from the 23-block on Thirty-fifth Street to the 24-block on Fiftieth Street. I asked the dispatcher what address I gave them, and sure enough, I had mixed up the house number and they pulled in down the street.

We forgot all about the umbilical, as the dispatcher and I directed them back to the right house. And *that* is always Kelly's favorite part of the story.

Amanda was over her initial shock and very helpful that whole time. She was one of those kids who never met anyone that she didn't act like she already knew, and when the ambulance guys came in the four-year-old talked their legs off.

"Man! It was crazy. Stuff everywhere! We used a bunch of towels! They told me it would come out, but I didn't know it would come out of *there*! Wow! Hey Mom! Did you know it was going to come out of your—"

"*Yes*, Amanda. Yes, we knew."

The EMTs loaded up Kelly and Abby and off they went to the hospital.

I remember thinking it was odd: "We" meant there were four of us now!

Amanda and I stayed back and cleaned. When we got it in good-enough shape for the relatives, who were now on the way, we headed down to meet them at the hospital.

Kelly was looking good. The labor had been painful—*no* anesthetic (Wow!)—but it had been short, so she said it was a lot less rough than the first one was.

I did paperwork with the nurses and told them her name. We were sure she'd be a boy and picked "Sam." We had discussed using that even if it was a girl, but we also liked Abby, and so Abbigail it was (although I spelled it oddly).

When Amanda was born, I was told to follow the nurse back into another room, where they cleaned her up and weighed her.

"What are you going to name her?" said a nurse who was filling out paperwork.

"Spike!"

I let that hang for a beat or two for extra comedy.

She turned to me and deadpanned, "You will not name this sweet little girl Spike. Give me something else, or I will ask her mother."

I folded.

"Amanda," I said sheepishly.

"That will do just fine."

A few months after Abby was born, we received a bill from the hospital that charged us for services that included "delivery of the baby."

Wait, what?

Kell spent a few days arguing with them on the phone and finally went down and showed them the ambulance bill, which read "Mother and Child," so they backed off that charge.

One of my regular customers at the photo lab that I managed owned a company that makes memorial bricks, the kind you buy to honor grandma in the sidewalk at the zoo. I had him make a brick that says, "Abigail Randle was born at this house." We set the brick in concrete in the sidewalk in front of the house, before we moved to another neighborhood in 1998. The current resident was as surprised as we were when we visited and showed it to him, still there after 20 years.

Another of my regular customers from then was a dentist. He heard our story, and then called me "Doc" for the rest of the time he knew me. I was a big hero with family and friends for a little while, and had a few drinks bought for me on the merits of this story. But there isn't really any reason for that.

I just stood there while Kelly very calmly had a baby right there at our house.

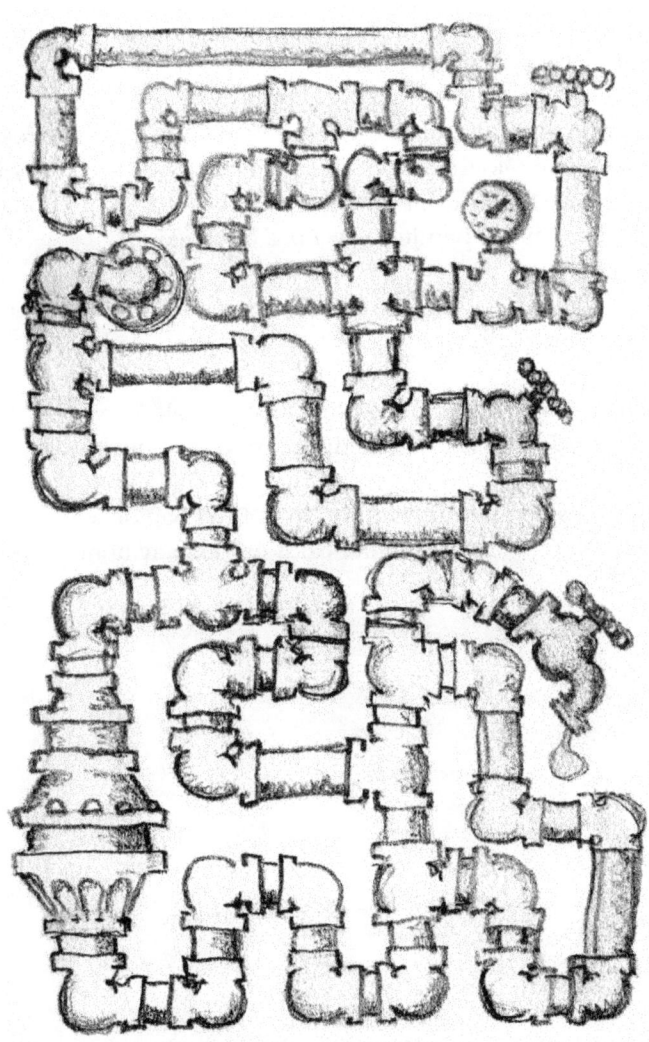

Observations While Following the Wife Around the Grocery Store

just trying to stay out of her way

They should have a brand of cat food called "Ungrateful Little Bastard."

Lay's should make pasta-flavored chips. That way, you could just buy a bottle of Prego and dip 'em.

The wrinkly ones could retain the name Cheetos, but the smooth ones definitely should be called Cheefingers.

In the '70s, Sweden had fantastic cheese in their grocery stores, and all I remember having in Oklahoma was Kraft singles. We have really upped our cheese game since then: even small-town grocers have imports. And the Swedes finally got more than just *one kind* of cereal.

Walking through the baking section always makes me wish Amanda and Abby were with us.

Beef Jerky, Jeef Berky, Jerf Beeky, Berf Jeeky, Beek Jerfy, Jeek Berfy, Berk Jeefy, Jerk Beefy, and a jar of those dry-roasted peanuts, please.

If the cashier asks you if you want her to put the bag of cat food in another sack, tell her, "Nah, we're just gonna eat it on the way home."

A Bank Robbery!

everyone on the floor

When I had explained to my boss that Abby was due in December and that I'd need time off, they were itchy about me being gone from work during our busiest season. But when I called and told the story of having her at home, they laughed and congratulated me and let me take some time.

A few weeks later, and back at work, I got a call at the lab from Kelly. She sounded shaken, and after hanging up I told the boss I needed to take off early to go get Kell and drive her home.

"My wife was just in a bank robbery," I explained.

"Gawd. This better be true," they said. "You are my all-time champ at crazy reasons to get out of work. Just go."

When I arrived, the scene at the bank had calmed down considerably, and so had Kelly. A news crew was just arriving and there were about ninety-seven cop cars in the parking lot.

Kelly told me she'd been standing in line in for Marge, our favorite teller, when she heard a gun go off behind her. She thought it had been a lot louder than a handgun, and everyone in the place hit the floor and flattened out.

She heard a scuffle, and then heard the bank's front door bang open, then close, then silence. After a minute or so, someone announced that it was all over, and they slowly rose. She had been asked to stay so the cops could interview her but hadn't had much to add.

Kell was calm enough to drive, so we headed home. We still had that deposit to make, so a couple of days later I went down to the bank. I was curious to hear Marjorie's side of the story, too.

We had done business with that bank since their early days—when their only location was a modified mobile home. Since they were very small, we knew everyone and they treated us like family, which is an unusual commodity in the big city. Once, when we were in a tight spot, their president worked us a small, low-interest loan and guided us through that lean time. One of his conditions was that we come by and talk to him each month when we made our payment. By the time of the robbery, they had grown enough they were in a brand-new red brick building. Marge had been our teller through all of it, and she greeted me when I came in.

"Ah, I see she sent you this time! I don't blame her. It's been weird coming in to work the last few days."

It was a slow day at the bank, so I asked her for the story.

She said that a guy with a mask had walked in the front door with a shotgun. The bank has a recessed waiting area near the entrance, kind of a cubby, with a bench seat and a popcorn machine, and the robber must have been intent on his task, because he walked right past a security guard sitting there.

Marge said that the robber just happened to pick the day when the biggest, burliest off-duty cop she knew was pulling security duty. The cop walked up behind our thief, put one arm around his neck, and grabbed the shotgun barrel with his other hand, jamming its muzzle against the wall. The shotgun went off, blowing a big hole through the wall, which had been repaired but not yet painted when I went in. The cop lifted Mr. Robber off his feet and pulled him out to the parking lot, and it was all over just like that.

Over the years, the little bank grew. One at a time, the bank officers moved on, and eventually so did Marge. When we moved further west, we changed to a closer bank, but we miss the people there and how well they treated us.

They Burned Our Church

what's so funny about peace, love, and understanding

We were shopping for a church when we visited the little Presbyterian we wound up at (which was neither Kelly's Baptist nor my Methodist). They had a brand-new, good-lookin', regular-guy pastor who was our age, and after a couple more visits, we found they were very accepting: Living up to their name in the Christian sense of the word.

They preached that Jesus loved everyone—Yay! They embraced racial diversity—Yay! They welcomed people with developmental disabilities—Yay! We joined, and over time, we became active. In a church with a hundred members, you will be called up eventually. I was made an elder and Kelly a deacon.

We liked their version of The Word, and in the ten-or-so years we attended, I only heard maybe two half-mumbled references to any kind of politics. On the surface, they were very tolerant. However, I think the congregation as a *group* might have been pushing the members as *individuals* a little bit out of their comfort zone.

Somewhere deep within the by-laws of the governing body of our branch of the church was a passage that said that to be ordained, you had to be "celibate or in a monogamous, heterosexual relationship." Well, sometime during the previous year the presbytery subtly changed that passage by removing just one word: heterosexual.

Around the same time, our pastor was "called by God to a different mission" (a nice way of telling us he got a better-paying gig at a huge church). This left us at a loss for leadership and forced to decide what qualities we wanted in a new preacher. As word of dropping "heterosexual" from the passage grew from a whisper to a rumble, people split into three camps:

A. A group that expressed the desire to embrace diversity in all its forms.

B. A group that expressed worry that the church could wind up with a gay pastor.

C. A group that just wondered why the two sides couldn't work things out.

The Bs decided that if the presbytery couldn't be talked out of their renunciation of Good Christian Values, they would pack up and leave. Never mind the point of order that our congregation would have to vote on the new pastor, so we could never end up with someone that a majority hadn't vetted and agreed to. They saw it as a matter of principle.

There were several congregation meetings (called by the Bs of course, who else cared?) to talk the rest of the members into joining a much more conservative branch of the Church. Kelly and I went to the meetings and witnessed people who were good friends screaming at each other about whose interpretation of the Bible was more correct.

Everyone loved our youth pastor, but when he let it slip that he was in group A, he was suddenly let go for "unrelated" reasons. As the arguments dragged on, we just stopped going to church. Thankfully, our girls had both moved on to college and missed this sorry display.

Church politics were involved, naturally: We were a tiny congregation, so everyone had been an elder or a deacon at one time or another. Everyone knows what's best when they have been king-for-a-day. Additionally, we just had too few members to survive a split.

The presbytery felt they needed us, and it had bent over backward to keep us afloat in the past. It also owned the mortgage on the building, so if they cut us loose, what would become of the building?

On a Wednesday, around three o'clock in the morning, someone broke into the church. They only took a couple of X-box sets and games. The office and other valuables were untouched. In the sanctuary, they moved chairs, piled up cushions from couches and chairs in the other rooms in one corner, and set it on fire.

The fire department put it out before it did structural damage, but everything in the building was ruined by smoke. We went to help clean up and there were lots of sideways half-references about "they wanted it to look like kids" and distrusting mumbles about "one of us or one of them."

We loved our friends there, and we miss them. Some who we miss have left for good, and we're still disappointed that the argument reached the level it did. We have been away for long enough that we don't know what they did as far as splitting, moving, staying, or letting it go. We drive past the place we went to on so many Sundays, and wonder.

Sometime after we stopped going, they sent out a request for information as to whether we were still members. I didn't know enough about what they had become to tell them.

Zapped

volts, amps, ohms, and watts

For some reason, I have lived through more jolts of electricity than I should admit to. Maybe I've been very lucky, or maybe it's as Tony says, I have opposite polarity from the universe. Maybe it's both.

The first good zap that I remember, I very much brought on myself. I was in my dorm room (the one where I painted the wall) after a shower wearing only a towel, using a shopping cart as a stepstool to reach a ceiling fixture with a burned-out fluorescent bulb. How much more setup do you need to be shocked? My hand slipped down to the metal sleeve on the bulb.

POW!

The next thing I remember I had an awful headache from hitting the tile floor.

I worked in a pump repair shop pulling apart electric motors, worked in a print shop with its machinery, and spent years in restaurants, which are full of stainless-steel equipment with wires running through it.

The worst (aka most life-threatening) charge I ever took was during a busy lunch at the restaurant. The big electric broiler shut down while we had orders to fill, and I knew from the way it behaved it had blown a fuse. I opened a panel and found it: As big around as your thumb and three inches long, with copper tips.

I had to change it NOW!

Half of my lunch-crowd was waiting for hamburgers. If I shut the broiler down, it would take half an hour that I didn't have to get it back up to temperature.

I grabbed a pair of rubber-handled pliers and went at the fuse. The broiler's power supply was 220-volts out of the wall and that was enough, I suppose, to jump past the rinky-dink rubber handles and get me. I woke up with my head and shoulders jammed under the drink station. The jolt had instantly straightened my crouched legs, which shot me away from the machine (thank goodness) and across the room. My arm was numb up to the shoulder, and I wound up shutting the danged broiler down anyway.

For a long time, I told people the electricity had tasted like copper pennies, but Doctor Dad said it might have been a little blood from the capillaries in my sinuses.

That joint was full of electrical surprises: A loud *pop* somewhere and the lights would go out, leaving an eerie silence and twenty people holding their breath. We became very familiar with the layout of the breaker box in the dark.

One afternoon, the *pop* was more of a *BOOM*, and when we flipped the breaker, we found that the meat slicer had welded itself to the roast beef oven. When it started back up, the slicer yanked the oven around, dragging it back and forth on its casters.

One or the other was grounded badly, and when a cook opened the door, the two met. I found a broad screwdriver and chiseled the weld apart.

It is common to encounter bad wiring when you are in a band. Play a thousand shows and you'll have found five hundred dives with crappy grounding.

Some places have plugged their buzzy-ass neon beer sign into the same circuit as the stage outlets, and more than a couple times we've had to run extension cords over the dance floor to the other side of the bar.

I don't know that I've ever understood the relationship between volts, amps, and watts. I do know that if your 500-watt bass amp and the PA amplifiers are not copacetic because the bar has bad grounding, the connection point is your *lips* and the microphone. The result is that when you sing your first line, you wonder why the lights seemed to flicker for a second, and suddenly your *whole face hurts*.

You'll sometimes see seasoned band guys walk out onto the stage and hold their guitar up close to the microphone. What they are doing is getting their strings close enough to the microphone-ball to see if it arcs between them. In the dim stage light, you can actually see the little lightning-bolt of the trouble you are about to be in. We played one joint down on Campus Corner, and while rolling around on the floor in a sweaty shirt (all part of the show, folks) I wondered what was poking me in the back. I hadn't seen any obstacles before I dove.

Bzzt-bzzt. What could it be?

Well, you know enough now to tell me that the bar's grounding was wonky, and the entire floor was just a little bit ... live.

Many guitarists use wireless packs, and not for just the mobility it gives you. Being disconnected from your amp by a radio signal is your best defense against the bar-owner's brother-in-law's wiring job.

Getting shocked is a strange feeling—one you remember vividly, and forever.

I'm told that the human body runs on electricity. Your nervous system is a conduit for the tiny sparks that run through it, actuating muscles and carrying information about maintenance or pain. Your mind and thoughts may be nothing more than the combined storage of these electrical impulses. Being zapped will make you believe these postulations, as if the current has connected with your *soul*—or momentarily disconnected it, perhaps.

A good hit seems to take a bite out of time. Like you've been rebooted—shut completely down and born again all in a split second. It is a very strange loss of memory. A small jolt produces a buzzing numbness in your hand, and the tinglies seem to be tiny creatures pulling on your arm, drawing you into the wiring to flow along with them to the next outlet. That it sometimes makes your hand grab tighter, just reinforces the feeling that it *wants* you.

Weird, huh? Yeah as I said, maybe I've been zapped a few too many times.

I've been a

cage cleaner and veterinary assistant, farmhand (wheat and cattle), gardener/lawn care provider, feed store/grain cleaner hand, aluminum can factory machine operator, furniture factory machine operator, Swedish restaurant cook, hand blown glass factory apprentice, commercial print-shop gopher, medical doohickey molding machine operator, repair technician at a pump factory, fast food worker, and a bindery/small print-shop helper. A cook, cashier, restaurant manager, bass player in a rock and roll band, dad, live sound technician, songwriter, draftsman, warehouse dock hand, photo developer, photo processing facility manager, photographer, construction hand, air traffic simulator operator, recording engineer, record producer, air traffic simulation lab manager, program planner/personnel scheduler, and an interim control-account manager for an air traffic training contract, and an author now too, I suppose.

Maybe I can take comfort in that old Robert Heinlein quote:

"Specialization is for insects."

Captain of a Pirate Ship

loot, pillage, and make hamburgers

I worked at Hardee's restaurants for nine years. I met my wife, Kelly, there and made many friends along the way.

It started as kind of an emergency job while I was in college, and I worked my way up to being one of the managers at the store on the corner of Twenty-third Street and Broadway in Oklahoma City. It was the store closest to downtown and was also a few blocks from the State Capitol and other government buildings. Across the street from the biggest liquor store in the state, it was the most ghetto store in the whole city. When the company assigned you a tour of duty there, it was assumed you'd made someone at the office mad at you.

It was a wild place to work, and many of my craziest work stories happened there.

We had a thriving population of homeless guys. I started out with a lot of sympathy for them. Kelly and I weren't rich, and "but for the grace of God" it coulda been me.

I say I "started out" caring because they just wore me down.

My first encounter was with a guy who made a good point: If a burger that we'd pre-made at the end of a busy lunch passed its fifteen-minute hold-time, we threw them out. Couldn't he help me, and himself, out by taking one? It made sense, so I gave the poor guy a burger. Felt good to help someone.

Twenty minutes later, his friends showed up in twos and threes to hit me up for a "cold burger." But if you're running your lunch carefully, you make little waste, and when the next bum came in, I told him we were out. When he stone-faced told me that I'd better get back there and make him one, I threw his ass out and experienced my first little attitude adjustment.

Bums and panhandlers, like all people, come in many varieties. There were down-and-outs, there were professionals, some were decent guys, and some were just evil.

We had two who ran around together who were known as Soapy and Abe. Abe had a Lincoln beard, of course. They made their living collecting trash and sorting it. They looked for anything valuable to pawn (yep, we had a pawnshop two doors down), sold cans at the recycling place, and slept wherever they could. They were decent guys, and we knew them because they came in daily to exploit the loophole that we'd always refill a Hardee's foam cup with coffee, no questions asked.

If you kept up with Soapy and Abe, they'd get progressively hazier and increasingly grubby day-by-day, but then one day their scrounging would bring them into some cash, and they'd wash and shave, comb their hair, and come in and buy a burger and coffee in a new cup.

Side note: I also told my crew that cops ate free, all the time. It was a necessary investment.

We had another regular bum for a while. They called him Redbeard, and he was a dick. One day, he hid around the corner of the building where I couldn't see him and pressed customers stuck in line at the drive-through for money. When I went out to confront him, he started swinging.

"I'll knock you out, I'll cut you down, how dare you treat a veteran this way, I fought for your ass in the war, hey!" he yelled while spittin' and throwing punches at the air all around him.

After that, I started ordering the brooms that have thicker handles, so my people could defend themselves when I sent them to clean the lot.

A couple of bums started camping in the tall Johnson grass on the other side of the fence behind the store. The grass was high enough we didn't even know they were there until a customer ran in and shouted, "Fire!"

They'd set the field on fire while cooking and burned a big piece of our fence down.

We had a clinic nearby where you could donate plasma for cash. It got so I could recognize people who had just been there by their impoverished look and bandage around their arm. They seemed to always come toward the first of the month, on a day when the clinic was open. I had a young couple with a baby come in that fit that description exactly. I asked, and yes, they were temporarily rich from their donation.

"Look, I really don't want to sell you hamburgers," I said. "Take it to the grocery on Tenth and get some bread, a can of soup. You could get a couple weeks' worth of stuff if you're careful. Just go away, please?"

Toward the end of my time there, I got so jaded that I would remember that it was plasma day and tell the cooks, "Put in some cookies! Them

Plasma-donors can't resist the smell of baking cookies! *Woo-hoo*, gonna make my sales goal today!"

Just shameful.

I saw two deaths there: A high-speed chase ended in a fiery crash in our lot, and on another occasion a street person died quietly in the lobby. I also saw two robberies and one attempt.

One night at closing time, a guy came in with a big knife, jumped the counter, and grabbed one of my favorite people to work with. He brought her back to the office, with the knife to her neck, and told the night guy to give him the money he was counting. She quit the next day.

Another was a drive-through robbery. At the tail end of a busy lunch, a guy ordered a burger, kept his head low while in line, and then pulled on a mask just before the window. He stuck a handgun in the window and asked for the cash drawer. The cashier turned to me with her eyes wide.

"Be slow, be careful," I said. "Give him what he wants."

I heard that they caught that guy. He'd driven his own truck and we gave them the plate number. I recently told a cop friend the story of the knife-to-the-neck lady, and he pointed out that in a case like that, it isn't uncommon for the victim to be an accomplice of the thief, who helped plan the robbery. I really liked that lady, but in that joint, it wouldn't surprise me.

We served breakfast, and back then, Hardee's made their biscuits from scratch, for real. Flower, shortening, buttermilk, etc. I can still do it, probably in my sleep, because the managers had to be good at it so they could teach. They also had to fill in and get a batch going if the biscuit maker didn't show up first thing in the morning.

"First Thing" meant five o'clock in the morning, so it happened a lot. Five pounds of flour, two pounds of shortening, roll, cut, bake, get on the phone with dough on your hands, and get a cook in here now!

One of the times I opened, I pulled into the parking lot and the biscuit maker was super-animated—just beside himself.

"I am so sorry," he said as I walked up. "I wanted to explain but I just don't have time I gotta go sorry!"

A taxi pulled up as he was talking, and he got in and shut the door during his last word. The taxi sped off leaving me scratching my head, and as I unlocked the door, a cop car roared up behind me and rolled down its window.

"Does John Smith work here?"

I pointed toward the taxi, and the cop squealed his tires off after them.

Whelp, guess I'll be makin' biscuits today. Better go ahead and do John's out-process, too.

Another time I arrived when the biscuit maker was AWOL, I went in and started things up just to have him finally show up forty-five minutes late.

Most of my employees walked or rode the bus to save money. This guy explained that on his way in, cops had stopped and frisked him and asked questions that sounded like someone had robbed the Q-Mart down the block just that morning.

We got things going, and my next employee arrived half an hour late with a similar story—and the next employee, and the next. They had stopped my entire crew, one at a time, and caused the whole place to be late. Since all ten of my guys had been stopped, I made a blanket proclamation that I wouldn't count today against anyone's attendance.

I just needed to keep things rolling!

I'd had to fill in and work the missing positions all morning, and pretty soon we got lunch set up and I could catch my breath. As they came in, each brought another piece of the story, and I put it together as I relaxed a minute and drank my coffee.

Someone had robbed the Q-Mart. It was an armed robbery. They were on foot. They were wearing brown polyester with an orange stripe. I looked out at my busy crew, humming like a well-oiled machine in their brown and orange uniforms, and realized that one of those SOBs had just robbed a store with a gun!

I decided to be a real nice boss for the rest of the day.

A week later, I was busy working the counter during lunch when three cops I didn't know walked up to the counter

"Do you have a Jim Badarski working here?"

I knew the sound of the back door by heart and heard it.

WHAM!

"*Uhh* ... kinda sounds like he's heading west," I said.

They hustled out the doors on both sides of the place, and I went back and erased Jim from the schedule.

We had a few outsiders rob us, but we had a lot of loss from within, also. We kept tight accounting on the cash drawers and still lost money. There are countless schemes to skim cash, but sometimes they'd just red-handed steal.

We worked hard to get our cash shortages down, then the inventory shortages would go up. We kept the freezer locked even while we were doing business, so employees wouldn't walk out with stuff. We lost ten cases of bacon one day.

That's 140 pounds!

We caught the guy, and when he confessed, we asked what on earth he did with a trunk load of bacon. He said he'd sold it to a local restaurant, for half of what it was worth.

It was like being the captain of a pirate ship. *Arrr*! Tie me to the yardarm, but don't steal me bacon.

One of my fellow managers was a Vietnam vet. At his core, Ned was a good person, and it shined through many times, but he could be a rollercoaster to deal with on a day-to-day basis.

His service left deep scars, and his stories were sometimes dark, even when he meant to be funny. He'd tell tales of jumping out of a Huey into gunfire and told me that the only way to convince yourself to do such a thing was to decide that you were already dead. Sometimes he'd get lost in the story while he was talking.

One morning, I arrived at the store about the same time as Ned. Our breakfast supervisor had opened the store, and Ned walked in about fifteen feet ahead of me. The morning supe was a smallish, older lady named Barb whom Ned had hired as a favor for a friend.

She was up at the counter and so nervous she was vibrating.

"Don't go back there," she said to us, almost crying. Then to Ned, "Charles has a gun! He says he's going to shoot you!"

This was in the late '80s, long before workplace shootings had become commonplace. None of us had experience with that sort of thing, let alone worked out what to do if it happened.

In this case, Charles was our biscuit maker, and Ned had been back at his table the day before, giving him hell about his work. He had poked his chest and told him he'd be fired if he couldn't put biscuits out any faster. I guess the next morning Charles decided he'd bring a gun and see what happened.

Ned's reaction was to blow a raspberry, and ask her, "Where?"

Barb pointed back to the biscuit table.

"No, ninny, where's the gun?" Ned said.

She made a motion indicating that it was under his work tunic behind his back. It was a slow part of the morning, and only a few customers sipped their coffee in the corners of the lobby. I stopped on the customer side of the counter and hung back in a spot where I could see what would happen. I know, these days we'd immediately hit the doors, taking all of our employees and customers with us. But this was back when we were all fresh innocents.

Ned stepped quietly back to the biscuit table where Charles was angrily throwing a big ball of dough around, mumbling expletives under his breath. I could see a lump in the back of his tunic that seemed to confirm what Barb had said. When Ned pulled the back of his tunic up, Charles froze in place. The pistol was a Colt 1911, a big hog-leg of a gun. Ned pulled it out of his waistband, cocked the slide, and pushed the muzzle up against Charles' temple hard enough to cock his head over at an angle!

I was frozen in disbelief.

"You, and your f*cking pistol, get outta my store," Ned hissed through his teeth. Then he gave Charles the buggedy-eyes and handed him the still cocked gun.

At that point, I hit the floor. Everyone else watching did, too.

"You are one crazy mothaf**ker," Charles said.

We heard the back door open and slam shut. We all slowly brought ourselves up off the floor..

"What?" Ned said as he rounded the corner—and it genuinely seemed he didn't know.

Hardee's headquarters was in North Carolina, and our payroll was administered from there. We received a package by registered mail each week with physical checks in it (no auto deposit in those days, although it was soon to come).

This process delayed payroll by ten days, so the check you got on payday was for your work two weeks prior. This wasn't good for relations with our employees, because it caused misunderstandings about what we owed them and when we could pay it.

I had fired a guy, I don't remember for what, and he showed up to be paid four or five days before he should have. It was a very busy day, and the lobby was jammed with customers eating and thinking about their afternoon. Kelly had a day off and came down to have lunch with me and was waiting in the lobby while I talked with the angry former cook.

I explained that I didn't have the check on the premises, and even if I did, I needed to follow the rules and give it to him on the regular payday. He went ballistic, yelling and gesturing wildly in front of his captive audience of burger eaters. I told him to come back on payday, and sat down with Kelly, who was seated at a table close to the door.

Our guy fumed for a minute, then went outside to pace up and down the sidewalk. Each time he came to our end of the sidewalk, he pointed at me and shouted epithets that, thankfully, were muffled by the glass. On his last trip he stopped, unzipped, and exposed himself to my wife and me (and the whole lobby full of people).

I got up and told Hal, one of my fellow managers, to go out and tell him to wait, that I'd decided to give him a check. I continued past Hal to the office phone and called the police. The cops came quickly, and I went out to press my complaint. It was obvious who they were called for, and my former employee took off running when they pulled onto the lot. As they put him in the car, he yelled over his shoulder that I was a "Short-d*ck honkey motherf**ker" and that when he got out he was going to kill me.

He hasn't yet, so that's cool.

Hardee's and the Terrible, Horrible, No Good, Very Bad Day

any bad week could be worse

Any time I'm having a tough day, it only takes thinking back to three days while I was a manager at the Hardee's on Broadway to realize that whatever today tried to do to me, it could have been worse.

That store had the strangest sales pattern of all the ones in our system. The area west of the store has had a revival since then, but at the time it was a rough neighborhood, so we did almost no business after seven o'clock in the evening and closed at eight on weekdays. However, it was also the nearest fast-food joint to the State Capitol complex at the time, so our breakfast and lunch sales were phenomenal.

Shortly after I was transferred to the store, they began construction of the overpass for a new highway, and it passed almost right over the store. That construction closed the roads of our intersection, in one-to-three directions at a time and cut us off from the Capitol.

Our sales plummeted from very competitive to the worst in the region. I didn't mind. It gave us a chance to work on the problems inherent to that place. We reduced the food and cash drawer theft to minimal while we waited for the road to be finished.

One Tuesday in the middle of breakfast, a man in an expensive suit and carrying a leather briefcase walked up to the counter and handed me his card. It said that he was an auditing accountant for Imasco Ltd. in Canada.

He explained, in what I thought was an unnecessarily grumpy tone, that Imasco was the parent company of Hardee's, that he had flown here from Montreal to do a full audit of the store's activities, and that he was going to "live with" me for three days.

The store had three managers at the time, Ned, Hal, and me. Ned was in the hospital. He'd had a very bad week, and his demons were getting the better of him. He went to get some help, and I am glad he wasn't there for this one—being Ned all over the place would not have helped us at all. That left two of us in charge. I picked up the opens, and Hal closed every night.

Day One: With only that sketchy introduction, I was reluctant to let The Accountant come any farther than my counter. I called my district manager, Charlie.

"Do whatever he tells you to, and I'll try to find out what the hell is going on," he said.

The Accountant (his name has been lost to time—maybe it's trauma-induced memory loss) marched me back to the office and demanded my keys. He said that we would be pulling the sales tapes for the last five years and instructed me to open the safe.

The safe had an inner compartment that required an additional key. I explained that it had been closed, with the key broken off in the lock, for all of my tenure. He told me that if I couldn't open it for him, he had the power to fire me on the spot and would.

I called a locksmith. Then, I pulled boxes of sales records out of the ceiling for him, while he worked on an inventory of the food we had in our freezer and coolers.

When he was done, he took up a position at a table in the front of the lobby, and I ran records and coffee out to him, as he needed them. The locksmith showed us that the mystery compartment in the safe had been empty the whole time.

Lunch went smoothly under his watchful glare. That is until a customer came to the counter,

"I think you might want to look under the table in the back corner," the customer said. "There's a man back there, and he's *not* moving."

I went back to look, and sure enough, the homeless guy we called "Redbeard" had crammed himself under one of the bench-seats with his back to us, and his skin was cold as a drainpipe.

Like a stray cat, he'd found a warm place to give up and died where he lay. I called 911, and they got a cop and an ambulance out to us. For service's sake, I kept it all low-key, although The Accountant eyebrows danced the whole time.

I handed the shift off to Hal, who said later that The Accountant stayed until closing time, a long day for him. Charlie called me when I got home and said that something big was going down, and I should follow company rules to the letter. His boss had forbidden him to go near the store, and I was on my own. I told him about Redbeard, and he belly-laughed on the other end of the line

"*Hahaha! Ha* ... Jeezus, Randle," he said and hung up.

Day Two: In the wee hours of Wednesday, would-be burglars chose that morning to throw a car battery through the glass of the drive-through window. The thieves crawled through and tried to rob us by yanking all of the boxes that hold the cash drawers out from under the counter. They got away with nothing. We always emptied the drawers and put all of our working cash in the safe after balancing out for the day.

When I arrived, I saw from my parking space that the window was out and opened the door to a mess of glass and wires. Their attempt wrecked all five of our computer-based cash registers. The Accountant arrived to a scene of glass repair people working in the drive through, a computer tech under the counters, and me giving a statement to the same cops who had been there the day before.

Our cashiers filled orders and made change all through a busy lunch using hand-held calculators and writing what they sold in spiral notebooks. They had to figure tax by multiplying each order by 1.0785, and The Accountant was buzzing from station to station with a look of distress.

What he didn't know was that we'd had problems with the computers a few times before, and we kept a box of calculators and notepads ready and had a good bit of practice running that way. We usually did a $3,000 day at that store, and to their credit, my guys came within $1 of balancing.

I was proud of them.

The highway construction crew changed the barricades yet again and the store went quiet for the rest of the afternoon. The cops came back for a follow-up after the computer guy restored our registers, and The Accountant went back to his work of filtering through five years of hamburger money.

Hal called later and said The Accountant left right after I did. That night was very windy. They'd predicted storms, but none materialized.

Day Three: Thursday morning, I opened the door and knew something was wrong. The safety lights were on in part of the store, and I smelled smoke. I tried to call 911 to have a fire crew check the place out, but the phone was dead. No extinguishers had gone off in the kitchen (what a blessing—the cleanup for that takes half a day), but the floor got wetter with each step.

All of the drains were backing up.

As I arrived at the back of the store, I saw that the mop room next to the office had a six-foot half-circle of black ceiling tiles above its door. The door was cold to the touch, so I opened it.

Everything inside was burned and wet.

Like most restaurants, we had an industrial, gas fired, hundred-gallon water heater that sat just off the floor in that room. The night before, someone left the mop on the floor, and had pushed it a little too far under the water heater.

The high winds that evening had blown across the top of the water heater's chimney, and made it flare out and light the mop. The mop lit some cleaning supplies, and the resulting fire would have burned the store down, had the Culligan equipment not cycled at just the right time.

The fire had melted through its hose, so the resulting rush of water and very animated hose-end sprayed down the room and put out the fire!

I took some quarters to the payphone on the corner and saw The Accountant pull up as I made some phone calls.

We opened the store for business while the firemen explained the mop/water heater/Culligan puzzle to us. Electricians repaired the wiring that ran through the mop room ceiling. Plumbers said that the plastic mop bucket had melted down into the drain directly under it and had clogged the city sewer pipe. The City plumbers brought a jackhammer and made a horrible racket through half of lunch. The Southwestern Bell telephone guys said that we (and half the neighborhood) lost service because the junction box for our side of the street had been placed in our mop room.

The thousand dollars for a new water heater was above what I could spend on my own authority, so Charlie finally got authorization to come out to the store, though he was not allowed to say much, or stay while The Accountant did our debrief.

Around three o'clock that afternoon, The Accountant summoned us to the table he had been occupying for the last three days. Hal and I sat opposite him, with his briefcase opened between us. We waited, not able to see his face, for him to finally tell us what the hell all of this had been about. He said nothing, and it seemed like he scratched at his paperwork forever as we nervously shifted from cheek to cheek.

He moved some papers around where we could see them and said, "Sign this. Here, here, and ... here."

A taxi pulled up as we signed. He took the papers, closed his briefcase, and got up to leave.

"Hey!" Hal said. "What's the deal?"

He turned and said, "Oh. You idiots are clean. But this is the godamnedest circus I ever saw in my life."

He sped away in the taxi, and Hal and I went back to work.

When the dust finally settled on the week, Charlie was able to explain just what had motivated the company audit: No one told them about the construction.

The sudden drop in sales at a very profitable store had made them suspicious that someone was embezzling. The store I had been transferred from had been suffering some puzzling losses, also (their manager probably *was* stealing, but they never proved it). I had transferred from one store to the other, and the losses had seemed to follow me.

He was there for *me*.

Charlie said that despite all that, The Accountant's report said that it was the construction that had choked our sales, and that we were running a good operation. Charlie laughed and said that had the store burned down that night, they probably would have had me arrested, *haha*!

Not funny.

Your Mother Can Roll

and she could ride, too

We lost Mom to cancer. I know too many people who can say something like that, and they all have memories of hospitals, chemotherapy, and how it affected them or their loved ones. Mom's was a long battle, and she fought hard.

Watching her fight made me wonder if I would do the same if I were in her shoes. Is a year or two with a very low quality of life worth the heartache and financial devastation it brings to the family? Maybe my speculation does a disservice to those who have fought hard, win or lose.

She and Dad did their homework and set up their insurance well so the cost of the health care wouldn't bankrupt them. I think it is criminal that in this wealthy country of ours you always have to consider sickness in terms of what it will cost. We need to come around to realizing that healthcare is a human right. Living in Sweden certainly influenced me in that regard.

Back in the States, when my father-in-law got sick, he let it come. And in his last days, Ernie seemed much happier than Mom was in hers.

Many people have a story with some spirituality to it, something that they can hold on to that helps with losing someone they loved or gets them through a dark night. Sometimes they're far-fetched: "A cloud looked like

Jesus the day Grandma died," or the woman who keeps a photo negative of her son's casket and hands out countless reprints because a reflection from the chrome makes the photo look like a spirit is rising.

I have one, too, and it might just be baloney, but that's okay. Don't tell me.

Our grandfather took his own life. The official story is that he had emphysema from a life-long smoking habit. He'd received a diagnosis that didn't look good. He decided that he didn't want to be a burden and would go out on his own terms. That he was a former fighter pilot and proud man fit this narrative.

My mom was devastated by his action. A few years later, she told me she was still mad at him. She was Daddy's Little Girl, and he'd betrayed her by not fighting for more time.

"How could he do that to me?"

That talk, and years later when she told me about her own final diagnosis, where the last times I saw her cry.

When Mom was sick, she fought hard, through rounds of chemo, through hope and disappointment, and through a last-ditch treatment. After it came down to home hospice, she stayed as long as she could, much longer than the doctors gave her.

She lingered long enough that it got very hard on Dad. He was a saint through all of it, caring for her at their house without a complaint, even after she'd stopped being able to communicate or move on her own. Barry, Jen, and I did what we could to help him. Still, she stayed.

One night, Jen and I met at their house and cooked dinner for Dad. After dinner, I helped Dad put Mom into her nightclothes while Jen did the dishes. I needed to start home soon. Dad had a certain way he liked the silverware put up, so he left me with Mom for a minute to show Jen.

I took the opportunity to tell Mom that I thought I knew why she had held on so long. I told her not to let *her* dad leaving early keep her here. She had fought her fight, and we were proud of her. She didn't have to stay if it hurt. I told her we loved her, and then I headed home. I didn't get three blocks away before Jen called me and asked me to come back.

Mom was gone.

A happier story: Dad called me one day during the time Mom was doing chemotherapy. He told me that Mom wasn't eating—she just had no appetite at all. I didn't understand it then, how could you not want to eat? Surely, hunger eventually brought your appetite around, and some instinct for survival would have you dig into a sandwich.

I held this disbelief until I was in the hospital for my appendix and was told I could go home when I ate something. As much as I wanted to go home, a sandwich sounded like the most horrible thing I could imagine.

Oops!

Back to my phone call with Dad:

"So, your mom isn't eating at all. She really needs to eat, and I've been looking for something to give her an appetite. I thought, you know ... well, I mean, uhm ... It's just that, uh, you're a musician and all ..."

There was an awkward pause while I tried to figure out what he was talking about.

"*Haha*! Are you asking if I have a connection?"

"*Haha*! ... Do ya?"

This was before medical marijuana was legal, and he wanted to know if I could score him some pot. I told him no, that I couldn't get it myself, but I knew someone who knew someone that could get us something. I mean, yeah. I *am* a musician.

"Does she need a way to smoke it?" I said. "Should I look for a pipe or something?"

"Nah, just pick up some papers."

Now it was my turn to be awkward with a long pause.

"Son, your mom knows how to roll a joint."

I was stunned. Mom?

"She graduated with a master's in art," he said. "In 1966."

Well, that made sense. And a presumption or two changed that day, if only by a tiny bit.

OK, another side story while we're here.

Dad's phone call surprised me a little, but then I remembered one of their college stories, about Mom having a friend who was not any bigger than she was (five-foot-zero), and the two talking themselves into buying a Harley (because they had an electric starter) so they would have a way to get to class without relying on their husbands.

Dad would laugh when he told about the girls roaring off on that huge bike but being only barely able to keep it standing when they were at a stop light.

Evidently, this arrangement lasted for almost a semester, until they dumped the motorcycle over on the way to school one morning and had to leave it there and run to class because they couldn't get it back upright.

The friend put an ad in the paper the next day and sold it soon after.

Warm Cup of Coffee

On an Elm Mills morning early

came a tan and fuzzy Squirrely.

Said, "Expect a Hummybird

to buzz up close and give a word,

to why your Mother sat upon

this porch to watch the early dawn."

They Found a Mammoth

feedlot paleontology

My grandfather had farmland next to the airport outside of Pratt, Kansas, and grew wheat on it when I was a kid. He sold a piece of it to a company that built a feedlot on the land just west of the aerodrome, and the approach plates for the runways say you should be careful not to mistake the lights of the feedlot for runway light.

If you aren't familiar with the term, a feedlot is an outdoor facility where they raise cattle en masse. This one's website says it maintains forty thousand cows at a time there. Well, moo!

The feedlot contacted Dad in '98 or '99 about leasing more of our land to install a "manure pit" for the cattle.

Yuck!

He signed the deal, and workers using excavators dug up what looked to them like a volleyball-sized bone. They stopped work, and the foreman told them to call Dad.

Dad drove up and identified it as the hip-end of a femur (leg bone). Its size convinced him he was looking at something bigger than an elephant. It was fossilized, so he contacted the museum at the university in Hays (about two hours north of the farm)

The Sternberg Museum of Natural History is smack in the middle of Kansas and has a first-class (and large) collection of dinosaur fossils and displays. Many of the specimens were gathered from that area by paleontologist George Sternberg.

Their collection represents many different eras of natural history on the Great Plains, and the museum is well respected for its research on the ancient Inland Sea. Their life-size mosasaur display is scary enough to sober you right up.

It is a great stopover if you are on the way to or from Colorado on I-70.

The museum sent Greg, their curator of vertebrate paleontology, who immediately identified our hipbone as from a Columbian Mammoth. He corrected us when we called it a "Woolly" and told us that Woollies lived up in Canada, while Colombians ranged all over the United States.

Greg brought out a small team to work the dig and invited our family to help. We went up a couple of times, spending a few days at a time, with Amanda and Abby staying the longest. Mom had some surveying experience, so Greg put her to work marking off a grid. She also helped set up the system used to catalog what we dug up.

Dad's veterinary background put him on the team identifying bones, as they were unearthed. The girls helped sift collected debris for small parts and got to dig the surrounding grid. Kelly and I took pictures and were gophers for the team.

Dad wound up telling everyone in town, so word got around. Television and newspaper people came from Wichita to do interest pieces. Dad was in his element: Identifyin' and educatin'.

Our girls enjoyed the experience, and it gave them a healthy interest in science. Abby went on to be a biologist and educator, and it inspired Mom to become a docent at the dinosaur museum in Norman. It was just one more thing she became an expert about.

The museum has a memorial for her, in their front walk.

That feedlot was close by, and it was *ripe* for our entire dig. The team slowly unearthed bones from the mammoth's pelvis and foreleg, and a giant tusk that was just under the surface. A jawbone appeared that even I was able

to identify as looking like an elephant, although it was the biggest I'd ever seen.

And it *was* big! Colombians are larger than Wooly Mammoths, and Greg said our pieces would be the largest examples they had in their collection.

What we found was not in good shape, though. The parts were crumbly, even by paleontology standards, and they scattered in a jumble. The museum folks speculated that the beastie fell near a creek, and parts of it (like the skull) were washed away, rolling downstream as the body deteriorated.

I asked if we couldn't look for the skull, and Greg pointed out that the tusk had been right under the surface for millennia without having been uncovered. The skull probably *was* there, but could be on the surface, or ten feet down. And it could be close, or two hundred yards away. We could scratch around for a decade and not find it. Such is paleontology.

We wrapped the fossils in foil in the ground as we uncovered them, and then poured plaster over the foil. It formed big white blobs the size of a dining room set, and these were lifted onto a palette. They loaded them in a truck, packed up their gear, and drove off.

It sure seemed quiet when they were gone. Still stinky, though.

We donated the lot of it to the museum. They already had several well-preserved mammoths, and one nice one is on display in the main lobby. I guess Kansas is stinkin' *full* of mammoths. They found another outside of Pratt in 2020.

Eventually, they decided that they'd just use our parts for research. A bit of it was displayed for a while in an exhibit about how fossils are collected. We stayed in contact with Greg until he moved to another museum, and we were invited to participate in any discussions the museum board conducted that involved "our" mammoth.

We were there when they presented their conclusions from the research. It was super-duper boring. But dinner was nice, and it is always fun to tour the museum again.

While she was digging in the grid, Amanda found a tooth from a bison of that same era. Her find was part of what made them decide that the area we were working was near a creek, where different animals came to drink. There was other evidence to that effect that Greg and his team could see in the layers of dirt, but I never could spot what he was talking about.

As little as we have left to show for our big adventure, I kind of wish we had told Amanda to put the tooth under the seat of our car.

I Have Seen a UFO

but no need to notify the Air Force

There is a distinct east-west line in Barber County in south-central Kansas where the geology changes. Drive south on Highway 281, though the legendary flat, treeless wheatfields of Kansas, and suddenly the plains drop away into green valleys and glens full of trees, creeks, and ponds.

My great grandfather Orville built a cabin there in the '20s, among the trees in one of those valleys, on the site of a former grain-mill. Grandma Shrack (Orville's wife) told me that people had been picnicking there since she was a little girl, and you can still find arrowheads left by the Kiowa that camped in that area before them. My dad's dad deconstructed a post-and-beam barn that had been in the family since the 1870s, and reused the huge walnut beams and flooring to build a new cabin on the same spot.

A creek runs through the yard and feeds a well-stocked fishing pond in front of the cabin. It is a quiet little slice of heaven, and Kelly and I are happy to be the next of our family to be its caretakers.

One of our favorite activities is to walk up on the hill behind the cabin and look out across the valley as we amble along and talk. My mom picked up botany, first as a hobby, then as a serious career, and then worked for Oklahoma State University as an extension agent. As such, she knew the name and taxonomy of every bush and flower on that hill. A year or so after she passed, my dad and I wandered up on the hill to talk and look at "Mom's wildflowers".

It was a summer evening, just before twilight, in that strange calm when the day creatures have all begun to turn in and the night critters have yet to wake up. It was so quiet, that the *pocka-pocka-pocka* of a pumpjack's motor a couple of miles away came and went, carried on the breeze from the south. The horizon fell away for miles under an endless, cloudless blue dome.

As our ramble turned north, we saw something in the air, about twenty degrees (two fist-widths) above the horizon. A round orb, two or three times the size of a full moon glowed an eerie orange and seemed to hover at a fixed altitude, drifting first left, and then right, in a random back-and-forth motion that made it seem almost alive. The object made no sound, which made the whole scene even weirder. Dad was spooked.

"Look at that!" he said. "What do you suppose it is?"

"Oh, I imagine it's a weather balloon."

"It's not acting like a balloon. Have you ever seen a weather balloon?"

"Well yeah, but deflated."

"So, you've never seen one flying," he said.

"Uhm, no. But—"

"So, you can't tell me what *that* is. It's a UFO, don't you think?"

"Well, it *is* unidentified." I said.

"Well, I think it's weird."

"Yeah, it's weird all right."

When we were kids, my buddy Walt had a weather reporting transmitter land in his backyard. It had a white plastic housing the size of a car battery with a large cylinder shape protruding from one side for the antenna. It had writing molded into its side with contact information to notify authorities of recovery. I remember a deflated balloon attached and asked him about it after my encounter with Dad.

"Sadly, no offer of a reward," he wrote. "I did take it apart and it was mostly battery. I vaguely remember lots of cordage but have no recollection of a balloon."

I remember seeing a dead weather balloon somehow, somewhere. It's possible that it wasn't Walt's, but my memory of the balloon itself is pretty clear: It was a translucent tan, and the shape, color, and consistency of the biggest prophylactic I had ever seen.

What Dad and I saw that night had to have been a weather balloon at a low altitude. The sun had just dipped below the horizon behind us, and our UFO was at the right altitude to be illuminated like a sunset. Against the endless Kansas sky, that orange orb was the only thing in our view.

Its odd movement could be explained by the balloon traveling away from our vantage point on a long, shallow S-shaped path, drifting slowly left and right as it flew along above the wheat fields.

I think I was most surprised by Dad's reaction to it. I always thought of him as a scientific thinker, being a doctor and all. This time, he seemed genuinely weirded-out and not kidding me, as he was prone to do.

Well, it *was* pretty spooky.

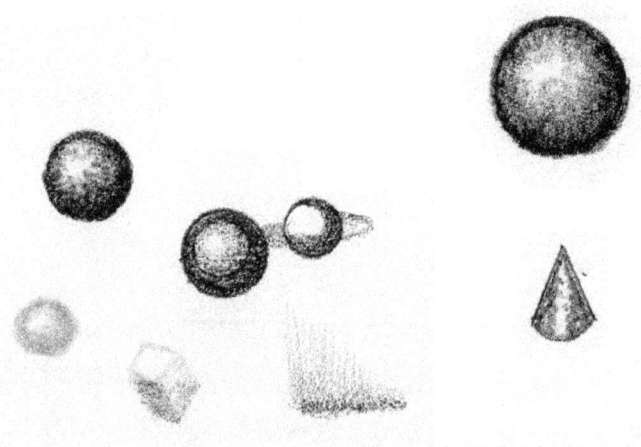

Alfred P. Murrah

9:02 a.m. April 19, 1995

On the morning of April 19, 1995, I was working in the retail photo lab I managed in Edmond, Oklahoma. As I was loading another batch of film into the processor, the front door opened just enough to ring the bell, then closed again.

Immediately after, I heard a low frequency "whump" and the frames hanging on the west wall clattered. There was a crew building out a coffee shop next door, and I had seen men on scaffolding, so I assumed that a worker had fallen against the wall. I started to go check but was busy finishing the work on an order.

A few minutes later, a customer came in and said, "Have you seen any news? They blew up downtown!"

"Downtown Edmond?"

"No! Oklahoma City!"

My store was thirteen miles away.

We turned on the small television we kept in the back room and tuned in the news. Early on, they didn't know that it was a disillusioned American who had done it, so the media, and all of us talking about it, assumed it was Middle Eastern terrorists.

When I read about World War I or World War II, where the men and boys marched right down in a big group to sign up to fight, it correlates directly with the mood of that day. We all wanted to volunteer immediately for something. To help, kick some butt, or do anything that would get us involved. Those times were pre-internet, so the meager news we got that afternoon didn't tell us how to help.

When I finally got off work, I went home and put on my big brown coveralls and told Kelly I would go to the Red Cross headquarters close to downtown and volunteer, and don't stay up late waiting for me.

We knew that a massive bomb had exploded in front of the Alfred P. Murrah Federal Building, and it had devastated the block north of Fifth Street downtown. Traffic on the way there was terrible. When I arrived at the Red Cross building, a lady wrote my name on a list on her clipboard and told me they had an overflow of volunteers and didn't need me. I was disappointed, and as I turned to go, she stopped me.

"You know what," she said. "I really need a break. Could you stand here with my clipboard and do what I'm doing for a while?"

I did. As I turned volunteers away, it started to rain a light mist. She was gone for an hour and a half, and I didn't mind. But my coveralls were getting soggy and heavy.

The crowd that milled around the headquarters, and people coming and going, kept us informed as news unfolded that night.

When my relief came, I wandered back to a meeting room where a scattering of people sat in rows of folding chairs watching the news on a big-screen TV. A team lead asked if I wanted to help distribute coffee and sandwiches down at the site.

I wanted to see first-hand what it looked like down there, so I jumped at the chance. Our van stopped a couple of blocks north of the building, and I grabbed my box of sandwiches and got out with the group. It was a strange sight.

The Southwestern Bell building had the windows on its south side blown out. There were venetian blinds, the old wide '50s-style, shredded and scattered all over the wet lawn. It had stopped misting and there was broken glass everywhere. The garage-door of a car repair shop had been blown in, and its cinder block wall was cracked.

Gawkers milled about and got in the way.

As a backdrop for all of this, the floodlights that were trained on the Murrah building reflected off the clouds in the rainy sky. There weren't many vantage points from the north where you could get a good look at it. A peak around the side of the *Journal Record* building while standing in the street was the best I could manage.

It was so brightly lit that I had to let my eyes adjust in order to pick out what I was seeing. The side that faced us two blocks away was a gaping maw of ripped cement, exposed floors, and dangling cables, with firemen crawling over the rubble while cranes lifted and lowered platforms and chunks.

The police, firemen, and EMTs heading south into the site were all very intense, and few were interested in a sandwich. The coffee gal was faring much better.

News trucks lined Robinson Avenue for blocks, and one of the camera crews was taking a break, so I handed them the last of my sandwiches. I found out later that the Asian lady I talked to was Connie Chung.

I was out of things to do again, so I decided to see if anyone from the Red Cross was down close to the building. I wanted to help more, but I also wanted to see if I could get a better look.

I stepped south into a parking lot that seemed oddly empty. Just as I crossed some invisible line, a repeating noise, like a car alarm, started pinging off in the distance. Surely that couldn't be for me.

It was.

Three ATF agents appeared out of nowhere and stopped me in my tracks. After a short interrogation while I showed them my sandwich box, they told me that I was not authorized to go any further, and then grumped off into the darkness.

I decided to give blood, so I walked to a clinic that some gawkers directed me to. The clinic was overwhelmed and told me to come back another day.

I was surprised to see that even the C. R. Anthony building, many blocks north, had some of its windows blown out. I couldn't imagine what it was like near the epicenter. I headed back to the Red Cross building, got some cold coffee, and flumped down in a chair in the TV room.

It was getting late, and the room was deserted. My coveralls had dried out, but my white and red "volunteer" sticker was all smeared. As I sat, a feeling of accomplishment came over me. I had signed up for something important and done all I could.

On the TV, the networks were still clueless about who was responsible, and they were concentrating on what information they could relay about the damage and the dead.

Someone came in and made a bunch of noise sitting down behind me. I paid him no mind until he started asking questions.

"What were the news stations saying? How many survived? How many got out?"

Ugh! I didn't know the answers to his questions. I told him what I could without turning around because I was tired, and I was trying to find those things out myself.

"Did any of the kids get out alive?"

Kids? I hadn't heard anything about kids being there.

I had worked hard and walked all over creation, and you know, if this goober is going to show up late and ask a bunch of dumb questions, I'd just turn around and tell him ...

When I turned around, I saw a fireman in his gear.

He was covered thick with dust and wasn't in a chair, he was sitting exhausted in a heap on the floor against the back wall. His helmet was next to him, and his sweaty hair stuck to his head. His tired eyes looked through the wall at something ten miles away. I realized that he didn't know any details because he had been nowhere near a TV.

He'd probably been digging people out, alive and dead, from the rubble all day. And I suddenly realized that I really hadn't done a damned useful or important thing all night long.

I know others who volunteered and have one friend who spent weeks down at the site. They have a lot better stories than mine.

Mark, the drummer from our band, is more famous as a photojournalist. He was on an assignment for a local paper on that Wednesday morning, and was heading into the city in his jeep. He told me he must have been in a valley when the shock wave passed, because he didn't remember hearing or feeling it. Facing downtown as he topped the next hill, he saw smoke rising fast. It was light colored at first, like what might have come from the blast, then it turned into the thick black smoke of burning tires and office furniture.

He looked for a spot to park, jumped out of his jeep with his heart racing, and took off at a dead run toward the scene. He said he suddenly realized he was operating on adrenalin and slowed to a stop to check his gear. Camera, flash, extra film, all there.

He told me the site was chaotic. He shot a couple of rolls, helped a couple of people, then loaded more film and took his other two rolls. In those days, he shot all black and white, and developed his own film. When he finished the rolls he had, he headed for his office at the paper, shocked but excited to see what he captured.

After developing his negatives, he and three other reporters returned to the scene. That afternoon, a guy from *Reuters* national news service came by the office and scanned one of his shots of the bombed-out building.

Days later, Mark got to cover President Clinton's arrival, and the memorial service he led. *Life* magazine wanted to jury Mark's bombing negatives for their next issue. He made a bunch of prints and FedExed them to New York City—the big leagues! They told him that the Bombing story had received so much press that they'd shifted their focus to the Ebola outbreak in Africa, so they decided not to use any of his shots. He handed the check from *Life* over to the paper.

Sometime close to one of the big anniversaries of the tragedy, Mark and I were having lunch downtown and passed by a newsstand selling a "special edition" of *Life* that commemorated the event. We picked one up and thumbed through it, while he told me about that day. He stopped several times, looking closely at this or that black and white picture, and remarked,

"You know, that is right where I was standing," he said. "That *could* be one of mine."

Another sign that it was probably his: It was a damned good shot.

Les was a regular customer at the photo lab, who I was always happy to see. He was an upbeat guy and always fun to talk to when he brought in the several rolls of film we did for him each week.

He worked for the local power company, documenting the work done in our region. He traveled from job site to job site, wrote up what was done, and took pictures of the men and the work. He was a good photographer, and the company sometimes used his shots for advertising and other media releases.

He happened to be on duty downtown when the bomb exploded at the Murrah Building. He had his camera ready and took many pictures. He sold his shots to the big magazines of the day, and you have seen at least one of them. His was one of the pictures of the fireman holding a baby that was widely distributed.

Les' company took him to court for selling his shots. The company's argument was that when he took the shots, Les was on the clock, in their truck, using their camera to take pictures on film they paid for. As such, they owned and controlled the rights to the pictures.

The company said that they did not intend to make money from the pictures. They said they would have donated the proceeds to victims. They did not want to appear to have profited from the tragedy and were willing to see a court battle through to prove it.

Les was sure that he was right, but there is a mountain of precedent in copyright and patent cases like this, and he lost handily. Les didn't have the deep pockets that the company had, so his court costs and whatever penalty the court exacted broke him financially. I saw him only one more time after the court case. He had found religion and moved on. His outgoing, fun demeanor was gone, also.

The aftermath of the Murrah Bombing had broken his spirit, as it did a few others that I knew.

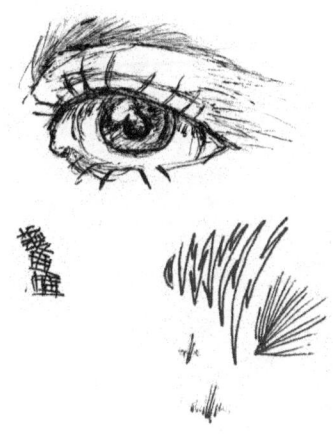

A Saint Croix Christmas

Single shelled mingled Swells

Crinkling the Cay:

Mollusks hide the bed beside

the beach on Christmas day (Hey!)

The Randle Christmas Curse

Surely it's not us. Is it?

Mom loved to go to live sports events, and one spring while she and Dad were planning a trip to Dallas to visit my brother's family, Barry suggested they catch a pro baseball game.

A couple of months later, at the Texas Rangers game in Arlington, a foul ball screamed into the stands and shattered Mom's forearm. They sent her the ball that did it.

"Why on earth would I want that?" she asked.

Her arm took a long time to heal, and it ached for even longer. So, while planning for the following Christmas, we decided to do something that would keep Mom from exerting herself.

And thus began a tradition of traveling somewhere interesting every few years for the holidays.

The first time we did, someone suggested New Orleans as a place with a Christmas tradition, fantastic food, and guaranteed good weather. And we did have fun! We hit the voodoo shops on Bourbon Street, took the midnight ghost tour, and ate a dress-up formal Christmas Eve dinner at Broussard's.

That was the winter right before hurricane Katrina devastated New Orleans, and our visit held some foreshadowing of the spring's crazy weather.

As we arrived, a winter storm dipped far below the usual latitudes where that kind of thing happens and bore down on New Orleans from the west. We heard it was coming while we were on the road. We had been paying attention to the radio, so when we checked in, we asked the desk if they had heard it was coming.

"*Awww*, that never happens here," he said. "No need to worry."

I asked if he'd been outside. It was starting already. Kelly asked if they had extra blankets available.

"Oh, no need for blankets, it's always warm here."

Our room was French Quarter gorgeous, with a courtyard garden, wrought iron bed frames, and an ancient exposed-brick wall behind the bed. It didn't take us long to find that the windows leaked freezing air, the door had a huge gap under it, and that brick wall had grown frost.

Mr. Desk was slow to react. They took a couple of hours to find some blankets and turn on the seldom-used heating system. But the next morning, the beignets at Cafe Du Monde were still fantastic, even if it was cold and gray. The palm trees drooped while we sipped our coffee.

We exchanged gifts on Christmas Eve with the whole family around us.

Kelly, Amanda, Abby, and I had driven the eleven-hour trip down. I needed to be back for work right after Christmas, so we planned to start our trip home on Christmas Day.

After a breakfast of calas fritters and chicory coffee, we said our goodbyes and hit the road. It began snowing almost immediately, and our pre-excursion stop to gas up was hectic. The snow was confusing the hell out of the native Orleanians, and a bunch of them crowded inside the small station.

It was so busy I skipped a bathroom visit, which would come back later to haunt me, and walked out to find the snow had turned into huge flakes. Big fat blobs were hitting our windshield and obscuring visibility. The guys in the gas station said that it hadn't snowed in New Orleans in twenty years.

There were only a couple of routes out of New Orleans on our map. They headed west, inland from the delta, and to make it out of town we'd have to pick one of the only two bridges shown.

The authorities were quick to close the north bridge out of town, citing safety reasons, and we ran into that roadblock almost immediately. We switched to the south route but needed a better map of the town.

We pulled into another convenience store, and as I put a map on the counter, I asked about a restroom. The woman running the place moved over into the entrance for the restrooms, folded her arms.

"No restrooms!" she exclaimed.

The cold wind had blown away all Southern Hospitality, and the Big Easy was turning mean. I chucked her map at her and decided we'd navigate on our own. We found the other route, and as we came closer to the bridge the traffic slowly ground to a halt, becoming literally bumper-to-bumper.

We were trapped.

Two lanes of cars stretched up and over the hill in front of us and for as far as we could see behind us. The curb was too high for a car to jump, so there we sat, *for hours.*

The radio mentioned the local sheriff's phone number, so we called it. They acted as though they had no responsibility for those of us on the road, other than *closing all of the ways out of town* (sounds a bit like how they handled Katrina a few months later).

The guy at the sheriff's office tried to educate me about black ice, and I'm glad they didn't have caller ID back in those early flip-phone days, because I called the guy an asshole.

It slowly occurred to Kelly and me that our only hope was if everyone on that piece of road put their car in reverse and backed up a half-mile to the previous exit, where we could all turn around.

Miraculously, we all figured that out at the same time, and a hundred cars crept for a thousand yards, slowly and in reverse.

All those cars had been stopped for a couple of hours, and once we all turned around, we *all* needed to pee. There was a Walgreens close to the next exit, and fifty of us descended upon it—all with the same mission.

The manager saw the mob marching to her door, and despite their marked holiday hours, she walked up and locked it in our face. The mob turned temporarily ugly, cursing and pounding on the door, until one of us spied a port-a-potty at a construction site next door.

The snow had stopped, and our holiday spirit kicked back in. We formed a line, joking and laughing at our predicament. The Randles got back on the road, but what to do? Head back into town, or head home?

A mile later, we saw a Ramada Inn by the airport, pulled in and booked a room. As the lady at the desk ran our credit card, the phone rang. She answered, gasped, and then hung up.

"You lucky you got a room," she said. "They just shut down the airport."

When we came back to the desk to ask about dinner, we couldn't get through. The lobby was shoulder to shoulder with angry travelers yelling at our desk lady.

The hotel restaurant was closed to observe Christmas Day, and we hadn't eaten since our big breakfast. We were starved! We bundled up, walked down to the corner gas station, and bought the kind of sandwiches that come in a plastic triangle box, and a big bag of Funyuns.

We sat on the beds, munched, and watched *The Sound of Music*.

Some would consider it a blessing to be able turn any yule into a white Christmas. For us, it always seems to involve a car trip and an *amazing* amount of snow.

The year after Mom passed, we planned to go down to Norman on Christmas morning to spend the day with Dad. Amanda was engaged to Keith, and we got first dibs in the in-law rotation to have the new couple at our place for Christmas.

I worked day-shift on Christmas Eve, and for the previous couple of days the weathermen had been predicting a white Christmas. Sometime that morning, the snow rolled in and hit with a fury. The site managers where I worked *finally* decided to close after lunch, and by the time they did, the wind was whipping up a whiteout blizzard.

A newspaper article from that week in 2009 said that it snowed fourteen inches in twenty-four hours, with winds greater than thirty-five miles an hour!

My normal half-hour commute slogged on for two hours.

Nevertheless, it wound up being a beautiful night. After dinner, we built a fire and had hot cocoa in our pajamas, then snuggled into our warm beds.

We woke on Christmas Day determined to make it down to Grandad's. He'd just lost Mom, and it was something we needed to make happen.

That decision wasn't easy though, fourteen inches of snow in Oklahoma is a roadway disaster. We had an ace in our hand: Keith had driven his all-wheel-drive Subaru to the house, and he was confident that he could get us over the river and through the woods.

The ride was not without its challenges. We passed a surprising number of accidents. There were cars abandoned all over the highway, at every crazy angle imaginable. We went carefully around several that had been deserted in the middle of the highway.

A Hummer bumped up over a couple of snowdrifts and onto the road, then zoomed off out of sight, confident in his four-wheeled abilities. We got a laugh when we passed him a mile later hopelessly stuck in a ditch, blasting mud and snow everywhere with all four tires.

Keith had saved the day.

We had a great visit with Dad, and the trip home was much less exciting.

Two wacky snow disasters at Christmas! The kids began to make jokes about a Christmas Curse …

You may remember from a previous story that Abby's birthday, as well as my mom's, is very close to Christmas. Mom never liked the proximity of the holidays. She had strict rules about making sure her presents were wrapped in *birthday* paper.

One year, when I got some time off for the holidays, we drove out to the Grand Canyon to celebrate Abby's. Though she tried not to show it, we could tell that Abbs thought it was the dumbest thing she'd ever heard of. That is until we got there!

The Canyon is unbelievably huge. The view from one of the lodges on the rim is a painting of mountains, composed in stripes using every possible shade of brown and red. The winter sunlight accentuates those colors.

That year's hike, and dinner after, still counts as one of Abby's favorite birthdays, and pinyon pine in a fireplace always reminds us of it.

When The Sibs (as Jen, Barry, and I call ourselves) got together to plan our next adventure, it was easy to agree with Kelly's suggestion that we spend Christmas Eve at the Canyon.

On this trip, it was *Keith* who wasn't impressed at first. We started our first day with a hike along the edge, and after all my poetic description during the drive, the Canyon was now filled with a layer of clouds that completely obscured our view.

It was a huge painting of *soup*.

Only when we hiked down below the cloud cover to "Ooh-Aah Point," did he get to see the real Canyon.

Barry's family arrived that evening, and we planned an activity we thought would be a perfect way for the whole family to get a good view.

The national park and lodges are on the South Rim of the Grand Canyon. The North Rim is extremely remote and at a higher elevation, so it's often snowed-in, and the Park Service closes it down all winter. We had visited the Desert View Watchtower on the eastern edge of the park during Abby's trip, and I told Barry that would make a great day trip, as the view there is spectacular. The posted schedule said the buses would be running all day, so we decided to take advantage of them.

We had breakfast in the Maswik Lodge restaurant, a big hall that has been there since the '40s and was recently remodeled in the obligatory Southwest theme. It feels like you might see Cary Grant with a tray, waiting in line to tell them how he wants his omelet.

As we ate, we read a story in the local newspaper about a family that was stranded in snow the day before on the road that goes to the North Rim. The temperature had crashed to negative one, and the mother had set out and hiked for *thirty hours* in the snow, saving the family's life, but suffering frostbite.

Wow, harsh!

After breakfast, we asked a ranger about the bus schedule out to the Tower, and she looked at us as if we were crazy.

"Oh! They're not running out *there* today," she said.

That should have made us wonder why. We thought that maybe we'd misunderstood their Holiday Schedule—it was Christmas Eve, after all.

We explored the rim for a while, then after lunch, we loaded up our rental cars and drove out. A two-lane road goes from Grand Canyon Village twenty-five miles out to the watchtower. It parallels the South Rim and is a typical mountain drive: Slightly dangerous, with steep hills and tight curves. Views of the canyon peek through the pinyons as you travel along.

The national park itself is remote, and Desert View is even more so. The lodges are a forty-minute drive from the tower, and the nearest other civilization is two hours away (in *good* weather) at Flagstaff. And there is not a peep of cell phone reception out there.

Barry said he had snow in his ear.

The snowstorm came out of nowhere when we were about halfway out to the tower. When we reached the parking lot ten minutes later, the snow turned heavy. By the time we walked to the top of the tower it was a danged blizzard. Because ... *of course it was.*

A lady at the gift-shop counter was one of the only people left.

"Go get in your car and leave," she said. "Go right now. Go! They're gonna close the road."

I asked if she would be okay.

"Honey I live here," she said. "And you are *not* doin' Christmas at my house. Now *git*!"

We staggered out through the wind to our cars. Barry's family got theirs going before us and took off down the road.

Our rental was a Dodge family van, and it had a lot of windows to clear off. As we were loading up, we saw a park ranger trying to keep his Smokey hat on with one hand and walking the big metal bar of the gate closed with the other—he was about to shut us in!

I sent Keith to talk to him and brought the van's nose right up to the bar. Keith walked toward him, inching him backward as they shouted over the wind.

"You can't shut us in."

"The Park is closed!"

"Ok, but we're staying *in The Park*."

"THE PARK IS CLOSED!"

By then, I had nudged the van through the entrance and yelled, "Keith, hop in!"

As we drove off, I saw the ranger in the rear-view mirror shake his fist at us, yelling into the gale.

Our van was handling the slick road very well, but the windshield wipers were barely keeping up. We'd gone five or six of the twenty miles to the lodge when we came around a bend and saw a long, steep hill ahead of us. Spaced out on the hill's climb were five vehicles, all pointing a different direction, and at the bottom was Barry's rental.

Barry told us that the line of cars had slowed to a stop to avoid running into someone at the top of the hill that we couldn't see, who was sideways across the road. Now, they were all stuck on the slippery slope.

Barry, Keith, and I trudged up the hill, stopping at each car to talk to its occupants. There was a young Aussie couple in a Mini Cooper, who were cheerful. There was a family of five in a van who were okay but worried. The next vehicle was full of Groovies who were taking the opportunity to hotbox their van. They were happy, but not too helpful. A Ford Fiesta held a pair of Asian college girls, who were grimly quiet. They had worried eyes and only nodded as we spoke. At the top of the hill was a pickup truck with three hillbilly-types who were just finishing putting chains on their back tires.

As we walked up, they hopped in and skittered away in a cloud of snow, with a middle finger salute for us out of the passenger window. Everyone else was stuck, in one way or another. Most couldn't get any traction, and Barry was the same—his tires just wouldn't bite.

Our having communicated with everyone somehow put us in charge, and our Council of Three needed a plan. A little time passed while we talked it

out, then a ranger truck with snow tires on it pulled around the corner at the bottom of the hill.

The guy who we later dubbed "Grumpy Ranger" hopped out and started in on us. We all needed to "turn this little parade around, and head back where you came from!"

We told him, as though he wasn't aware, that the Tower gate was closed.

"Well then you just keep on going until you get to Flagstaff," he said.

Dumbest danged idea I'd heard in a long time: Flagstaff would be eighty-two miles of winding, icy, desolate road in a snowstorm—to arrive in a place one hundred miles from our beds and fancy dinner reservations.

Abby asked if he couldn't just transport us in his truck. He said no, and that civilians weren't allowed in the truck unless he had arrested them. Abby stuck out her wrists to be handcuffed.

"Ugh! No!" he said. "Look, I don't have time for you people. We have folks who are in real trouble to worry about!"

He jumped in his truck and roared off, back around the corner. We stood in the quiet that he left. I could see dread creeping in on the guys' faces. His "people in real trouble" comment had reminded us of what happened to the family on the North Rim just the day before.

Grumpy Ranger hadn't given us much. We got out a map and figured out why he wanted us to go to Flagstaff—the park grounds end just east of the tower, and we would no longer be their problem.

There was a glimmer of hope, though. It had stopped snowing, and at least the rangers knew we were there.

The Council of Three decided that to get everyone out of there, they'd have to bring a sand truck through, so all of the cars needed to move over to make that happen. We put together a crew to push, drive, and drag everyone as far over to the right side of the road as we could.

When they finally answered our knock on the hippie-van door, a dense blue cloud rolled out.

"Wow. Uh wow, hey," Groovy-dude said. "Hey, are, are y'all Gingers? 'Cause we love Gingers."

We told them yes, if it got their van moved, we're *all* Gingers.

Keith came down to the group from the college girls' car and told us that they might be a problem. The driver had just passed her license exam that week, and the passenger didn't drive at all. They were super worried and getting spooky.

We decided that we could get them out if everyone pushed their little car up the hill, and then we'd let Keith drive them back to the lodge. We didn't want to lose his help, but it was worth it, to get their panic away from the rest of the group. We waved them off and waited.

We had now been stuck for a few hours. The sun was beginning to set, it was getting *cold*, and we were quietly worrying about the minus-one temperature prediction from the newspaper story.

The girls designated a ladies bathroom area and formed a line. Barry had let his daughter, Ann Francis, come over to our van to hang out with Auntie Jen, and the rest of us in our van marveled at Ann Francis' ability to fall asleep immediately.

A second ranger arrived just when morale had dipped. Happy Ranger told us not to worry, that he would radio for a sand truck, and that we'd done a fine job keeping everyone calm and moving the cars over.

Sand-truck Guy arrived soon after, at the bottom of the hill. He spread a couple runs of sand, then turned his truck around and told us to follow him. We ran to our cars, and he took off fast!

Barry and I kept up with him, but we were kicking up a huge cloud of snow—enough that we saw no one else from the group behind us. We assumed that he would lead us back to the village, but he turned off somewhere, vanishing into the woods.

We pressed on as fast as we dared. Just when we were nearly to the village, Barry and I skidded to a halt. There was a gate across the road like the one at the tower, with a lock on it barring our way. We both jumped out of our vehicles and ran over to find that the lock was not completely shut.

Salvation!

When we drove into the village, our phones blew up with all of the S.O.S. messages that we'd tried to send. Keith had sent a text that he was safe at the lodge and having a beer.

We had reservations at the fancy restaurant in the main lodge, and we didn't bother showering or changing. We just went in our jeans and sweatshirts and sideways hair and had lobster bisque in the sweet arms of civilization.

As for the Randle Christmas Curse? Well, if we ever invite you somewhere exotic for the holidays, be sure to check the weather.

Christmas morning was a winter wonderland.

295

This book is set in the ITC Garamond typeface family.

www.ingramcontent.com/pod-product-compliance
Lightning Source LLC
Chambersburg PA
CBHW032102090426
42743CB00007B/204